"AN IMPORTANT BOOK." —*Publishers Weekly*

"Lawyers in their greed . . . legislators by their negligence, courts by the relaxation of rules . . . and the U.S. Supreme Court by its failure to protect due process are all flushed from their bunkers under Olson's withering salvos."
—Walter Guzzardi, *Fortune*

"A SPLENDID BOOK . . . Correctly analyzes the causes of the sickness of our litigation system and presents prescriptions for a cure."
—Robert H. Bork, *Washington Times*

"A persuasive case for reform of the civil litigation system and for ending the abuse of litigation." —*Kirkus Reviews*

"What Adam Smith was to free marketeers and Karl Marx was to revolutionaries, Walter Olson is to court reformers. *The Litigation Explosion* is a superb work of advocacy that catalogues every mistake the court system has made in the last fifty years. This book is the entering wedge for a serious reassessment of civil courts."
—Richard Neely, Chief Justice, West Virginia Supreme Court

"Will appeal to anyone wondering why the litigation explosion developed and what it means . . . recommended." —*Library Journal*

WALTER K. OLSON was born and raised in Detroit, graduated from Yale University in 1975, and studied economics at UCLA. A senior fellow at the Manhattan Institute, he has written for *Fortune*, *Barron's*, and the *Wall Street Journal*.

WALTER K. OLSON

THE
LITIGATION EXPLOSION

WHAT HAPPENED WHEN AMERICA UNLEASHED THE LAWSUIT

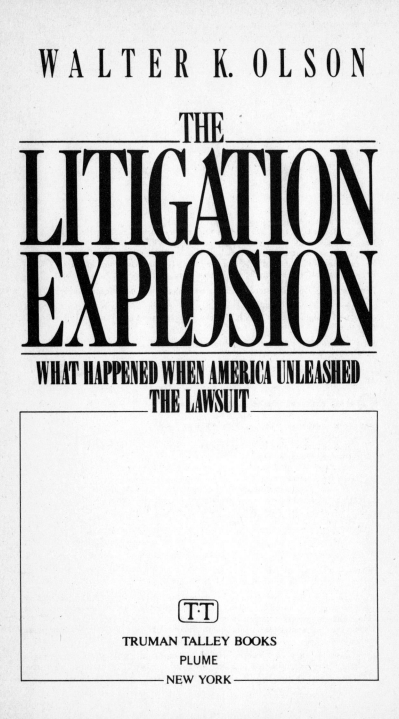

T·T

TRUMAN TALLEY BOOKS

PLUME

NEW YORK

PLUME
Published by the Penguin Group
Penguin Books USA Inc., 375 Hudson Street, New York, New York 10014, U.S.A.
Penguin Books Ltd, 27 Wrights Lane, London W8 5TZ, England
Penguin Books Australia Ltd, Ringwood, Victoria, Australia
Penguin Books Canada Ltd, 10 Alcorn Avenue, Toronto, Ontario, Canada M4V 3B2
Penguin Books (N.Z.) Ltd, 182-190 Wairau Road, Auckland 10, New Zealand

Penguin Books Ltd, Registered Offices: Harmondsworth, Middlesex, England

Published by Truman Talley Books/Plume, an imprint of New American Library, a
division of Penguin Books USA Inc. Previously published in a Truman Talley Books/
Dutton edition.

First Truman Talley Books/Plume Printing, July, 1992
10 9 8 7 6 5 4 3

Ⓟ REGISTERED TRADEMARK—MARCA REGISTRADA

LIBRARY OF CONGRESS CATALOGING-IN-PUBLICATION DATA
Olson, Walter K.
    The litigation explosion / what happened when America unleashed
  the lawsuit / Walter K. Olson.
        p.   cm.
    ISBN 0-452-26824-9
    1. Justice, Administration of—United States.   2. Actions and
  defenses—United States.   3. Frivolous suits (Civil procedure)—
  United States.   4. Legal ethics—United States.   I. Title.
  KF384.O45   1992
  347.73—dc20
  [347.307]   92-4636
                                                           CIP

Printed in the United States of America
Original hardcover design by Steven N. Stathakis

To my parents

CONTENTS

THE LAW

THE CONSEQUENCES

THE WAY OUT

FOREWORD

Why do Americans spend so much time and money fighting each other in court? Why are lawyers in this country so numerous, so powerful, and so widely feared? Is litigiousness somehow part of our national character? Can anything be done—should anything be done—to change matters?

America's litigation explosion was not inevitable, and it can be stopped. This book tells the story of how, in a series of specific changes over decades, we changed the rules in our courtrooms to encourage citizens to sue each other. The trend proceeded gradually over decades and then quite suddenly moved into high gear in the late 1960s and 1970s, amid little real public debate. Taken together, the changes amount to a unique experiment in freeing the legal profession and the litigious impulse from age-old constraints. America has deregulated the business of litigation.

The experiment has been a disaster, an unmitigated failure. The unleashing of litigation in its full fury has done cruel, grave harm and little lasting good. It has helped sunder some of the most sensitive and profound relationships of human life: between the parents who have nurtured a child; between the healing professions and those whose life and well-being are entrusted to their care. It clogs and jams the gears of commerce, sowing friction and distrust between the productive enterprises on which material progress depends and all who buy their products, work at their plants and offices, join in their undertakings. It seizes on former love and intimacy as raw materials to be transmuted into hatred and estrangement. It exploits the bereavement that some day awaits the survivors of us all and turns it to an unending source of poisonous recrimination. It torments the provably innocent and rewards the palpably irresponsible. It devours hard-won savings and worsens every animosity of a diverse society. It is the special American burden, the one feature hardly anyone admires of a society that is otherwise envied the world around.

This disastrous experiment had at its origin a revolution in ideas. America's common law tradition, like the legal tradition of every great nation, formerly viewed a lawsuit as an evil, at best a necessary evil. Older lawmakers and judges tended to recognize litigation as a wasteful thing, in its direct expense and in the demands it placed on the time and energy of people with better things to do. It was grossly invasive of privacy and destructive of reputation. It was acrimonious, furthering resentments between people who might otherwise find occasion to cooperate. It tended to paralyze productive enterprise and the getting on of life in general by keeping rights in a state of suspense. It corrupted its participants by tempting them to harass each other and to twist, stretch, and hide facts. It was a playground for bullies, an uneven battlefield where the trusting, scrupulous, and plainspoken were no match for the brassy, ruthless, and glib. For all that, it was sometimes the least bad of the extremities to which someone might be reduced; but society could at a minimum discourage it where it was not absolutely necessary.

These views shaped the most fundamental features of the old legal system. First and most obvious were the ethical rules set up to control the legal profession itself. Yesterday's lawyers were specifically forbidden to "stir up litigation." Unlike ordinary tradesmen they were expected to sit passively waiting for clients, smothering any entrepreneurial urge they might feel to drum up business; they might sometimes be the instruments of suspicion and contentiousness, but they were not to be its instigators. Social pressure backed up these restraints. So did tough laws.

The rules of legal procedure, until not long ago, provided a second line of defense. Their consistent theme was to narrow and focus a dispute within close limits. It was made hard to drag someone to court without laying out a plausible case against him, and hard to use legal compulsion to pry into his papers and private affairs except for good cause under the watchful scrutiny of a judge. Geographic barriers to litigation were also important: briefly put, a citizen's fundamental liberty included the right not to be sued except in his own court and under the law of the place of his action. The law also kept within tight bounds the supporting evidence litigants could deploy against each other and the tactics they could resort to along the way.

The third line of defense against litigation was the most subtle yet vital of all. It consisted of a certain unmistakable approach to writing and interpreting legal rules. Judges and lawmakers alike took care to spell out clear, definite lines of responsibility. Courts in particular tended to yield to the spirit of private contract—of letting people shape their own legal rights, relationships, and duties. Most collisions could be headed off, it was thought, if people were given (or better yet, could write for themselves) specific marching orders. By following cut-and-dried rules for a sale of land, a hiring, a rental, or a loan, you could be fairly sure that the deal would not end up in court, or at least could know which side would win if it did—which meant it would probably never get there. There were always a few gray areas at any one moment, but normal dealings by their very normality stayed out of court.

The overthrow of the old barriers began with a simple idea. Squinted at from a distance, litigation would appear to have a brighter side. When successful, it brings some benefit ("relief") to the instigator: money, rights to visit a child, the cessation of some local nuisance. So it might be seen as a generous sort of social welfare program, by which people who crave an infusion of money or some less tangible commodity can get it from other people who (perhaps) could well afford to give it up. By the same token, those who get sued and lose must (in a court's view) have done something they oughtn't: broken a promise in business dealings, practiced medicine below a certain standard of care, held on to a child that would be better off in someone else's custody. Maybe litigation is also a tough form of punishment and example-setting, which teaches those who misbehave an emphatic, not-soon-to-be-forgotten lesson.

The idea of treating lawsuits as vessels for "compensation" and "deterrence" is seductive. In no time at all you get to thinking of them less as a personal tragedy and more as a policy opportunity. You begin to imagine that the more people sue, the more will find happiness; while the more people get sued, the more responsibly everyone will behave for fear of sharing the same fate. The more lawsuits there are, in short, the closer to perfect the world will become.

By the 1970s the climate in the law schools had turned around on the subject of litigation, first to ostensible neutrality and then to admiring support. One oft-cited article on legal ethics struck a typical note when it assailed as "distinctly medieval" the view that litigation is "at best a necessary evil" and litigiousness a vice. Lawsuits increasingly came to be described as litigious persons themselves describe them, as assertions of rights—and who could disapprove of asserting rights, or giving everyone his day in court? The process culminated in 1977 with a five-to-four decision by the U.S. Supreme Court officially endorsing the new idea that a lawsuit was no longer to be considered an evil.

That Court opinion was in the nature of a ratification; the wider trend had been in progress for some time. Step by step the old procedural barriers to the litigious instinct had been dismantled. The controls on running litigation as a no-apologies, profit-making industry soon came off as well, since if a product is wholesome and desirable, what better way to get it produced in bulk than by deregulating its providers? America's lawyers began breaking free of the humdrum role of hired middlemen—much as Wall Street's investment banks were doing at around the same time—to become "players" who thought up the deals, or in this case the fights. They began identifying likely grievances and approaching potential clients with the happy news of their lucrative right to accuse someone of wrongdoing. Some took a percentage stake in the outcome, so the size of the deal weighed heavily on their minds. As time went on, many of the increasingly passive clients were reduced to little more than figureheads, as lawyers found ways to litigate more or less openly on their own account.

With each step along the way critics predicted and supporters seldom bothered to deny that more lawsuits would result. And that is exactly what happened. America did not begin litigating more and harder because its population suddenly took it into its head to become more contentious. We got more lawsuits because those who shaped our legal system wanted more lawsuits. The American litigation explosion was no enigmatic Big Bang from out of a void. It had a long, traceable fuse.

Personal injury litigation, long one of the more marginal and ethically problematic areas of legal practice, was first to be transformed. The rags-to-riches story of malpractice lawsuits is by now familiar. New York officials have estimated that payouts in suits against doctors and hospitals in their state have risen 300-fold in a generation—not 300 percent, but 300-fold. By 1990 many New York obstetricians with good records were paying liability insurance rates of $100,000 and more a year, although rates were for the moment in the soft phase of their periodic cycle and the "insurance crisis" was off the front pages. Miami neurosurgeons with good records paid $220,000.

Most malpractice lawsuits have nothing to do with genuine negligence. Preliminary figures from a new and exhaustive study by Harvard researchers indicate that in four out of five lawsuits filed the care given was not in fact negligent. And as the legal firestorm sweeps through the profession patients as a group are being left worse off, not better. A major National Institute of Medicine study found that "defensive medicine"—the taking of steps not considered clinically justified in order to fend off charges that doctors had not done everything they could—had seriously compromised the quality of patient care, leading, for example, to the performance of millions of unnecessary Caesarean sections. The study also found that one in five rural doctors had stopped delivering babies in the past five years, with liability the overwhelming concern.

Other lines of injury litigation have followed a similar growth path. New York City, which self-insures and is thus immune to the vagaries of the liability insurance business, saw its lawsuit payouts soar from $24 million to $114 million between 1977 and 1985, with the size of an average settlement rising from $7,100 to $31,700. The increases were found consistently among various city functions and departments: highways, schools, parks and recreation, hospitals, police, and more.

Lawsuits over allegedly defective products have been another great area of growth for the litigation business, with results equally inimical to the welfare of society. In each manufacturing industry to come under sustained courtroom assault—prescription drugs, vaccines, contraceptives, sport-

ing equipment, small planes, small cars, insulation materials—products that represent a valuable choice over some of
the remaining alternatives have been either driven off the
market or not introduced for fear of liability, with increasingly
tragic results for the public health.

No other country's legal system operates remotely like
ours. The British scholar Patrick Atiyah examined the statistics in a 1987 *Duke Law Journal* article and concluded that
America had almost three times as many lawyers per capita
as Britain, with American tort claims running at least ten times
higher, malpractice claims thirty to forty times higher, and
product claims nearly a hundred times higher, in each case
per capita. One survey found that America spends five times
as much as its major industrial competitors on personal-injury
wrangling as a share of its economy, and that the gap is widening rather than narrowing. The survey concluded that over
the last two generations the cost of injury litigation rose four-
teenfold after inflation, while the size of the real U.S. economy rose threefold.

By now much of this story is familiar. What is striking
and ominous is that the techniques perfected in personal
injury lawsuits are fast being rolled out to a hundred other
areas of courtroom combat. Inflated damage claims and speculative legal theories, scorched-earth procedural tactics and
calculated appeals to emotion over reason, contingency fees
and client solicitation—all are being successfully adapted to
divorces and patent fights, employment suits and securities
cases, will contests and debtor-creditor wrangles. Lawyers
who got their start advertising on late-night television are
moving from car-crash and slip-and-fall cases into commercial
litigation, today's fastest-growing category of litigation and
the category that consistently brings the highest verdicts.

Litigation and its threat have begun to metastasize to
virtually every sector of the economy. Retailers sue manufacturers, franchisees sue franchisers, commercial tenants sue
office and mall developers, and everyone sues accountants.
Litigious borrowers have forced banks to cough up more than

$1 billion under new theories of "lender liability" virtually unknown a few years ago. Corporate dealmaking now routinely winds up in court, a state of affairs which is not inevitable but which dealmakers are coming to accept as if it were. "Originally, I thought British laws [on corporate takeovers] were tougher than [ours] over here," a New York businessman told *The Wall Street Journal*. "But now I think it's easier over in England. It's just a jumble of litigation over here. All you need is a good lawyer and you can tie up somebody's bid for a year."

Lawyering is transforming the American workplace as well. The California courts have lately been trying to quell a surge of more than 100,000 employee suits accusing employers of such offenses as wrongful firing, wrongful failure to promote, and departure from policies spelled out in company employment booklets. The giving of bad references is routinely sued as defamation and on a half-dozen other theories. One survey found California employer-defendants losing 78 percent of the cases that went before juries, at an average verdict of $424,527; a worker fired for refusing a drug test, for example, was awarded $480,000. A second California survey by Rand Corporation researchers found that wrongful-dismissal cases brought an average of $646,000 at trial; a national survey by the Bureau of National Affairs found the average age-discrimination verdict to be $722,000.

Formerly doctors but not many other professionals had to worry about buying insurance against being sued. Now it is a crushing expense for many accountants, nurses, amateur sports umpires, and local charity volunteers. Most hairdressers and veterinarians reportedly buy it. It is the coming thing among social workers, school counselors, and the clergy, who have been sued in much-publicized cases for giving wrongful advice. Lawyers pay dearly for their own coverage, and judges have been added to the list in the wake of rulings that they may now be sued in some circumstances for handing down wrongful decisions. And now, as always, many of the most devastating kinds of legal jeopardy, in family law, real estate law, employment law, and elsewhere, are risks against which people cannot normally insure at all.

It may come as no surprise when the bunglers and ethical edge-skaters in every walk of life, the hell-for-leather drivers, abusive ex-spouses, and chiseling tradespeople, get taken to court. But the rest of us used to imagine that if we took care to know the law and behave ourselves we could stay out of legal trouble. No longer. Honest, careful, competent people now get sued in huge numbers, and lose with some frequency. Between 70 and 80 percent of obstetricians have been sued, as well as, reportedly, every neurosurgeon in Washington, D.C. No degree of care or honesty can "lawyer-proof" the siting of an apartment complex in many cities and towns, or the sale of a radio station anywhere. And for all the talk of no-fault divorce, even marriages between otherwise reasonable people increasingly end in Grand Guignol legal battles.

As the hazards of litigation have multiplied Americans have begun to feel (and often quite rightly) that they dare not enter an important transaction without lining up a lawyer's backing. Which inevitably has given the legal profession a more and more prominent role in the running of the business and medical worlds, academia and public service, entertainment and sports—virtually every walk of American life. The profession's power and influence, if not its share of public affection, have risen apace.

As has its income. In 1989 freshly minted law school graduates were climbing aboard the major New York firms at starting salaries of between $80,000 and $83,000, higher than the average for veterans and novices alike in the much envied securities business. As for lawyers who make it to the top, a 1989 *Forbes* survey found a prosperity that was impressive by any measure. Dozens of corporate lawyers earned million-dollar salaries, putting them ahead of the CEOs of many a large corporation. But that was table sugar compared with the Big Rock Candy Mountain of today's American law: the contingency-fee industry, the business of suing people for a share of the proceeds. At least two dozen elite lawyers of this sort, according to *Forbes*'s estimates, took home $4 million or more apiece in 1988. Houston's Joe Jamail bagged an estimated $450 million, most of that from the famous Texaco/Pennzoil case. Those with mere million-dollar incomes were too numerous to count.

Pots of money like these have a way of attracting young talent. Applications to law schools continue strong, as does the number of lawyers, which in July 1989 stood at 725,574, with 35,000 more joining each year. Lawyers, like good prize fighters, are sometimes said to create each other's demand: as the old saying goes, a town too small to support one can provide a decent living for two and a feast for three. But more likely the great influx of talent into the profession in recent decades has been a response to, rather than the cause of a steady expansion of demand for lawyers' services. Despite the occasional slowdown in one or another specialty, that expansion has continued.

The promise was that the more lawyering went on, the better and fairer life in America would be. The signs are otherwise. As the volume and intensity of their output has risen, our courts, rather than converging with new confidence on important truths, have become more random and inconsistent in their pronouncements. Private and public institutions, as they are sued more and more, become more adversarial and bureaucratic in their workings. As for the bar itself, leaders of the profession lament a sad erosion of ethical standards, a decline in civility and honesty, and a growing incidence of harassment and intimidation.

And the expense is astonishing. Rand Corporation scholars have found that most of the money spent on injury litigation is chewed up in the process, less than half getting through to claimants. Other respected observers, such as Professor Jeffrey O'Connell of the University of Virginia, believe that when all costs are counted only around 15 percent of the cost of injury litigation goes to compensate claimants. For every dollar spent on litigation itself many others are spent up and down the line on negotiations, preventive legal counseling, and other measures short of war.

Litigation's expense and distraction, its acrimony and destruction of privacy, the corruption of its participants, were for a long time derided by partisans of the new legal order as a "parade of horribles." Yet the parade is now marching down Main Street in full regalia. It never had to start, and it can be stopped. Turning around America's legal culture will require the help of persons both within and without our legal system. This book is written primarily for the nonlawyer, and by one.

By now the accumulated force of self-interest and ideology have given America's litigation industry an extraordinary institutional momentum. Legislators have repeatedly come up with sensible plans to reduce litigation, but most of those plans are soon swallowed up, subverted, or knocked on their ends by the immensely raging force of the adversary tumult.

Yet there are some grounds for optimism. A great many judges, lawmakers, and lawyers themselves are fed up and ready for a change. Several promising reforms have been introduced piecemeal in the past few years. By pressing the logic of those reforms, building on them in coming years, we can start to make America's litigators accountable for the hurts they do to those who are drawn involuntarily into their power. We can work toward a law that provides a remedy both to those who are mistreated in the wider society and to those who are mistreated by the workings of the law itself.

The reader in search of hopeful signs will, however, have to be patient in the following pages, while we take a long look at how our law got into its present predicament.

· T H E ·
INDUSTRY

1

⚖

LET'S YOU AND HIM FIGHT

Come to Major Hopkins to get full satisfaction. I win nine-tenths of my cases. If you want to sue, if you have been sued, I am the man to take your case. Embezzlement, highway robbery, felonious assault, arson and horse stealing, don't amount to shucks if you have a good lawyer behind you. My strong point is weeping as I appeal to the jury, and I seldom fail to clear my man. Out of eleven murder cases last year I cleared nine of the murderers. . . . Come early and avoid the rush.

> —*Possibly mythical advertisement of late nineteenth century Arizona lawyer,*
> *quoted in Murray Teigh Bloom,*
> The Trouble with Lawyers

The doctor at a large Long Island hospital was still shaking his head in disbelief. He had just been sued over the delivery of a baby more than twenty years earlier. To be precise, the lawsuit arrived twenty years, ten months, and a few days after the child itself arrived on this planet. Like many obstetrics lawsuits, this one charged that bad handling of the delivery had caused a birth defect. And like many long-delayed suits it was going to be tough to defend, not because the doctor thought he had done anything wrong, but because the facts would be hard to reconstruct after so long. All he had done was assist at the delivery; the doctor who had actually delivered the baby had died years ago. But as usual the lawyers had sued every doctor in the file.

How people decide to become litigants is not a matter of public record, but it is very unlikely that the family that filed this lawsuit sat around thinking of suing for two decades before finally making up its mind. By 1990 litigation over birth defects had emerged as a source of immensely profitable business for trial lawyers. Some of those lawyers had responded by learning one of the classic techniques of the expansion-minded business: the cold call. They got access to registries of handicapped children, approached the families, and warned that the statute of limitations (a long one where children are concerned) would soon expire. And they proposed filing a lawsuit.

For a long time in America, down through the 1970s, it was thought that lawyers should not drum up their own business. They were not to volunteer their services even to someone who had definitely resolved to hire a lawyer. Much less could they approach him to make the case for hiring one. Nor could they engage in promotion or public relations, however restrained and dignified, to market their particular brand of services. Occasional experience with lawyer advertising in nineteenth-century America had served to confirm the general feeling. Through most of this century American lawyers could not advertise at all. Similar rules were and are found in other nations.

Like many ethical rules, this one was widely if covertly evaded. The socialite whose marital problems figured in the gossip columns might open the mail to find the business card of an enterprising divorce lawyer. The department store, having lost the deadbeat customer's trail, might get a quiet call from a collection lawyer in a far-off city suggesting he could be of use.

The most colorful and outrageous ethical violations were

always those of the personal injury lawyers. Most big cities could boast a rowdy underworld of paid "runners" who hustled accident business. Some sprinted to the scene of a calamity to press a card into the hand of the dazed victim. Others cultivated cops, reporters, or attending nurses who, mindful of the occasional gratuity, would sing the lawyer's praises or get him into the recovery room for a direct pitch.

The lawyer who drummed up business in this way could actually be sent to jail. "Ambulance chasing," as the papers always seemed to call it, had been punishable by jail terms since the early days of the common law, and prosecutors launched periodic crackdowns with what now seems ferocious zeal. Thomas Dewey, in his days as a crusading district attorney in Manhattan, helped put fourteen members of one such "ring" (to use the papers' word again) behind bars; the prescribed sentence in New York was one to three years. As late as 1954 Gotham authorities broke up a circle of eighteen lawyers and nine accomplices operating with "all of the efficiency of a supermarket."

Injury lawyers were not the only ones punished with severity for chasing business. In the early 1930s a Los Angeles lawyer took out newspaper ads inviting readers to send away for a leaflet on what were then the distinctively liberal divorce laws of Mexico and Nevada. Bar officials promptly tracked him down and suspended him from practice for a year; when he continued his activities unrepentant, they got the California Supreme Court to disbar him. (Under California law, which was typical, it was illegal to offer help in procuring a divorce, even if the offerer was not a lawyer and no money changed hands.) In a 1954 Kentucky case, the errant lawyer was disciplined for combing through court records to find unsatisfied judgments that he then volunteered to collect.

The clean-up campaigns were always temporary. The profits in solicitation were too tempting to be ignored for long, and when it worked as intended no one complained. Many doubted for that reason that it would ever be suppressed entirely, but that it was reprehensible nearly everyone agreed.

Henry Drinker's standard 1953 treatise on legal ethics noted in passing that "ambulance chasing" was "so well-known and so obviously improper as to require no extensive comment."

Occasionally, however, an outspoken accident lawyer or maverick law professor would question the ban on solicitation. Their arguments ran somewhat as follows.

The ethical lawyer was supposed to sit back passively and wait for clients to come around. All well and good once a practice was established; but what about the fledgling lawyer, the immigrant who had struggled through night courses? Once he had exhausted the legal needs of his friends and relatives by drawing up a few wills and leases, was he to starve?

It was all too easy, the argument ran, for the leaders of the bar to dispense their timeless wisdom. These WASPy eminences (Drinker himself was one of the famous Philadelphia family of that name) mingled constantly with potential clients in the boardroom and on the golf course. They kept their names in circulation by leading charity drives, running for public office, serving on prestigious committees. Behind the easy disdain for hucksterism, it was hinted, was the complacency of an elite who had already promoted their careers successfully and didn't want their client lists raided.

And what of the clients themselves? Of those who knew they wanted legal help, some went back to a lawyer they had used for years because they didn't know any better. Others chose the first name that seemed familiar from the phone book, or picked one entirely at random. Too often, it was said, they wound up with some sleepy, high-priced practitioner when a hungry newcomer might have handled the same work with more skill, vigor, or economy.

Many others never hired a lawyer at all. Some of these naive nonclients were badly wronged for want of competent advice. While the lawyer waited in vain, barred by an antiquated code from making the first advance, they were signing the grossly lopsided business deal, taking the insurance adjuster's low-ball offer, accepting the dangerous reconciliation with the hot-tempered spouse.

This critique was heard sporadically over the years, but it did not kick into high gear until the 1970s. It was helped along by a shift in the way American opinion makers came to view advertising and its allied promotional arts. Earlier popular writers like Vance Packard and John Kenneth Galbraith had made much of the idea that advertising pandered to the weaker side of human nature, luring consumers to buy on impulse things they might be better off without, or even "creating" wants among the gullible. Besides, didn't the price of products have to be kept high to cover the cost of ad campaigns? Now a different and on the whole more sophisticated school of thought came to the fore, especially among economists. The new thinking emphasized the benefits rather than the dangers of sales promotion. Advertising teaches novice buyers what goods are available on the market and how they can best be used. It spurs comparison shopping, putting extra pressure on sellers to provide what consumers want or lose business. Mass marketing paves the way for mass production, with its enormous economies of scale. On the whole, paradoxical as it may seem, ad spending probably lowers product prices more often than it raises them.

A series of real-world studies strikingly confirmed the central insight. Several learned professions had historically forbidden advertising by their members but were forced to lift those rules in the 1970s under government pressure and court order. When opticians, optometrists, and druggists began taking to the airwaves and the local newspapers, the cost of eyeglasses, eye exams, and prescription medicines dropped almost at once. All indications were that customers were delighted with the new state of things. Symbolizing the turnaround in reformist opinion, the Federal Trade Commission, known as a scourge of Madison Avenue, led the way in agitating for the lifting of professional ad bans.

The coming of advertising had boosted consumer demand for eyeglasses and the like, and no one doubted it would do the same for lawyers. "How much new legal business this would generate is something perhaps incalculable, but there is little question that it would be considerable," said one typical commentator in the *A.B.A. Journal.* "In fact, legal business might increase by geometric proportions." Many favored the change for exactly this reason. A writer in *Barrister* saw an "absolute and compelling need to increase the demand for legal services," in part because large numbers of newly trained lawyers would have to be absorbed.

More plentiful eyeglasses and eye exams, most of us will agree, are an unmixed blessing. More plentiful prescription medicines are not quite so easy a case; most will benefit, but some people take more pills than is good for them, and making cheap drugs available with less fuss will pull a few over the line to abuse and addiction. But what happens when society gets more "legal services"? How many of the newly recruited clients will be better off? And is society's interest the same as theirs?

Few of the reformers of professional advertising gave these questions much thought. Most tended to lump the lawyers in with the optometrists and the rest. As for the organized bar, although it resisted advertising stoutly, it was singularly unsuccessful at reaching the public with its case, perhaps because it was squeamish about explaining why not all lawyering might be worth promoting. Instead it fell back on the plea that advertising would be a mortal blow to the profession's dignity. One despairing member of a District of Columbia ethics panel foresaw a proliferation of neon signs, balloons, and catchy jingles. Others warned that price-cutting operators would stick foolish customers with shoddy bills of sale, ineptly drafted prenuptial agreements, and half-baked secured transactions.

These were the very arguments least likely to convince the general public. Hopes had been raised that advertising would help cut lawyers' fees by unleashing competition within their ranks. Most customers were willing to brave whatever dangers there might be in fee-cutting. As for saving face for the bar, arguments from lawyers' professional dignity tend in this country (unfair as it may be) to raise a hoot from nonlawyers.

As antitrust enforcers started making menacing noises, the organized bar began to back off its longstanding ethical tenets, as other professions had done before it. In February 1976, amid signs of utmost reluctance, the American Bar Association relaxed the ethical canon that had forbidden its members to advertise. The grass roots continued resistant, however, and not one state bar saw fit to do away with the major bans. Then came two sudden strokes that finished off the debate before it had really begun.

In May 1976 the U.S. Supreme Court threw out a Virginia ban on advertising by druggists. This time it announced, momentously, that the ad ban had violated not just the antitrust laws—which would have left the issue open to compromise and adjustment in Congress—but the Constitution's First Amendment guarantee of free speech. The next year, in 1977, came the utter downfall of the old order.

The Phoenix law firm of Bates and O'Steen was trying to carve out a niche serving clients of modest means. It took an ad in the *Arizona Republic* listing its fees, which were reasonable enough, for four kinds of routine legal work: uncontested divorces and adoptions, name changes, and bankruptcies with "no contested proceedings." The state bar tried to discipline the firm, it resisted, and the case made its way up to the high court. Justice Harry Blackmun, writing for the barest five-to-four Court majority, declared that the Constitution protects lawyers' right to advertise the availability and price of legal services, at least those that are routine.

Overnight, the most drastic sort of change came over America's legal profession. On June 26, 1977, in every state of the union, lawyer advertising was kept under close wraps if not banned altogether. On June 27, from Kiska to Key West, no combination of public discomfort and peer opposition could stop it. Because lawyers' newly discovered right to advertise was found to be lodged in the Constitution, it could not practicably be revised (short of a change of heart on the Court) no matter what lessons experience might turn out to hold.

Many states and bar associations have sought to control the form and content of lawyers' ads, usually by curbing techniques thought to pack a greater emotional punch. Some have tried to confine ads to print rather than broadcast media, forbid the use of dramatizations reenacting the heartbreak of the sports injury or birth defect, or ban testimonials from celebrities or from the happy customer for whom the lawyer won a gigantic settlement. Again and again these rules have been withdrawn under antitrust pressure, struck down by courts, ignored in practice, or simply let drop. Nothing came of the *Bates* opinion's suggestion that advertising might be restricted for services that were not "routine."

Within a decade, late-night TV was keeping up a steady drumbeat of messages that with but a little reading between the lines invited one and all to dump their hubbies, stiff their creditors, and take their bosses to the cleaners. "Tony Patterson received $50,000 for his auto accident. His attorney: James Sokolove" runs one Boston ad. Other spots by the same attorney have featured crutches and an empty bassinet. An attractive young woman in a New York ad, her voice sinking to breathy Marlene Dietrich tones, confides that the lawyers being touted had procured for her a "sub*stan*tial cash settlement." Many ads stoke feelings of moral righteousness. "Tired of being pushed around?" asks a Phoenix ad. "We think people should pay their debts," reads a New York subway ad for lawyers who go after ex-husbands for child support payments.

These methods work. Boston's Sokolove, he of the empty bassinet, is a former VISTA lawyer in his early forties who started an injury practice from scratch. Within five years, backed by a monster $1.1 million annual marketing push, he made himself into the leading handler of medical-malpractice claims in New England, according to a *Wall Street Journal* report. He was reported to be fielding four hundred new calls a week, with his practice growing at a rate of 25 percent a year. According to the report, Sokolove farms out much of his nineteen-hundred-case inventory to other lawyers for actual representation in exchange for a share of the winnings.

Not surprisingly, other lawyers feel strong competitive pressure to get on the promotional bandwagon. Television ad spending by lawyers jumped 29 percent in 1989 to $82 million, after rising at a 40 percent annual clip through the 1980s. The biggst area of growth was personal-injury litigation. The Sunday Los Angeles *Times* has reportedly run close to a full page at a time of ads inviting people to, in sample wordings, "sue for money and benefits" if they have job-related "headaches, stomach aches, or poor sleep" or are "injured or harassed at work."

In 1985 the high court was asked the next, inevitable question: if lawyers could advertise for particular kinds of cases, could they solicit cases against a particular defendant?

Some lawyers had long made a de facto specialty of suing particular opponents. If there is only one big railroad or sawmill in town, it is not hard to predict who will have to respond to the filings of the local labor lawyer. But for lawyers to go around openly trying to drum up litigation against a particular opponent—against IBM, or the Roman Catholic church, or the NAACP—caused some queasiness. Grudge matches could be at best poorly policed through a separate set of rules against malicious litigation. And the targets themselves could get the same unsettling feeling as a small city when it learns that halfway across the world there is a ballistic missile with its name on it.

The case of *Zauderer* v. *Office of Disciplinary Counsel*, like so many landmark cases, presented the facts in a seemingly sympathetic light. The ad in question had solicited claims arising from the Dalkon Shield, manufactured by perhaps the world's most hated corporation, the A. H. Robins Company. The injury claims over the Shield had already been widely publicized, and Ohio lawyer Philip Zauderer could have recruited many of the same claims by wording the ad a bit more generally. When he won, however, the precedent made it clear that henceforth lawyers could recruit "specific legal business" against any sort of institutions, good, bad, or otherwise.

By now the advance scouts of the plaintiff's bar had the big target in their cross sights. Their next, ineluctable question was: if opponents can be selected one by one, why not clients? If it is all right to advertise to a million readers, why not to just one—in brief, to solicit business in a direct instead of roundabout manner? Why not, after all, let the lawyer hightail it along behind the speeding paramedic's vehicle, or slip into the hospital room afterward?

The solicitation of individual clients, in the old system, had been the arch-offense of the catalogue, much worse than advertising in general because it so directly stirred up claims. But the logic of the line of decisions was now carrying all before it. Back in 1978 the Supreme Court had ruled that solicitation with a primarily "political or ideological" motive could not be banned. Other victories followed, culminating in a ruling ten years later that lawyers have a right to send targeted letters to solicit the business of persons known to have legal interests that could be exercised.

The major taboo that remained was in-person solicitation, the actual uninvited visit to the hospital room, and there was a good deal of doubt as to how long that would last. Or whether it could be any longer enforced. From ferryboat sinkings to mine cave-ins, every disaster around the country and indeed the world seemed to be followed within hours by a raven-like descent of American tort lawyers boldly stalking the airport lounges and hotel lobbies where flown-in relatives waited for news of survivors. After a 1987 Northwest crash in Detroit, one enterprising runner reportedly dressed as a priest to mingle among grieving families. Others posed as Red Cross workers after a store roof collapsed in south Texas, helping dig out victims and sign them up.

Lawyers began descending on the Alaskan town of Valdez even before the oil from the 1989 Exxon spill had hit the beach, in what was quickly dubbed "tanker-chasing." An account by *Wall Street Journal* reporters Charles McCoy and Ken Wells caught the flavor: "Liability lawyers and prostitutes fresh from nearby Anchorage are said to prowl the dark, smoky bars in search of clients. Townspeople aren't as concerned about the prostitutes as they are about the lawyers. Sue Laird, a salmon fisherman from nearby Cordova, says she got twenty calls from lawyers within hours of the disaster. 'They are like cannibals. They bite into you and they don't let go.' "

Even the injury lawyers' lobby, the Association of Trial Lawyers of America, was embarrassed enough to throw together a code of conduct for accident scenes; whether it has had much effect is another question. But if some lawyers have shown signs of a bad conscience, others are boastful and strutting. Prominent tortster John Coale, arriving in Bhopal after the lethal gas leak of December 1984—on the same plane with Mother Teresa, no less—was asked whether some might not see him as an ambulance chaser. "I don't care what they say," was his reply as quoted by the *Washington Post*. (Coale later disavowed it.) "If I come in from the airport and two days later have seven thousand clients, that's the greatest ambulance chase in history."

Like other savvy publicists, lawyers also learned ways of getting "free media." The old ethical code had frowned on contacts with the press except in a fairly narrow range of circumstances, mostly involving comments on behalf of particular clients who needed their affairs explained to the public. As recently as the 1960s, when Martin Mayer was writing his classic survey *The Lawyers*, he kept finding that attorneys refused to talk about their exploits for fear of Canon 27 of the A.B.A.'s ethics code, which had been interpreted to forbid such things as "furnishing or inspiring newspaper comments" or "acquiesc[ing] in the publication by a magazine of a laudatory history of the firm."

Now the full arsenal of public relations tactics could be

deployed. New York City injury czar Harry Lipsig, according to a *Wall Street Journal* account, sends reporters gifts of Chivas Regal and keeps two publicists for his firm. Even such conservative firms as Sullivan & Cromwell and Willkie Farr & Gallagher have hired publicity advisers. "P. R. firms came out of the woodwork" when *Business Week* reporter Paula Dwyer was doing a piece on patent and copyright litigation: she talked to nearly a dozen firms in all.

One thing journalists soon learned was that no one is a better source of negative tidbits about an institution than the lawyers who make a habit of suing it. Sometimes the incitement to litigate in the resulting articles is subtle, the lawyer remaining in the background without being quoted by name. And sometimes it is quite blatant. "Burned by broker? Lawyer: Fight! Fight! Fight!" was the *USA Today* headline over a Dan Dorfman column about a pugnacious New York lawyer who urged investors to file claims against Wall Street firms in the wake of Black Monday. "Don't be a sap," the lawyer told readers. "If you've got something to fight about, do it."

On an infinitely more dignified level, hundreds of law firms have hired marketing directors to coach practicing lawyers on how, as part of their interaction with a client, they can subtly make a pitch for him to give the firm more business. "In general, I tell them not to think of it as selling, think of it as meeting someone's needs and solving their problems," said Cathy Petryshyn, who handles marketing for a Cleveland law firm.

Others took a more gregarious tack, hanging around Parents Without Partners meetings to find likely family law litigants, or organizing clubs to promote fathers' or grandparents' rights. Some set up groups of pitifully disabled injury claimants to make an emotionally gripping case for more draconian liability laws and, not incidentally, field calls from the newly aggrieved. Official-sounding disease associations were launched to publicize suitworthy illnesses and steer call-ins to lawyers. Two industrious operators sent out vans with x-ray machines to park in front of factories and union halls and diagnose workers with asbestos-related dysfunction. A University of California researcher found later that the diagnoses contained "an outstanding number of errors," but the campaign helped triple the number of asbestos lawsuits filed in 1987 from the previous year.

Direct-mail solicitation was soon brought to a high pitch of efficiency. "You may be in danger of death" was one attention-getting line in a Detroit lawyer's mass mailing to merchant seamen who might or might not have been exposed to high concentrations of shipboard asbestos; the letter told of damage awards "in the six- to seven-figure range." Like the mobile-clinic campaign, this one pulled in new litigants by the thousand. Houston criminal-defense lawyers have pitched their services to mailing lists of the newly indicted.

The fall of the old rules was widely hailed as a victory for the public welfare over the organized bar's crass self-interest and pompous concern for its dignity. Mysteriously, however, the profession began to prosper mightily after the self-interested rules came off, and to become vastly more powerful and widely feared after suffering this blow to its dignity.

The truth is that the old rules had not been meant merely to preserve the bar's dignity or suppress competition within its ranks. They were aimed at evils of broad public concern. Filing and threatening to file lawsuits—to name two things lawyers do—were not activities that an earlier society was at all eager to deregulate. Although "extensive advertising would doubtless increase litigation," Drinker declared, "this has always been considered as against public policy." Blackstone was more pungent, warning in his *Commentaries* about the "pests of civil society, that are perpetually endeavoring to disturb the repose of their neighbors, and officiously interfering in other men's quarrels."

Over many ages the solicitation ban had been enforced not just through private arm-twisting and associational discipline, but by stringent prosecutions amid signs of widespread public support. And few if any of those prosecutions

were aimed at the "poacher" who lured active clients away
from a fellow lawyer. The heavy enforcement was instead
directed at the "ambulance chaser" who expanded the uni-
verse of legal customers and thus actually created new business for other lawyers. This made no sense as a way of
protecting elite lawyers from competition. It made perfect
sense as a way of protecting society from aggressive lawyering.

Of course lawsuits are not lawyers' only products. Much
lawyering, maybe most of it, can be seen as preventive, nonadversarial, or defensive. Viewed in the most favorable light,
this activity need not contribute to the ambient level of conflict, tension and strife.

Nonadversarial proceedings, such as adoptions, are often
conceived of as benefiting all sides. Preventive lawyering—
tax planning, contract negotiation, document drafting—can
help keep people out of court by preventing missteps or mis-
understandings that might have led to later squabbling. And
it might seem that a lawyer does not stir up any new kind of
trouble when he offers to defend someone from serious legal
charges; the target commonly wants legal advice, and the main
question is where he will get it.

The early cases that shattered the old ethical code
aroused public sympathy because they involved services of
these descriptions. Bates and O'Steen, in their Arizona *Republic* ad, offered to perform name changes, adoptions, un-
opposed divorces, and bankruptcies with "no contested
proceedings." Another of the early antitrust challenges was
to fixed fees for title searches, a standard preventive procedure
whose usual outcome is to confirm expectations and increase
confidence on all sides.

Truth to tell, few lawyerly services are entirely free from
at least a slight tincture of adversarialism and assertiveness.
Hiring a lawyer to help negotiate a contract can improve its
clarity and completeness, or it can lead to a cycle of new
demands and suspicions that cause the transaction to fall apart.
(The Japanese reportedly consider it a hostile act to bring a
lawyer to a business meeting.) Cooperative or preventive

transactions can easily turn into something else if lawyers take a strongly adversarial approach, urging clients constantly to stick up for their rights. Thus also can uncontested divorces or bankruptcies turn into contested ones, and the defense of arrestees into the filing of "excessive-force" suits against arresting officers.

Even the most peaceful preventive specialties, like corporate and tax law, can shade gently from letting clients know how to obey the law to letting them know what they can get away with. "I'm a poor speaker," said Mr. Dooley's lawyer. "But if iver ye want to do something that ye think ye oughtn't to do, come around to me an' I'll show ye how to do it." By requiring people to exert some initiative to arm themselves with the law's weaponry, we improve the chances that they will act from settled conviction and for reasons of some weight.

Still, some routine types of uncontested lawyering—will drafting, title searches, adoptions—are innocuous enough that advertising might seem to promise some good and little mischief. A number of commentators in the years before the *Bates* decision suggested drawing such a line, allowing advertising of some services but not others. The writer in *Barrister*, who endorsed advertising in principle, said, "Regulation should prohibit practices that would encourage unnecessary lawsuits."

But the Supreme Court majority showed no interest in doing any such thing. Justice Blackmun's opinion deplored the "underutilization" of lawyers' services. Lest anyone imagine that by this he meant only nonadversarial services, his first point, in a passage about how advertising could "offer great benefits," was that it "might increase the use of the judicial machinery." And in a footnote he tied it all together by noting that the Court's emerging approach would be hard to understand "if a lawsuit were somehow viewed as an evil in itself." Justice Byron White, in the 1985 Zauderer case, struck the same note: "We cannot endorse the proposition that a lawsuit, as such, is an evil."

The Court, in other words, had endorsed the emergent legal ideology of the era. That ideology encourages each citizen to be fully educated about, the better to seek complete vindication of, his set of legally defined interests. "Will such a position, if implemented, stir up litigation?" asked the writer Jethro Lieberman in a discussion of solicitation. "Of course. . . . But what of it?"

The *Bates* opinion relied on a newly developed theory that the First Amendment's guarantee of free speech protects advertising as "commercial speech." Some imagined this new idea would be applied in an across-the-board, evenhanded way to protect all truthful advertising in the commercial marketplace. No such luck. The Court has shown very little interest in using the doctrine to protect ordinary businesses that advertise. In 1987 it announced that Puerto Rico, where casino gambling is legal, could after all ban casino ads in hopes of protecting citizens from their presumed corrupting influence. (Cigarette ads, it was widely predicted, would be next on the okay-to-ban list.) The Court knew good advertising from bad when it saw it. And whereas advertising for slots might well be bad, advertising for suits was surely good.

Some consistent libertarian thinkers have argued from principle that government in a free society should never keep private parties from advertising a product or service that it is lawful to sell, whether it be cigarettes, political candidacies, or mood-altering prescription medicines. Even on that view, the real question is whether lawyers as a class that is delegated certain quasi-governmental powers to initiate compulsory process might not be asked in exchange to follow certain rules to prevent its overuse. At any rate, some of the results of lawyers' advertising have been wholesome enough: it is nice that the home buyer can shop around for a title search and that the born procrastinator can learn where a will may be drawn up.

Perhaps society can learn to live with the demise of the formal restraints on legal solicitation. Not so easy to live with is the collapse of the underlying principle. Had strong disapproval been leveled at the lawyer who fomented litigation, had newspapers indignantly rejected his ads and law school professors held him up to the scorn of their young charges, the disappearance of the old legal sanctions might have been of incremental rather than drastic significance. As one set of floodgates opened, some of the earthworks downstream might have been bolstered to hold off any litigious inundation.

Just the opposite happened. On the matter of promotion, the American legal profession did not just relax its old ethical strictures, which would be a common enough sort of thing, but stood them on their head. Down through the mid-1960s the A.B.A.'s ethical canon number 28, against "stirring up litigation," was still very much intact. Within a few years many had come to see stirring up litigation as an inspiring public service, in fact morally obligatory. By 1975 one of the most quoted of the newer legal ethicists, Monroe Freedman, could write provocatively but in all seriousness of a "professional responsibility to chase ambulances."

The train had pulled into reverse; litigation had become a goal to be sought rather than a danger to be fled. And so the chasers had become the vanguard.

2

⚖

A PIECE OF THE ACTION:
The Triumph of the Contingency Fee

Karen Michaels: You'd do all that . . . just for a part in a play?
Eve Harrington: I'd do much more, for a part that good.

—All About Eve *(Twentieth-Century Fox, 1950)*

For years the New York City firm of Morris Eisen P.C. ran one of the nation's biggest personal injury law practices, employing fifty lawyers and handling hundreds of cases at a time. Like all big law firms that specialize in injury lawsuits, it worked on contingency—keeping a share of its clients' winnings, if any ("no fee unless successful").

It all came undone in 1990 when a federal grand jury indicted Eisen and seven persons associated with his firm on charges that included bribing witnesses and court personnel, suborning false expert testimony, doctoring photographs, and manufacturing other physical evidence. Among those charged along with Eisen were two lawyers, a former office manager, and four private investigators who worked regularly with his firm.

U.S. Attorney Andrew Maloney of the Eastern District

of New York detailed the charges. "They produced an eye-witness to two automobile accidents," he said. "The witness was never at either accident and, at the time of one accident, he was serving time on a forgery charge." In another case, where one of Eisen's employees claimed to have tripped at a racetrack parking lot, Maloney said one of the suspects used a pickax to widen a pothole so it could be blamed for the supposed incident. Two of the group were charged with causing a witness to give false testimony in another lawsuit where an injured woman claimed that a bus driver had signaled for her to cross the street into traffic; New York City settled that case for $1 million. Altogether the nineteen lawsuits where wrongdoing was alleged had brought in $9 million in awards and settlements, of which the lawyers had pocketed an estimated third as contingency fees, along with some additional sum to cover their reported expenses.

Around the rest of the country a wave of similar scandals was breaking. A front-page series in the *Miami Herald* told how a North Miami legal practice had conspired to manufacture and exaggerate injury claims. Florida prosecutors followed with a thirty-two-count indictment of three lawyers, two doctors, and three others. A federal indictment charged two New Jersey lawyers and a doctor with fifty-eight counts in an alleged scheme of massive fraud in auto-accident claims.

One reason lawyering has always been treated as something of a special line of work is that lawyers come under such intense and varied ethical pressures. They face countless temptations to exploit opponents and clients alike. Huge amounts of money can hang on the choices they make when no one is looking over their shoulder. Few occupations offer such chances for dishonest persons to become very rich.

A job that offers enormous returns to unscrupulousness will attract many unscrupulous persons and corrupt many persons of ordinary character. Most of the possible ways to sort out the bad apples are not very promising.

Criminal prosecution, disbarment, and other heavy-duty disciplinary measures can help in the few cases where abuses can be brought to light and proved conclusively. In practice only a few relatively flagrant cases of lawyer misconduct (mostly embezzlement of client funds and the like) are caught and corrected in this way. Advance screening of bar applicants for "good character" is a subjective affair that can imperil the merely unpopular applicant along with the shady one; it has fallen largely into disuse. Civil lawsuits against lawyers, as we shall see later, provide occasional recourse for victimized clients but next to none for victimized opponents.

Finally there is the idea of reducing the temptations for dishonesty within the practice of law itself.

The ethical rules of many professions share a common underlying principle: if temptations are allowed to get out of hand, many will yield. To put it in raw dollar terms, if under system A people can grab a thousand dollars by telling a lie, and under system B they can grab a million by telling the same lie, more people—not all, but more—will tell the lie under system B. No system could block all chances to profit from lying, cheating, and corner-cutting; that would be hopelessly utopian. What a practical system of ethics can do is fence off the steepest and most slippery slopes, lowering the rewards for dishonesty not to zero but to a point where most people can be trained in the habit of resisting.

One ethical rule commonly found in professional sports forbids athletes to bet on their games. There are obvious reasons for not letting them bet against their own teams. The reasons for not letting them bet in favor are in the end no less compelling. Some athlete-gamblers would throw their strength into certain contests at the expense of the season as a whole. More generally, kneeing and below-the-belt gouging of opponents would run wild: badminton would soon get as mean as hockey, and who can think what hockey itself would be like?

Likewise doctors have never been allowed to charge contingency fees—in effect to place bets with their patients on the success of their therapies. Under a system of medical contingency fees, doctors would dispense with their fees if a patient remained sick. If he rallied, they would charge higher-than-usual fees. And if he got well enough to go back to work, they might even arrange to take a share of his future earnings, to reflect the value of their efforts.

Why would this be unethical? One reason is that it would open up so many temptations for doctors to depart from honesty. Under such a fee arrangement some doctors would portray transient maladies, best treated by doing nothing, as life-threatening to scare patients into promising a whopping contingency. Some would cure an illness with harsh remedies that left the body vulnerable to worse assaults later on. Some would allow patients who were still sick to believe they were cured, perhaps administering feel-good potions toward that end, although their best judgment would otherwise be to recommend drastic measures to stave off an imminent relapse. Falsification of test results, bedside charts, and autopsy findings would go on constantly. Even doctors of ordinary integrity would feel their objectivity subtly disoriented, and the truly unscrupulous would find chances to become very rich indeed. Observing this, more unscrupulous persons would enter the medical profession instead of other lines of work.

And so the custom arose of paying doctors by the hour, as work went along, whether their patients recovered miraculously, feebly, or not at all. By achieving a surprise cure a doctor might hope to get valuable word-of-mouth and repeat business. But that is the difference between more and some, not between feast and famine. Many of the subsidiary rules of medical ethics, such as the separation of medicine from pharmacy, follow similar lines. By shielding doctors from a sharp financial interest in drug dispensing, we avoid clouding their decision whether to prescribe or withhold drugs in borderline cases.

The ethical rules of the medical profession, however, carry some very real costs. Medical contingency fees would offer at least two enormous advantages over the familiar hourly-fee way of paying doctors. One would be to spur productivity. The evidence from every other line of work is overwhelming: when people are exposed to very sharp incentives, when their compensation is tied directly to their results, they really hustle. Salesmen who get paid on commission scramble to set volume records, while those on straight salary are taking long coffee breaks and chatting with friends. Garment workers paid for piecework far outperform those paid by the hour. Most doctors already work hard, but they would set an even more impressive pace were their paychecks tied directly to the medical outcomes of the cases they handled. Of the extra cures they provided, not all would be fake; many would be real.

The second advantage might appear even more tempting in an age that places a high value on equality. Medical contingency fees might seem the ideal way to bring medicine within the reach of persons short on ready cash. It is just the person who stays sick, after all, who most needs to have his doctor's bill forgiven. And it is just the one who gets well enough to go back to work who can best afford to pay a larger or proportional fee. Many patients would be glad to accept that deal. Some would propose it themselves. The doctor's contingency fee, if allowed to spread, might also relieve the medical profession and society at large of a good part of the burden of providing care on a charitable basis to poorer persons. No doubt it would soon come to be extolled as the "key to the hospital" for the working man.

These are not advantages to be laughed at. Ethics rules are not free, and we give up some real benefits, as well as some illusory ones, as the price of keeping doctors (more) honest. The medical profession itself gives up what would probably be a ticket to vastly greater wealth and influence; under a contingency-fee system many doctors would become instant millionaires just by finding the right patient to treat at the right time.

In virtually every other country in the world, the case of lawyers is seen as very much like the case of doctors. The near-universal view is that neither clients nor (especially) opponents are very good at looking out for themselves; that no direct means of policing lawyers' misconduct is likely to be even halfway effective; and that the first line of ethical defense for lawyers is therefore to insulate them from a direct stake in the outcomes of their fights. The tradition of the English common law, the French and German civil law, and the Roman law all agree that it is unethical for lawyers to accept contingency fees. In 1975 British judges strenuously opposed even a closely regulated version of the fee, in which a contingency suit could go forward so long as leading lawyers verified its reasonableness. They explained that lawyers would no longer make their cases "with scrupulous fairness and integrity."

Why is America the glaring exception? What has emboldened our lawyers to accept this sort of fee?

The American exception on contingency fees seems to have developed naturally and inevitably from a wider and more profound American exception on legal fees in general, an exception that is central to understanding the problems of our legal system. America is the only major country that denies to the winner of a lawsuit the right to collect legal fees from the loser. In other countries, the promise of a fee recoupment from the opponent gives lawyers good reason to take on a solidly meritorious case for even a poor client. Oxford's Patrick Atiyah notes that "the reality is that the accident victim with a reasonable case should be able to find a lawyer with equal ease in England and America." The obvious result of not allowing recoupment is that clients must find some other way to compensate their lawyers. Unless the client has independent sources of cash, the only place for the fee to come from is out of the recovery itself.

At first much of America tried a not-very-promising substitute for the contingency fee: volunteer legal service. Lawyers were supposed to make a reasonable effort to handle a poor person's claim for free when it appeared meritorious. When a suit of this sort was a money claim and it succeeded, the now not so penniless client might offer the lawyer a grateful recompense but was not obliged to do so. The system was supposed to work on two-way altruism, first from the lawyer, then from the beneficiary.

Systems that depend too heavily on pure altruism to work do not tend to chug along forever. Without a legal right to recover fees in case of victory lawyers did not donate enough time to these *pro bono publico* cases, and some meritorious claims slipped through the cracks. The straightforward solution of shifting fees to the losers of lawsuits was obstinately resisted. So, amid misgivings and reluctance, the contingency fee was admitted state by state; Maine was the last state to legalize it, in the 1960s.

Restrictions hedged in the use of the fee, confining it to the necessary cases. The arrangement was to be discouraged unless a client was too poor to pay the normal freight. Crucially, lawyers could represent only plaintiffs on this basis, and never *defendants*, either civil or criminal. And although contingencies were permitted for most money claims, they were disallowed in many other kinds of lawsuits, divorces in particular.

A further web of swaddling rules protected lawyers from dealings by which, purposely or not, they might end up obtaining stakes in the cases they pressed. They could not buy up a promissory note to collect at a profit, or buy businesses or parcels of land to which lawsuits attached unless their primary aim were to acquire the property rather than the incidental share of its value represented by legal claims. They could not give money to their clients for free for fear of the appearance that they were paying to keep a lawsuit alive (which, as the offense of "maintenance," was punishable at common law by imprisonment). In fact, to avoid pitfalls of this nature, they were advised not to enter into business dealings with their clients at all.

The older American legal ethicists emphasized the need

for vigilance against the special corrupting dangers of the contingency fee. Lawyers were to recognize that taking a share in the spoils subjected them to a sort of moral vertigo that should be shunned when not necessary and handled with tightrope care where it was. They would have to cultivate a special humility and detachment when they worked on this basis, trying harder than other lawyers to remember that winning wasn't everything, struggling to forget that victory in the case at hand might bring personal riches or that loss might come as a financial blow. In short, the system was asked to run on a new kind of altruism, the self-restraint of lawyers with fortunes at stake.

Just as salesmen paid on commission step forward and make eye contact when the customer walks into the store, so contingency-fee lawyers have a strong incentive to get clients interested in the merchandise. And sales pick up. The standard American text on legal ethics, by Judge George Sharswood of Pennsylvania, said the fee gave "an undue encouragement to litigation." Street-level views could be much more scathing. By the 1920s one federal prosecutor was calling the fee the "arch tempter to the ambulance chaser" (as well as the fount of "false claims, witness fixing and perjury"). Henry Drinker, a relative pussyfooter, described it as "somewhat inconsistent" with the lawyer's duty not to stir up lawsuits.

With their incentive to go for volume, volume, and more volume, contingency-fee lawyers, exactly as one would expect, have long done far more than their share of advertising and solicitation, both lawful and un-. "MY CUSTOM T.V. ADS CAN MAKE YOU MILLIONS" promises a full-page pitch on page three of the December 1985 *Trial,* the magazine for injury lawyers. "27 Lawyers have become millionaires while running my custom T.V. commercials; 9 are multi-millionaires and 22 are close (net worth between $450,000 and $975,000"), asserts independent ad producer Paul Landauer. "Some started with less than nothing! One borrowed $6,000 to go on the air and took in an off-shore injury case the second week that settled for $3.8 million." Smart lawyers, he explains, know that attracting clients "in bunches and droves" increases the odds of getting a "big one." "I give you an elegant, 100% custom, 'dream lawyer' image the TV audience can't wait to call."

Getting potential clients, elegance-impressed or otherwise, to dial the operators standing by to receive their call, may be the initial step in the encouragement of litigation. But it will not be the last step. The encouragement naturally extends to every later stage of the dispute. The true cultivator of discontent does not sow the seeds of grievance and then retire while the seedlings grow or wither as Nature ordains. He waters and fertilizes the tender shoots to a state of garish bloom.

The popular television show *L.A. Law* has made famous the character of divorce lawyer Arnie Becker. A woman comes in who is thinking of splitting up with her husband: they haven't been fighting, but they seem to have drifted apart; maybe it's time to work out a parting of the ways. As Arnie drops a word here and a hint there, her mood subtly changes. She begins to feel annoyed at her hubby, then downright aggrieved; by the next commercial she is howling for his scalp on toast.

This edifying style of consciousness-raising or client education can be applied to virtually any legal problem. Someone walks into the office in a far from combative frame of mind, feeling there is something to be said for both sides, not at all in the right mood for litigation services. The entrepreneur can artfully lay out the full gravity of the other side's conduct. The client who wants help in rescheduling overdue bills can begin to appreciate how irresponsible the banks were to send him so many credit cards. The frightened tenant behind on the rent can realize, the thought coming as if unbidden, that the landlord's delay in repairing the sink is really little short of depravity.

None of this would have surprised old-time lawyers in the least, and it was one reason for the insistence on detachment and passivity that runs like a shot of lidocaine through their writings on the lawyer/client relationship. Yes, lawyers were to apprise clients fully of their rights and options, but it was best done clinically, so as not to inflame any latent feelings of fear, rage, envy, or avarice. If the case did proceed to litigation, the client as "master of his suit" was to provide the impetus not only for the initial filing but for any major escalation of the battle. Given a client of lawful intent, the ideal lawyer did not try to shape even his attitudes, let alone his story.

If you have hired a contingency-fee lawyer you surely know already about the great advantage of giving him a piece of the action: he gets a powerful incentive to bring in the absolutely biggest cash amount. But when you think about it the absolutely biggest cash amount may not be what you want.

You may not, for example, be feeling angry enough to fire off every arrow in your quiver of legal rights. Maybe it strikes you as a little rough to sue the nurse as well as the doctor and hospital just to get a few dollars more, or brand your ex-business partner as a racketeer as part of your action seeking a fairer division of the enterprise property. You may not want to pry into the other side's private life or invite prying into your own. Then, too, litigation can end in many ways. The bitterest marital fallings-out have been known to end in a miraculous reconciliation. (Most states still forbid contingency fees for obtaining divorce decrees because they so clearly give the lawyer a reason to sabotage any such development.) A new management might take over at the workplace where you were fired and offer you a job instead of a back-pay settlement. The magazine you sued for libel might print your side of the story. In a University of Iowa study of libel complainants interviewed after their suits were over, a substantial majority said they would have been satisfied at least initially with a correction or retraction instead of cash damages.

But there is a new dynamic at work to take the decision

out of your hands. If someone else fronted the money to get you into court, the action is no longer yours alone. You have a new partner in your lawsuit, maybe a senior partner, to whom words of forgiveness butter no parsnips and gestures of mercy pay for no beachfront condos. You may be pushed toward high-ticket strategies, though they end in hatred and self-reproach.

Timing is a common source of conflict between lawyer and client interests. Most litigants tire of their fights, if not at first, then after a while, and at some point would rather get on with their lives than hold out for a little more. The incentive of the lawyer with a big war chest can be to make you wait in order to go for the extra money. Every so often the roles are reversed: some clients have complained, and at least one legal-malpractice suit has charged, that lawyers settled too early for a low figure because they needed help with the cash flow in their own office.

Hiring a lawyer on an hourly fee puts you in control of the direction of your affairs, much as a taxi fare gives you wide discretion to name your own destination and hop off when you want. The contingency fee takes you along for someone else's ride, aboard a high-powered machine typically geared to breaking altitude records. With luck, it might be a ride to riches. But it is best not to complain about the steering. And although you may think you have the right to change lawyers in mid-lawsuit if things get too ugly, just try it.

There is no point denying that contingency fees have certain productivity advantages. Paying people only if their efforts culminate in success definitely coaxes more effort out of them, but the question is always whether the effort is aimed in the right direction. Much of the economy is run on a fee-for-results basis. Farmers get paid for cabbages based on how many edible cabbages they come up with, not how many hours they spend in the cabbage patch. Realtors and travel agents work on straight commission. So, for that matter, do authors who hope to make royalties past the advance on their books: if the product doesn't sell, they may get no recompense for an extra hundred hours of work.

Not all occupations are like cabbage, house, or book selling. Contingency fees tend to be disfavored in professions to whom the interests of others are helplessly entrusted, where misconduct is hard to monitor. Accountants have long been barred from accepting contingency fees ("I'll pay twice your normal rate if my taxes go down, the bank stays happy, and I survive the next annual meeting without being voted out"); we hope they will stay independent enough to tell the client unwelcome truths. Salesmen are not always paid on commission because the hustle factor in salesmanship can be turned in a destructive direction: commissioned salesmen, although they outperform the hourly variety, are also more tempted to use high-pressure sales techniques and manipulative tactics that "make their numbers look good" to the boss.

Contingency fees are particularly frowned on where the costs of abuse fall on third parties who are not taking part voluntarily. Giving traffic cops contingency fees by hinging their bonuses on whether they make a ticket quota arouses widespread anger because it so obviously tempts the officer running under quota to be unfair to the motorist. The same is true of giving tax collectors contingency fees by hinging their bonuses on how many deductions they disallow or how many assets they seize. ("Tax farming," the old system where private parties were deputized to collect taxes and keep some of the haul for themselves, was abolished long ago in well-run countries, not because it was the least bit inefficient—it was a favorite way for Roman emperors to extract revenue from conquered provinces—but because it encouraged brutality and trampling of due process in tax collection.) Giving soldiers contingency fees for successful attacks, by letting them loot the towns they capture, was long favored as a way of encouraging warlike zeal but came under gradual ethical control as civilization progressed; we now give out medals and ribbons instead of the contents of civilian homes.

Which interests are helplessly entrusted to lawyers? Their clients', of course, in many cases. In the classic underworld injury racket, the operator, after pocketing the defendant's tender of settlement, gives the accident victim whatever pocket change it is thought should satisfy him, or just dumps him back on the street with no money at all. (Any back talk from the victim and he is in trouble compared with which his original accident was minor.) Most clients of today's litigation industry fortunately do not get treated that badly. But many are quite surprised to discover at the end of a suit that the lawyer's claimed "expenses"—copying, filing costs, expert witness fees and so forth—have somehow ballooned to represent a huge share of the settlement on top of the contingency fee itself. (Some naive souls never find out for themselves how much the defendant paid to settle, but take the lawyer's word for it.) If the client gets any real accounting of the expenses, it can be extraordinarily hard to challenge.

Although contingency-fee lawyers face many temptations to exploit their clients, the worst dangers of the fee do not rest primarily on that ground. Alert clients can be on guard against being exploited by their own lawyers; as the abuses are more widely publicized, more may learn to avoid the lawyers who get too greedy in bill reckonings. The real problem with the contingency fee derives not so much from the conflicts it creates between the interests of lawyer and client as from the even more dangerous identity it creates between their interests as against everyone else's. In truth, many clients are delighted to find a lawyer who is much more ruthlessly committed to winning than the hourly-fee lawyer who represents their opponent. They seek out the operator who knows how to turn a worthless or low-value claim into a cash bonanza even if he keeps most of the extra money for himself. If they are made to cooperate in truth-shading or worse, they are not bothered. Some are only too glad to think up new embellishments of their own.

The case against the contingency fee has always rested on the danger it poses not to the one who pays it but to the opponent and more widely to justice itself. As other nations recognize, it can yoke together lawyer and client in a perfectly harmonious and efficient assault on the general public. There are things lawyers will do when a fortune for themselves is on the line that they won't do when it's just a fortune for a client. Taking all in all, we don't want them to do those things.

Contingency-fee law has made more overnight millionaires than just about any business one could name. *Forbes* surveyed the richest lawyers in America and found that the big fortunes were overwhelmingly made in contingency-fee work, not the corporate law and transaction planning that have always represented the zenith of prestige law practice. Among the top scorers on its list were a Detroit lawyer whose thriving practice takes in an estimated $100 million a year in settlements; a Brooklyn Law grad who specializes in suing doctors and carts home an estimated $12 million a year; a Wichita lawyer who sues vaccine makers and has made more than $5 million in each of the last ten years. Tucson's Richard Grand did not make the list, but Laurence Bodine of the trial lawyers' newsletter *Lawyers' Alert* reports that Grand has collected $200 million in verdicts and settlements over his career, with sixty cases exceeding $1 million. At a one-third contingency, that would add up to $67 million. Harry Lipsig, czar of lawsuits against New York City, has "been earning well into the seven figures every year for as long as anyone can remember," a spokeswoman for his office was quoted as saying in 1988. South Carolina asbestos-litigation king Ron Motley admits to earning a meager $1.5 million a year, but that is still reportedly enough to make his 255-employee firm the third-biggest employer in his section of the state, following a nuclear power plant and a large textile mill.

These men (very few are women) seldom seem to favor sober, understated ways of spending their newfound wealth. One has turned lawsuits against doctors into a villa in the south of France and a $2 million Paris apartment. A list of their known holdings is spangled with the ranches, jets, and very fancy cars that befit tycoons riding a cash wave with no end in sight. And indeed, no end is in sight. Something about today's contingency-fee system has made these lawyers very much richer than most of the doctors, hospital administrators, and corporate CEOs whose decisions they second-guess, and incomparably richer than the defense lawyers who oppose them.

There is a funny thing about this brand of lawyering: the more opulent it becomes, the more cloying an odor of sanctity it gives off. Self-righteousness is an occupational disease in several sectors of the legal profession, but injury lawyers top all. A spokesman for Morris Eisen had no apologies when he was indicted on charges of massive claims faking. Just the reverse. The charges, he said, were "a brazen effort to cripple the advocates of the men, women and children who have been crippled and maimed." Suing people for a share of the proceeds has become, like one or two famous television ministries, a venture in hellfire preaching and unctuous hand-wringing that enables its practitioners to live in the luxury of Babylon.

What is supposed to make all this okay is that it is done in the name of persons of modest means. Injury lawyers carry on endlessly about how their favored fee arrangement provides the "key to the courthouse" for the widow and orphan. But they seldom much care for the method all other countries use to provide that key: an hourly fee paid by the losing opponent. And it turns out that they happily charge contingency fees to middle- and upper-income and business clients that could easily afford to pay on an hourly basis. A group of companies stymied in efforts to build a coal slurry pipeline hired the big Houston firm of Vinson & Elkins on a contingency basis to file antitrust charges against several railroads for allegedly blocking the project: the law firm reportedly pocketed nearly $200 million in contingency fees from the resulting settlements. *The Wall Street Journal* has reported that the state of Massachusetts has hired private lawyers on a contingency fee of up to 30 percent to pursue some property-repair claims with an estimated value of $100 million.

In fact, mysteriously, the contingency fee has become the *only* way most individual clients can get a lawyer for injury cases, even if they would rather pay an hourly fee. Some clients suspect that a phone call or two from a lawyer, or a letter on his stationery, may be all they need to get a satisfactory resolution of their problem. Giving him a third of the amount won in such a case, they might feel, would be an undeserved windfall. But they are out of luck. A report from the Federal Trade Commission showed that 97 percent of lawyers took injury cases only on contingency, refusing to consider hourly rates, however generous. Lawyers seem to have come to the conclusion that a good injury case is a plum and, damn it, they have a right to a share, as befits a player rather than a taxi driver. They are also loath to undercut the "going rate" fee percentage, even when success in a case seems virtually assured. In some of the rougher towns like Philadelphia, Detroit and Kansas City, the going rates over the years have been reported to run at 40 and even 50 percent.

As lawyers have discovered how very profitable this kind of practice can be, more of them have gotten over their scruples. The contingency fee is coming to be seen as the basis of an industry boldly and openly run for profit, as an enthusiastic first resort for the general case rather than a troubled last resort for the special. Even big-name firms like Washington's Williams & Connally and Arnold & Porter are now reported to take work on contingency. And in a trend that is full of implications for the future, the fee is spreading to litigation over employment matters, child support, will contests, copyrights, taxes, and, perhaps most ominously, divorces.

In Texas, where the contingency-fee industry is unusually well developed, it is having a profound effect on commercial litigation. Texas lawyer John O'Quinn may represent a one-man wave of the future. His full-page Yellow Pages ad, as quoted in a *Wall Street Journal* report, says he is dedicated to "helping injured people obtain cash damages" and promises an "attorney on call 24 hours a day." State bar officials have accused him of illegally using runners to acquire injury cases. What makes O'Quinn an interesting and apparently a very, very rich man is that he also applies his methods to otherwise routine disputes between businesses, with astonishing success. His most startling victory came in 1988 when a jury awarded $600 million to one of his clients, an Ohio natural gas producer, in a contract dispute with the giant Tenneco Corporation.

O'Quinn believes the techniques of personal-injury advocacy are highly effective in these disputes over how the business world is run. "We tend to approach the cases in a common sense way—simplify it," he says. Avoid the boring details, and get personal. He depicted the gas-producer plaintiffs as "hard-working, honest Christian people—your basic small-town Americans" facing an impersonal corporation. "Business lawyers—they talk like they're talking to a bunch of lawyers. I think lawyers who do what I do are actually better equipped to do these cases."

In recent years the Texas courts have handed out a string of astoundingly large verdicts. A verdict in a second natural gas case nearly matched O'Quinn's $600 million bite out of Tenneco; another Texas jury hit five railroads with a $1.3 billion antitrust verdict; and yet another Texas jury, of course, gave Pennzoil a $10.5-billion verdict in its 1985 trial against Texaco, with lawyer Joseph Jamail taking a contingency cut of the eventual $3 billion settlement.

The tycoons of the lawsuit business emerged at roughly the same time as those of the 1980s investment-banking and corporate dealmaking boom, although their stratospheric earnings have continued year after year instead of falling back after a short, spiky peak. The parallels and differences are instructive. For a long time many Wall Street advisers were paid whether or not a deal went through, let alone whether or not the client's stock went up afterward. In the 1980s, Drexel Burnham Lambert led the Street into taking "equity kickers" and warrant packages that greatly sharpened the advisors' financial incentive to make deals come out with favorable numbers. From middlemen they soon graduated to "players," and their power and income surged dramatically, as often happens to highly talented persons who get to work on contingency. Of course their temptation to sharp practices also increased. Some succumbed.

Was the added productivity worth the added misconduct? That depends on the answer to two questions. Can an investment banker's own clients reap the benefit of the hustling without falling victim to it? And can third parties stay out of the way, or will some of the cost of the deals be dumped on them? One school of thought sees the clients of investment bankers as somewhat pigeonlike, and third parties (such as holders of earlier debt that loses market value when a company issues new junk bonds) as highly vulnerable. Those of this view tend to see the Wall Street dealmaking of the 1980s as an ethical disaster area. Another school of thought sees both clients and outsiders as competent to fend for themselves over the long run. Those of this view tend to applaud, as a move toward market efficiency, the undeniable torrent of energy and creativity that characterized the new, contingency-fee-oriented Wall Street.

Of course many injury lawyers would profess great outrage at being compared with Wall Street operators. With their constantly proclaimed identification with the "little guy," they often assume a marked moral superiority to mere business people, whose ethical corner-cutting, real or conjured-up, is a favorite topic of theirs before juries.

The comparison is indeed unfair, but not in the way they imagine. Entrepreneurs of litigation are middlemen not of commerce but of combat. They search out and sedulously promote chances for their fellow citizens to fight, not produce or trade. A better comparison might be with the impresarios of the boxing arena, whose productions, in pain and ringside drama, have so much in common with those of the courtroom. On second thought, that would be unfair to boxing promoters. In their spectacles, the contestants have come into the ring of their own free will.

3

ROLE REVERSAL:
How Lawyers Took Charge

As a general thing—as far as I could make out—these murderous adventures [of the Knights of the Round Table] were not forays undertaken to avenge injuries, nor to settle old disputes or sudden fallings out; no, as a rule they were simple duels between strangers—duels between people who had never even been introduced to each other, and between whom existed no cause of offense whatever. Many a time I had seen a couple of boys, strangers, meet by chance, and say simultaneously, "I can lick you," and go at it on the spot; but I had always imagined until now, that that sort of thing belonged to children only, and was a sign and mark of childhood; but here were these big boobies sticking to it and taking pride in it clear up into full age and beyond.

—TWAIN
A Connecticut Yankee in King
Arthur's Court

The brief Associated Press item seemed like just another routine business-litigation story. It reported that the management of CBS, Incorporated, while admitting no wrongdoing, had agreed to pay $6 million to settle a claim by a disgruntled stockholder named Roger Minkoff, a resident of the U.S. Virgin Islands. Minkoff had sued the giant broadcaster, charging that its management had harmed stockholders' interests by repelling a 1985 takeover bid from cable magnate Ted Turner and by paying too much for some of the magazine operations of the Ziff-Davis group in the same year.

Routine, yes, but just below the surface of the story were some odd angles. In the first place, rank-and-file CBS stockholders wouldn't be getting any checks in the mail; the bulk of the settlement, $4.5 million, was going into the CBS corporate treasury rather than, as one might expect, coming out of it. (In fact the settlement was being paid by an insurance policy, not by the corporation itself.) The next surprise was that the aggrieved shareholder was not, as one might expect, an investor with enough of his own money in CBS stock to make such a fight worth pursuing. Minkoff actually owned a mere fifteen shares, hardly enough to pay the postage in a lawsuit like this. As recompense for having gone to the trouble of suing he was to receive $15,000 from the settlement, not bad for a holder of fifteen shares (valued at $184 each) but only a sliver of the $6 million that was changing hands.

What happened to the other $1.5 million? Why, that went to Mr. Minkoff's lawyer, Richard Greenfield of Haverford, Pennsylvania, as legal fees per the terms of the settlement. And that explained everything. Mr. Greenfield is very, very well known in America's boardrooms. His firm has turned up as attorney of record in scores of other suits against American corporations whose common feature was that the legal fees billed vastly exceeded the sums recovered for the named clients.

For a long time people tended to see lawsuits as private quarrels between private parties for private gain. To the extent that the wider public had an interest in them, it was mostly in laying them to rest by clarifying responsibilities, so that the disturbance of the peace might end and life get back to normal.

This point of view was not very conducive to the emergence of an industry devoted to stirring up lawsuits for profit. But a new and much more suitable ideology now arose. Lawsuits (it now began to be urged) should be seen not just as ways to clarify the bounds between two private rights that might have come into conflict, but as campaigns to liberate people whose rights had been insolently trod on. In fact, even more important than to liberate existing victims was to deter future treadings-on of rights. The enforcing of good conduct through fear of being caught and punished was an acknowledged aim of the publicly enforced criminal law. Why not the privately enforced civil law as well?

Before long lawsuits were being praised to the skies as highly productive and public-spirited enterprises. To file one, it was argued, was to do a commendable service to the general populace, far over and above any incidental benefit to oneself. The more judicial scrutiny was applied to private dealings, the more responsibly everyone would behave for fear of being sued and losing. And as more cases were put through the mill of litigation, a finer and finer grade of truth and justice would issue forth, with more and more human relationships being reordered according to their merits. And who could be against the merits?

You might call it the invisible-fist theory. In Adam Smith's famous account, the butcher and baker are led in their self-seeking as if by an invisible hand to further the general welfare: private striving leads to public benefit. The bold new twist was the idea that private *quarrels* also lead to public benefit; the more fights you get into, the better a place you make the world for everyone else.

All this provided a sorely needed moral basis for the sue-for-profit industry, a basis that was to prove amazingly powerful in overcoming all sorts of nagging misgivings and lingering doubts legal entrepreneurs might feel about intensifying their efforts. If to litigate was to do the world a favor, then late-night lawyering ads were not at all in the same league as crass come-ons for vocational schools or wrinkle creams, but were more like public service announcements that broadcasters should probably be running for free. Direct solicitation? An even more commendable outreach program, providing door-to-door service. Just the same, the demand for litigation services still fell a long way short of what far-sighted promoters knew it could be. No matter how well the persuasive apparatus might be honed, most people with a potential claim, most of the time, still did not visit a lawyer to inquire about pressing it. Bathed in a constant stream of rousing ads and strategically planted articles, pelted with cus-tomized direct-mail appeals from experienced copywriters, assured of the moral rightness of their cause, reminded of their obligation to set their children up well in life, most persons with gripes still declined to fight, for the same varied reasons that people decline to fight with their fists: scruples, continuing relations with the designated adversary, disdain for the sport itself, or lack of stomach for its grueling ordeal.

If the cannon fodder was not volunteering in the desired numbers, one option was to offer sign-up pay.

The contingency fee had already promised to take care of the client's major financial risk here, by assuring him that the biggest expense of a lawsuit, the lawyer's time, was noth-ing he had to worry about paying out of pocket. ("No fee unless successful.") Officially, clients are still responsible for the other miscellaneous expenses of a losing lawsuit. If that rule were enforced it would discourage many lawsuits, per-haps including stockholder lawsuits against big corporations by owners of fifteen shares. So in practice it is widely ignored. All sides understand that in many of today's suits the lawyer is covertly gambling the expenses, as he is openly gambling the fee.

The next logical step is to pay the client cash on the barrel to sue or keep a suit going. Like so many promising promotional strategies in the litigation business, this one had been illegal under English common law: furnishing money in exchange for all or part of someone's right to sue was a criminal offense called "champerty." The law sometimes per-mitted outsiders to buy and enforce an obligation where the obligated party had consented in advance to make it assign-able. But experience with that process tended to confirm the mistrust. Dunning agencies that buy up overdue accounts and try to collect them are widely seen as several notches less scrupulous than the in-house billing departments of established merchants with good will to protect. There was little enthusiasm for extending the assignability idea to, say, divorce, libel, child support, or car crash claims.

And yet the logic of legal entrepreneurship points in that direction. Once lawyers feel comfortable taking a one-third share in a suit in exchange for forgiving their fee, why should they stick at taking a two-thirds share purchased by way of a direct payment to the client? After all, such a payment might enable the client to resist the otherwise seductive settlement offers of the opponent. In a widely cited law review article, Professor Philip Shuchman of the University of Connecticut law school has explained that viewed in a "contemporary social context," there would seem to be nothing "self-evidently wrong" with champerty, which after all allows the lawyer to "create some measure of equality in the economic staying power of his clients." Champerty has not yet been made lawful, but anecdotal evidence suggests that it is widespread.

Comparatively routine are fee-splitting arrangements in which the law firm that lands a client sells him to a second firm for a share of the eventual fee. This allows a division of labor between lawyers who are good at inciting litigation and those who are good at waging it. More creative financial techniques are on the horizon, as speculative legal practices find ways to secure outside financing for their inventory of grievance. A Los Angeles bank has joined with the local trial lawyers' association to offer a "client cost account program" to fund the costs of lawsuits. The line of credit is nominally taken out in the client's name but the lawyer is the one who guarantees it; in exchange for fronting the money, the bank gets a lien against any recovery.

West Coast entrepreneurs have also been pioneering something called the syndicated lawsuit, in which venture capitalists chip in to build a war chest for a lawsuit in exchange for shares of any recovery. Such syndicates have spread especially fast in the world of patents, where they appear only a slight novelty: if it is proper to buy the full rights to an invention, why not buy just the right to sue people for selling allegedly infringing products?

The syndication format is adaptable to many other types of lawsuit. Its most spectacular success thus far has come in a commercial suit. A syndicate bought a promissory note that the ComputerLand Corporation had issued in its start-up days and sued the company on the theory that the note was really intended to be convertible to vastly more valuable ComputerLand common stock. It convinced a jury of this theory and won a $125 million jackpot as well as a big equity stake in the successful retailer. Shares in the syndicate that had been offered originally at $10,000 skyrocketed to a trading value of $750,000. The organizing lawyer, rather like a Viking clambering aboard a rich merchant ship, even got to join ComputerLand's board of directors.

These trends have a logical culmination: unlimited public trading of lawsuit shares. Although a New York Verdict Exchange has not yet been set up to handle this new type of commerce, it may be closer than we think. For a while, investors who bought shares in Pennzoil were mostly buying a legal claim against Texaco to which a collection of refineries and miscellaneous assets happened to attach.

The decay of the rules against champerty and maintenance is one more way litigation is being put on a flourishing, deregulated business basis; it also represents the downfall of one of the more important old barriers to litigation. Claims can migrate from those who might be disinclined to press them to those most inclined to press them to the hilt. No longer need grievances remain stunted in their natural surroundings; they can be transplanted to year-round luxuriance in hothouses.

A stroke of legal innovation in the 1960s promised to go yet further in dislodging many inhibited claims.

The old law had long recognized an obscure type of lawsuit known as a bill of peace. It could be used when many persons had been harmed in the same way by the same offender. One of the earliest English cases, which perfectly illustrates the principle, was allowed against a shipowner accused of cheating a returning crew of its wages. The law could have handled the charges by holding a hundred (or however many) trials, and if the owner had lost the first cases he might not have fought to the bitter end. But why hold so many trials when the underlying issue was the same each time?

Situations of this sort did not come up often. Perhaps the most common use of the class-litigation format came to be in suits by investors charging misconduct in the running of public companies. If management had shortchanged one stockholder, the reasoning went, it had shortchanged them all. The first case of note here was filed by irate holders against Sir Richard Congreve for issuing shares in a venture to buy Irish mines but keeping most of the money for himself and some confederates.

By the time the bill of peace had evolved into what we now know as the class action, it had some peculiar attractions for the aspiring drummer-up of litigation. Class actions permit recruitment and solicitation not just by ones and twos, but by carloads and counties. A client with some smallish complaint walks in, having seen the lawyer's flashing sign or matchbook cover; he turns out to be a human Klondike, because his injury is the same as that of a host of others with whom he can be joined in a class.

But the rules made it hard to organize class actions. And so the rules had to be changed. A 1966 round of federal reforms made it easier to organize actions involving very large groups. In 1974 the Supreme Court did away with a rule that had required the organizing lawyer to show a significant chance of winning on the merits. Group suits began to burgeon in the antitrust, employment, environmental, and welfare-benefits fields.

The American class-action lawyer can represent thousands or millions of people who have never seen or dealt with him, or each other, in any way: all the soldiers who fought in an overseas war, all the buyers of a certain car, all the consumers who might not have bought Perrier water had they known it contained infinitesimal traces of benzene, and so forth. "It is not necessary that every class member be directly affected by the actions [of the opponent] or feel aggrieved by them," declares a leading treatise. After the brouhaha over the liaison between evangelist Jim Bakker and church secretary Jessica Hahn, lawyers filed suit against the Bakker ministry on behalf of three members of an Ohio family and no fewer than 500,000 other donors. The family had given the ministry $11,800, and wanted it back along with a nice round $1 million in punitive damages. For the class of donors as a whole the lawyers asked $100 million in compensatory and a tidy $500 million in punitive damages.

Under modern rules, members of a class are given a chance to opt out of the suit in their name by sending in a postcard, in the sort of "negative check-off" familiar to members of book and record clubs. Unlike other club members, however, members of the suit-of-the-month club do not save any money by opting out of the latest selection, and not many usually do so, especially since their own withdrawal would do nothing to prevent the suit from going forward in the name of everyone else. Like voters in one-party states, a few scratch the designated name off the ballot, and the rest get counted as client/supporters for no better reason than inertia.

The class-action lawyer does not of course have to pick as a client the first member of the outraged collectivity who happens along. In the age of legal solicitation, he can search out just the right one. Of the many class members, at least one may turn out to be the wonderfully obliging sort of client who leaves the case's management entirely in the lawyer's hands. It might be a cousin, an old college chum, or a colleague on the class-action circuit for whom the lawyer once did a similar service. The client may also have the grace to be qualified to sue in the state or judicial district that the lawyer considers most favorable to this kind of suit or hostile to this defendant. And through the miracle of the class action a million complainants who have never set foot in that sympathetic state or court district can also be brought in to benefit from its brand of justice.

Most notable was the class action's treatment of lawyer's fees. If the suit makes good, the lawyer can't very well (so the theory goes) negotiate with a hundred sailors or a thousand shareholders for his fee. Instead he asks the court to deduct an appropriate sum from the total award or settlement before it gets distributed among the plaintiffs.

Class action fee requests appear to be based on the standard per-hour format of a "taxi-hire" fee, but concealed just behind this facade is the actual structure of a contingency fee. In the first place, the class-action lawyer, like the contingency-fee lawyer, gets nothing if his client loses. It would be astonishing if the individual whose name went on the action, the stockholder, Perrier drinker, or Bakker donor, expected for a moment to shoulder the whole cost of the lawsuit should it fail. The suit in practice is understood to go on at the lawyer's risk.

The other major feature of contingency fees—the proportionality of the fee to the amount won—is a real though unwritten feature of most class actions as well. Judges are not as well situated to watch meters as paying clients, and when the fee request is presented to them at the end of the suit many feel uneasy about trying to reconstruct, without benefit of adversary process, how much lawyering should have been done in a case that may have lasted for years and has gone on mostly outside the courtroom. But judges do sincerely want to prevent abusive fee padding; there is still some discomfort about a string of cases in the 1960s and 1970s where the lawyers got nearly all the money and the aggrieved parties little or none. So what most of them do is try to make sure the fees do not exceed what seems a fair proportion of the recovery. Once lawyers figure out what a court will tolerate, they somehow tend to pitch their fee requests around that level, and the effective contingency fee is complete. A substantial literature in the law reviews urges courts to move to an open percentage or bounty system.

So long as the size of the client herds remained small and the interest of each member sizable, there was some hope that the class members could compare notes and collectively keep an eye on the lawyers, thus providing at least some check on the litigation. But the liberalization of the rules pushed in exactly the opposite direction. Some lawyers began collecting on cases where thousands of claimants had only a few dollars at stake apiece, and law school visionaries began working on techniques to lump into a viable action nationwide claims of a penny or two per person.

Thus was crossed a vexing barrier to the ambitions of entrepreneurial litigators: the unreliability of live clients. So long as lawsuits could emerge only from the spontaneous grievances of real people on the scene, the vagaries of those people would represent an endless source of lost business. Again and again live litigants settled for an apology or symbolic recompense early on before seeing what really vigorous rights-assertion could do. When they were willing to sue at all, they too often directed their anger at a party with nothing in the bank and flat-out refused to go after a solvent one. Or they would press only a minor claim when a much bigger one was ripe for the taking. Then they wearied of the battle and settled too early, or, contrariwise, rejected a lucrative settlement because they insisted on proving a point in open court.

Like many innovations making it easier to sue, class actions were recommended as a way to cut court costs. They soon grew monstrously expensive and complicated. As plaintiff groups got bigger they got more motley, and it got harder to pretend that the members had the same interest at all. A band of sailors after a voyage have a common and focused interest in getting paid as promised. But did all the female students in the Chicago schools really share an interest in ending the practice of having boys and girls play on separate sports teams?

Did each and every patient at a poorly run mental hospital—
to take another actual case—have an interest in closing it down
and being moved a hundred miles to another? The *reductio
ad absurdum* was reached when a court allowed a lawsuit
against a labor union to go forward as a class action although
every single member of the class except the named plaintiff
objected to it.

   Also hard to ignore were the growing clashes of interest
between lawyers and their supposed clients. What should the
private lawyer representing three hundred thousand federal
workers do when the government offers a settlement that
would be generous to workers with high seniority but stingy
to those with low? Take it and declare victory? Negotiate
away some of his clients' interests to get a better deal for
others?

   The law reviews began to silt up with a dense literature
on how to handle conflicts of class interest, but all the solu-
tions turned out to make things even worse. Some insisted
that what was needed was a case-by-case fight over whether
the lawyer had chosen token plaintiffs who were "typical"
enough, which begged the question of whether any subset
of wax-figurine clients could really contain the requisite mul-
titudes, and the larger question of what difference it made
when the clients exerted no effective control over the lawyer
anyway. Others, holding to a principle of one-figurehead-one-
frigate, called for the (self-) appointment of additional lawyers
to enter the fray on behalf of identifiable subclasses, greatly
complicating settlement negotiations and ensuring that even
more of the money changing hands would wind up in the
pockets of lawyers instead of the nominal beneficiaries.

Curbing clashes between lawyer and client interests has always been one of the preoccupations of the law. That was
one reason for the general insistence that courts handle suits
one at a time—group grievances were largely left to other
branches of government to handle—and that lawyers focus
their full attention on the client of the moment, with no

destination other than that chosen by the current passenger. The ideal lawyer would take clients as they came in to the office; in fact most practicing lawyers until recently could not even list on their letterheads or business cards their areas of preferred practice. In effect they were to forget about trying to pursue their own litigation goals at the expense of clients who might need them; they were to handcraft their services one at a time to clients' order, rather like the bespoke clothiers who turn out personally tailored suits of the other kind.

Barristers, the British equivalent of trial lawyers, follow a "taxi-hire" system to this day, still commonly switching off in case to case from management to union, landlord to tenant, debtor to creditor. Remarkably enough, they even switch back and forth between prosecution and criminal defense work, because the government farms out its prosecutorial advocacy to the private sector (for a flat fee, needless to say, not a fee contingent on convicting the defendant). The ideal is to be fully alive to the clients' situations but inert to their fortunes, recalling the extreme detachment sought by Sophocles' Ajax:

> Only so much to hate my enemy,
> As though he might again become my friend,
> And so much good to wish to do my friend,
> As knowing he may yet become my foe.

One result of the taxi-hire conception of lawyering is to discourage lawyers from assuming the Nemesis role of specialist in suits against one or a few opponents. With the combination of advertising, solicitation, and contingency fees, more American lawyers have found it profitable to begin specializing in just such a way. As a result many of them have come to settle cases in batches, which re-creates in the context of individual suits the same conflicts of interest with which class actions are so rife. Leslie Cheek III, who plays on the opposite side as an executive with the Crum and Forster insurance companies, explains how the game works.

A lawyer will come to us with twenty or thirty as-bestos claims. Of these, two or three are strong cases that would win something at trial. Several more are dicey, and others are so weak that normally we wouldn't make an offer. The lawyer won't settle the strong claims unless we settle all the rest, so we spread the money around without spending much more than we would have spent on the strong claims alone. Result: the lawyer can tell all his cases they won and get all his expenses back. It's fine for the weak claimants, of course; they come out ahead. But the two or three strong claimants come out with less than they would have gotten with a different lawyer.

The prospect of future cases, like the looming presence of other current ones, can distort a lawyer's settlement incentives. The opponent may offer a pricey sum to settle a claim that is unlikely to bring much money to this client, but could set a precedent for many more lawsuits to come. Will the lawyer snap up the offer in order to do best by the client at hand, or go for the long-run pot of gold by refusing? Or the opponent may offer a generous settlement at an early stage because it wants to protect the privacy of its internal documents; the lawyer may torpedo any such offer precisely because he wants to get his hands on the materials for use in future cases. (And once he gets them the opponent may no longer be willing to settle with this client, the damage to its privacy already being done.) Turning down a more than generous settlement in favor of a risky trial can also be a way for the lawyer to draw out the weaknesses of this opponent for use in future cases, or develop a flashy reputation for handling this kind of suit.

Under the old taxi-hire conception, where the point of litigation was to protect the legitimate interests of the named client, outright disloyalty to that client's interests was a high sin. As lawyers increasingly became the real players in class and batch litigation, as clients came to seem a bothersome obstruction, a new ideology was needed to justify what was going on. The invisible-fist theory fit the bill perfectly by shifting the focus to the need to chastise the opponent and deter future misbehavior by those in a similar position. A defendant who ponied up a stiff settlement, after all, was just as effectively chastised and deterred whether or not the named client ever saw much of the money. Litigation where the lawyer or his friends kept much or all of the proceeds could thus be idealistically reconceived as a new and higher form of litigation, on behalf of the interests of future victims in general rather than any one past victim. Davy Crockett, traveling through Tennessee on his way to the combat on the Texas frontier, was asked why he was going. "To fight for my rights."

Before long it was being argued that the legal entrepreneur was really a new kind of public servant, the "private attorney general," who represented the interests of the citizenry at large (without being subject to any actual public accounting or control, of course) and who should thus be free, like the elected or appointed public prosecutor, to file his civil charges without the prompting or perhaps even the permission of injured persons. Not all charges would pan out, but even a losing suit had its virtues: it showed a sort of police presence in a doubtful area, and by stopping and frisking this defendant showed others they were being watched.

A spate of new laws was passed embodying these ideas. Some gave any "citizen" (in practice, any lawyer) the right to sue anyone who had failed to comply with one or another part of some vast body of federal or state regulation. Other laws authorized outright bounties for successful lawsuits, aside from any damages to clients that might be proved. Hundreds of laws were passed doing away with the old "American rule" on lawyers' fees (each side pays his own), on the (not unreasonable) logic that prevailing plaintiffs should be allowed to collect fees from losers for going to the trouble of suing. But the laws did not allow prevailing *defendants* to collect for *their* trouble in having to prove their innocence; the fee shifting was to work in one direction only. That was a crucial distinction: as we shall see in the chapters ahead, the denial of recourse to vindicated defendants, no matter how badly they have been hurt by litigation, is what makes the whole profitable system go 'round for the plaintiffs' lawyers.

The same ideas helped push class actions toward the outer limits of their logic. It had already been observed in some of the wider, shallower class actions that after the litigators had cut a deal with the defendant and taken their fees off the top there was—whoops, sorry!—little or no money left for the class of clients. Why not go all the way, and admit that the class members, with their petty rights of notification and opting out, played an artificial and indeed dispensable role in the process? If the real point of litigation was to chastise defendants for their misbehavior, shouldn't it be done by the most direct path, without fussing with every piddling victim?

A milestone came when Minda Satterwhite, having flatly lost her individual claim of unfair treatment against her employer, the city of Greenville, Texas, was nonetheless allowed to go on pursuing an identical claim on behalf of a larger class of city workers—although if her lawyers succeeded in proving that the claim of the wider class was valid, they would only have managed to prove that she was atypical of that class. Dissenting judge Thomas Gee sighed that the court was finally giving in once and for all to "the notion that a class suit belongs to no one so much as to the plaintiff's lawyer."

But that was just the point, and pressure came from the law schools to proceed openly down this path. A piece in the *Harvard Law Review* called for judges to drop the named-client fiction entirely and allow lawyers to file class actions entirely on their own behalf, with courts screening the filers for ideological sincerity but not requiring them to line up any in-person clients. It seemed that before long the up-to-the-minute litigator would entirely leave off working the laborious vein of individual claims in favor of mechanized strip mining, with its enormous extractive capacity.

Every step along the way to the new system tended to elevate the role of the lawyer and depress the role of the client. Advertising—which now, as always, was addressed at the marginal and uncertain buyer rather than the one whose mind was firmly made up—brought in more clients who were ripe for taking in hand. Contingency fees put the lawyer fiscally and psychologically in charge of the suit, giving him a powerful incentive to tease and groom clients' attitudes and recollections into the desired shapes. In the class action the client was increasingly shoved off the stage altogether, his name alone being used. Finally, under the banner of the private attorney general, lawyers could start waging litigation purely and openly on their own behalf, for ideology, profit or both.

It took only a few years to turn the age-old lawyer/client relationship on its head. For centuries lawyers had been expected to cabin their formidable powers through a self-imposed passivity, aspiring to no independent dominion of their own, acting only at the behest of some person who needed a friend at court. Now a new ideology had been cobbled together that glorified clientless litigation as somehow cleaner, nobler, more disinterested, than litigation on behalf of someone who had actually been hurt badly enough to want to sue. The lawyer who meekly facilitated clients' interests began to be derided as a hired gun and a chump. The cutting-edge practitioner threw off all such shackles, and was a friend to no one but himself.

·THE·
LAWSUIT

HAPPIER HUNTING GROUNDS

When I was at home, I was in a better place.

—*SHAKESPEARE*, As You Like It

Ida Weitz of Victoria, Texas, had a son in the Marine Corps. She bought him a car to use at Camp Lejeune in North Carolina where he was stationed. One of his friends there borrowed the car and got into an accident with it, and the family of the accident victim decided to see a lawyer.

Injury lawyers spend a lot of time thinking about how to find new people to sue for old problems. In this case they could obviously sue the friend who drove the car and try to show he was negligent. Less obviously they could go after young Weitz, arguing that he should have known his friend was the sort of character who might get into an accident. The theory is called "negligent entrustment" and has made a lot of money for lawyers.

Trouble was, one young Marine was not likely to have much more money than another, and money, not blame, is often the real point of the exercise. Deeper pockets were needed. Why not Mrs. Weitz's? She had entrusted the car to her son knowing he might reentrust it to persons of unknown character. So she could be accused of negligence too. She had some insurance, and nothing says lawyers have to be content just with insurance either. In a 1989 case that provoked something of a public outcry, ninety-two-year-old Vermont widow Luella Wilson almost lost her house after lawyers got a $950,000 jury verdict against her; her offense, by coincidence also one of "negligent entrustment," had been to lend her great-nephew the money to buy a car that he later crashed.

Mrs. Weitz's lawyers hoped things would never reach that point, especially since they had what they thought was a very strong argument. It would be one thing to sue her in Texas where she lived, but these lawyers were trying to sue her in North Carolina. And she had never set foot in that state in her life. No matter, said a federal court of appeals in a landmark 1961 decision: she could properly be forced to come into North Carolina to stand trial under the state's "long-arm" law.

Over the centuries no legal rules were framed as loftily or guarded as jealously as the rules on whether a court could exert rightful authority over you. The law of jurisdiction had the special solemnity of law that governs law, law meant to bind the courts themselves. A court can get the factual details of a case wrong and its errors may stand as permanent findings. It can mistake the law it is applying and its blunders will still obtain some deference from other courts. But if it oversteps its jurisdiction—so runs the older rule, at least—its verdict is void, a mere nullity, entitled to no respect from other courts; given to the winds. The law of jurisdiction sets the ultimate limit, if there is to be one, on who is to rule over whom.

In private lawsuits, for many centuries, the chief rule of jurisdiction was clear and straightforward. To sue someone you had to pay him a visit. You could not just denounce him to the first court that seemed convenient; you had to go to a court that was in some sense his. The "most important principle of all municipal law of Anglo-Saxon origin," a Pennsylvania court sonorously declared in 1874, was "that a man shall only be liable to be called to answer for civil wrongs in the forum of his home, and tribunal of his vicinage." Actually the principle was ancient when the Anglo-Saxons came on the scene. The Roman law's pithy maxim was *actor forum rei sequitur*, "the plaintiff must pursue the defendant in his forum."

Why? Some thought it was a matter of consent. If you were nestling under a state's protective wing you could not complain about having to submit to its talons and beak. Others reduced the issue to one of raw physical power. Maryland courts took sole charge of suits against Maryland residents because their sheriffs were the ones who could compel them to stand trial. For much the same reasons they could hear a dispute over who owned a tract of land in Baltimore or a ship in its harbor, even if the owner were absent, because Maryland sheriffs could physically seize and dispose of the goods.

Framed thus in terms of the raw might of the sovereigns, the doctrine does not much sound like a bulwark of individual liberty. What was interesting was its corollary: by submitting to one sovereign, you could escape the whims of the others. By staying in Maryland you had nothing to worry about from the Virginia civil courts. Of course you might owe money in Virginia or have wronged someone there, and for that the Maryland courts and sheriffs would hold you to account. But first your Virginia opponents had to make proper application to the Maryland courts, lest Virginia entrench on the majesty of its sister state.

If the only courts that could try you were those of the place you *called* home, it would be too easy to frustrate your creditors by naming as your imaginary home some distant place. Instead a court's power over you was tied to your literal presence. The state you were physically in, even if just on a day trip, was the state where you could be sued at any moment. So a state line was something real and momentous. When you stepped across it the Indiana sheriffs lost their power over you and the Ohio sheriffs' power suddenly loomed large—however vexing that might be to you or your creditors.

The formality of these rights could (and sometimes still can) turn the "service of process" with which a lawsuit begins into a faintly ridiculous game of tag. Hard-pressed debtors retired to remote places, while syndicates of creditors kept agents at transit hubs who checked passenger lists and tagged unwary riders with process as they changed trains. (Long ago, when Sundays and holidays were off-limits for lawful tagging, much gadding about was done on those days.) A court upheld the tagging of a traveler at a Connecticut hotel although the whole point of choosing that place was to make the lawsuit hard for him to defend. Likewise held valid was the serving of a defendant with an Arkansas complaint while flying over the state in an airplane.

Fortunately, judges had ways of tempering the harshness of these rules for the innocent traveler. The judge in the place where you were tagged might let you go of his own accord, or your lawyers back home might get a judge there to order your hometown creditors to stop pestering you by use of distant actions. In either case, however, you got relief at the court's discretion, not by right, and one precondition would probably be your agreement to stand trial on the same charge at home.

Otherwise, a successful tag pretty much ended the jurisdictional game. If you skipped town after coming under a court's lawful dominion, it would enter a "default judgment" against you, and when your opponent tracked you down in another state you would have no chance to reargue the merits: the U.S. Constitution requires states to give "full faith and credit" to each other's duly entered judgments.

For all their occasional gamesmanship, the old rules of jurisdiction had some definite advantages. They were easy to understand and follow: they basically let you know off the bat where you could sue or be sued. They also discouraged litigation. In disputes between persons at a distance from each other, the cost of travel and the little inertias of life cut against suing. Many lawsuits did not seem worth the trouble of taking to a distant forum, and were not filed at all.

It never seemed entirely fair that some people had to drop otherwise good cases because travel was such a bother. It seemed even less fair that they might have to drop good cases because they feared that the strange court they would visit would be biased against outsiders. Trouble is, these two sources of unfairness cannot be done away with; they can only be shifted. In a long-distance dispute, at least one side always has to travel and be an outsider upon arriving, like the bride coming to Yellow Sky. Earlier generations of Americans were more frightened of being summoned before an unfamiliar tribunal as an accused wrongdoer than of having to go there as an accuser. Maybe distant states could not always be relied on to lend a neighborly hand to the visiting complainant. But if so, could they be trusted not to plunder the visiting defendant? At least this way if you saw the courts of some state as corrupt or biased against people like you, you could stay out.

Of course lawyers searched for loopholes that would let them pull outsiders into local courts; and many state lawmakers and judges would have been glad to accommodate them. But through much of American history the Supreme Court steadfastly upheld the right not to be abducted to a distant court. It considered that right a crucial part of the due process of law guaranteed each American citizen by the Constitution. In a much-cited 1878 case called *Pennoyer* v. *Neff*, the Court declared that a judgment entered without proper jurisdiction could not be enforced even in the state where it had been issued, let alone anywhere else.

The right not to be sued except at home was, in short, a full-fledged constitutional right, one that has never been rolled back by any constitutional amendment. Had the courts been vigilant against its infringement we would enjoy it to this day.

The beginnings were modest and reasonable, more an evolution than an erosion. Almost from the start special rules had been applied to corporations, which can be in more than one place at a time. The worry was that a corporation might send salesmen into a state to peddle its bogus patent medicines or whatever, and then pull its cash receipts out before anyone got around to suing. Individuals or partnerships might get away with the same trick, of course, but what seemed new and unfair was that the same team could come in under the guise of a different corporate shell the next month. A state could pass a law requiring the out-of-state corporation that wanted to do business within its borders to appoint an ongoing local agent suitable for future tagging. If a corporation simply ignored that requirement, the offended state could sue in the corporation's home state for the violation of its laws; but in the meantime it could not throw open its own courts to suits against the wrongdoers.

The other major target of discontent under the old rules was the out-of-state driver who got into a local accident and escaped the state too fast to be tagged with process. The problem as such was nothing new, having dated back to the days of the horse, but it seemed to be getting worse as the automobile made rapid interstate travel a pastime of the millions.

The first breaches were opened in the jurisdictional fortress by the creative use of ideas of tacit consent. Way back in 1856 the Court had ruled that if an unregistered corporation entered a state to do business, it could conveniently be *assumed* to have appointed a state official as local agent to be sued. And in 1927 it upheld a Massachusetts law providing that visiting motorists, like visiting corporations, tacitly consented to appoint local agents by the act of rolling across the state line.

There was something breezy in saying that a genuine bit of constitutional due process could be waived without any explicit consent. But the Court had closely limited reasons for its rulings. Driving on public roads was a privilege, and corporations were artificial creations. Since a state could keep people from driving or running incorporated businesses entirely, it could exercise the lesser power of allowing them on conditions. The Court emphasized that the Constitution protected people's natural liberty to go in and out of states for almost any purpose but these two, without fear of having to return to face suit. A 1918 Court opinion by Oliver Wendell Holmes reaffirmed that the Kentucky courts could not use the tacit-consent fiction to corral an unincorporated Illinois partnership that had done some business in the Bluegrass State.

Lawmakers, however, find tacit consent to be heady stuff. Even in this noisy world most people are still silent most of the time. If silence is consent, it would seem that the commodity of submission is being proffered in boundless supply. And now the long arm of the state courts, as it flexed more often, was growing muscular. New laws reached out to nonresident boat and plane operators as well as drivers. And lawyers began pushing at the bounds of what it meant for a corporation to have been "present" in a state and thus subject to its courts. What counted as being present? Hiring a full-time employee? Or would a part-timer do the trick? Keeping a regular place of business? Or would a single advertising brochure tacked to a bulletin board be enough? It was universally conceded that a company had not entered a state when it merely accepted orders from buyers there and shipped them the goods. But what if it sent in a troubleshooter to investigate a complaint that a shipment was spoiled?

In the early 1940s the International Shoe Company of St. Louis had (as it thought) carefully arranged its affairs to stay out of unfamiliar courts. It kept no offices or agents in the state of Washington. It paid commissions to traveling salesmen who visited the state, but took care not to let them collect money or enter contracts on its behalf. Instead it provided them with one sample shoe each of a pair in various styles. The salesmen would show the samples to the managers of local shoe stores, who then placed direct orders for shoes from the International Shoe factories in Missouri and elsewhere. The state of Washington claimed jurisdiction over the company anyway, and the case went up to the U.S. Supreme Court.

By now the Court had tired of the fiction-on-fiction game of widening chinks in the constitutional wall that protected defendants. In its 1945 *International Shoe* decision it simply took a bulldozer to the offending structure. It announced a new, all-purpose rule of jurisdiction that would apply to companies and just as momentously to individuals as well. From now on, any state court could haul you in so long as you had "certain minimum contacts" with its territory. What sort of contacts might those be? Those such that letting the suit go forward did not offend "traditional notions of fair play and substantial justice."

No one knew at the time what this language meant. No one knows to this day. Of course courts are supposed to aim for fair play and substantial justice, but a court whose orders stop there is a court left to its own devices. In the decades that followed the state courts began grabbing one outsider and then another and then another, and the Court turned down all chances to stop them. The lone exception for many years was a 1958 case where a Florida court had tried to get its hands on a Delaware trust fund, but that decision was criticized in the academic commentary and in time virtually ignored. In essence the federal court resigned control over its whole fractious state brood, like the beleaguered parent who was reduced to shouting, "Do whatever the hell you want—now let's see you disobey *that*."

The sudden overthrow of the old limits on jurisdiction vastly multiplied the options for filing suits. It meant people and businesses could be sued not only in places where they had been active in the past but also in places they had never visited at all but with which they had unspecified "contacts" as they went about their affairs. The only question would be whether taking them there would offend the sense of fairness of the court that would be trying them.

The business world felt the first effects. Courts quickly seized jurisdiction over enterprises that had never entered a state but did ship goods regularly into it, purchase supplies from within it, or accept checks from customers who lived in it. The most profound impact was not on the really big companies, which with their sprawling nationwide presence were already used to being sued in many places, but on the typical small to mid-sized firm that serves a nationwide market from a single location. Suddenly these companies found themselves defending suits in Skowhegan and Winnemucca, Kissimmee and Juneau. It mattered not how tiny a share of overall business they had done in a state: an Illinois company was made to go to the U.S. Virgin Islands to be sued though only $1,800 of its $35 million in annual sales came from that territory. A magazine publisher might find itself sued not just where its editing or printing took place, but wherever it had subscribers or newsstand sales.

Nor was there much hope of staying out of a state's courts by screening its citizens from one's customer list, because indirect contacts counted too. After a bus crash an English company that made component parts found itself compelled to stand trial in Hawaii even though it had no direct commercial connections with that island state. The court explained that a businessman should expect "to defend his product wherever he himself has placed it, either directly or through the normal distributive channels of trade." Everyone in the chain of commerce was vulnerable. Auto dealers and car rental companies began to be sued in distant states to which customers had driven their cars.

Surprising things were happening to individuals as well. Tennessee, Iowa, Washington, and California grabbed jurisdiction over out-of-state men who, it was alleged, had fathered children during time spent in the state. California passed a law providing that anyone who had sexual intercourse within its borders automatically submitted to later suit in its courts. Nor was it necessary, as Ida Weitz discovered, for an individual to visit a state physically to experience its justice. In 1984 the Supreme Court ruled that a Florida journalist, like the national magazine he wrote for, could be made to go to trial in California, where his allegedly libelous articles had circulated. New York collared a California man who had put in telephone bids at a Manhattan auction, and lawyers warned that a single letter or phone call into a state might bring you into its courts as a defendant. Tacit consent, it seemed, could now be given in the privacy of one's own home.

State judges and state legislators took turns pushing out the frontiers of their jurisdiction. It became common for the judges simply to announce that they were assuming this or that new power over residents of other states. Where they hesitated, state legislators passed "long-arm" laws. In 1973 California invented a vacuum attachment that worked beautifully to pull in loose cases from around the country. The state's legislature simply declared that its courts were empowered with such jurisdiction as was consistent with due process—or, as a cynic might have put it, with as much as they could constitutionally get away with.

Of course judges could still turn away suits when they felt like it. An Oregon court said no when a Portland movie theater operator wanted to force Elizabeth Taylor to come to town to answer his charges that her off-the-set shenanigans had hurt the box office receipts of the film *Cleopatra*. Similarly, a federal court rebuffed a woman who had moved from South Dakota to Idaho, gotten her doctor to renew her prescription by telephone, and then decided she wanted to sue him in Idaho. The court said it thought it would be too bad if every doctor had to worry "where the patient may carry the consequences of his treatment and in what distant lands he may be called upon to defend it. The traveling public," it noted, "would be ill served were the treatment of local doctors confined to so much aspirin as would get the patient into the next state."

But this was a mercy rather than a solid right. Either court could easily have ruled the other way had it been so inclined. All the Oregon court would have had to assert, for example, was that Miss Taylor should have foreseen that her alleged misconduct would harm the business of theaters in Oregon, as for that matter in the rest of the Western world.

One rule of thumb that emerged was that a defendant with a "pervasive multi-state business" could be taken pretty much anywhere. For everyone else, the general pattern was that if a court wanted you it could probably have you, at least for those of your activities that were connected with the state; if it could find a few contacts more, it might assert "general" jurisdiction over your misdeeds wherever committed.

One of the chief assumptions behind long-arm jurisdiction was that many long-distance lawsuits are filed against big businesses, or, as in auto accidents, against individuals who are for the most part defended by insurance companies. It was hoped that these deep-pocketed entities could make travel just another cost of doing business, passing it on to their customers. Whatever the merits of this view, it was soon noticed that not all the defendants being shanghaied by the new system were big, nor by any means were all the plaintiffs little. In fact larger plaintiffs very often succeeded in forcing smaller defendants to travel. There was no real way around this. A few courts announced that they would base their jurisdiction in part on how wealthy a defendant was, but most hesitated to introduce an explicit wealth test for depriving litigants of what had so recently been their constitutional right.

As the old right to be sued at home sank over the horizon, a new orb was sighted in the legal firmament, the right to *sue* at home. No state could quite establish that right in so many words, but many made it clear that they approved of the general principle. One implication was noteworthy. If a state wanted to provide full service for its own local plaintiffs, it could not stop at merely handling those troubles they had encountered while they were on its own soil. It had to figure out a way to get jurisdiction over cases that arose while they were visiting other states.

The California Supreme Court found one creative approach in a 1976 case. The Cornelison family of California was on the highway in the state of Nevada when its vehicle collided with that of a Nebraska-based trucker named Roy Chaney. Mr. Cornelison was killed. His widow, who survived the crash, lived close by across the state line in California and could have traveled back to Nevada for trial without apparent hardship, but her lawyers apparently wished to sue in the balmier judicial climate of the Golden State.

When the case reached the high court in Sacramento Justice Stanley Mosk, speaking for the court majority, conceded that the crash had not literally taken place in California. But, he pointed out, it had certain important connections with California. The victims lived in the state. Chaney, the Nebraskan, often visited the state on business. In fact, he was on his way there when the crash took place and only a short time later would actually have arrived. So the state had every right to make him stand trial within its borders.

Justice William Clark, later to serve in the Cabinet under President Reagan, dissented in a tone that betrayed a certain what-next exasperation. The only adequate excuse for grabbing an outsider, Clark observed, would be the outsider's California-related activities. And yet the "only conceivable connection" between those activities and this crash was that Chaney "was rolling toward (and plaintiff away from) its border." If being only a short drive away from the Golden State was enough to be sucked in by the gravitational field of its courts, how far away did people have to keep to know they were out of the orbit of jeopardy? Three hours' distance? Twenty-four? "Our busy courts," Clark said, "should have little interest in assuring each resident who leaves the state that he may return to litigate every wrong incurred in his travels."

These pshaws and faughs notwithstanding, many law

school commentators saw the direction the *Cornelison* case had pointed out, and approved wholeheartedly. Why not make an alleged wrongdoer stand trial wherever the consequences of his actions might be felt? And where more were they felt than where his victims went back to live after a mishap?

The states' newfound yen to hear out-of-state controversies when their own citizens were the ones filing the suits required a fairly stunning U-turn in the arguments that had been used to propel the jurisdictional juggernaut this far. It had been plausibly urged that local mishaps should be brought to local courts because that was where the witnesses, highway patrol, and hospital reports were to be found. Now that these arguments suddenly cut against the extension of jurisdiction, they were discarded without a second thought. The California high court allowed as how the police records of the *Cornelison* accident were located in Nevada, where Chaney preferred to be sued; but after all, Mrs. Cornelison "was also a witness to the accident and she is a California resident."

New York soon came up with an irresistible method of conscripting defendants that other states rushed to emulate. In 1966 its highest court asserted jurisdiction in a suit against a Quebec driver who had injured a New Yorker in a Vermont crash. Its reasoning was that the suit was really against the Quebec man's insurance policy, that the policy could be found wherever the company that issued it could be found, and that this company did business in New York. Before long New York was hearing cases against drivers across North America who had never allowed their cars to set tire in the Empire State. Driving along near your home in Moline or Little Rock or Spokane and grazing the fender of a passing car, you might find yourself the defendant before a Bronx jury. The cheerful assumption was that the suit should be of no concern to you personally, only to your insurance company—a notion of scant comfort when you found yourself summoned as a witness, or found your rates going up after a big payout was made in your name.

Had the new rule simply been that a case would always

be tried in the complainant's back yard and never in the respondent's, the impetus for litigation would have been strong enough. But the emerging order was actually much more favorable to plaintiffs and their lawyers than that. They kept gaining new options; seldom if ever did they have to give up any old ones. Mrs. Cornelison's lawyers won the right to sue in California, but they could still have taken her suit to Nevada or Nebraska if that had been more to their liking.

What happened was inevitable. Lawyers headed in droves for the courts with the highest verdicts, the least demanding rules of evidence, the most lopsidedly pro-plaintiff procedural rules, the laxest scrutiny of attorneys' fees. They searched out the judges and juries most sympathetic to their kind of client or hostile to their kind of opponent. Some things were not supposed to vary from court to court: Chaney's driving was supposed to be judged under Nevada highway rules no matter where he faced trial. But everything else did vary, and any lawyer knew that the intangibles of personnel and procedure could tip the balance in many a case.

The value of getting into the right court is quite tangible. Some years ago an experienced injury lawyer was quoted as saying that injury cases with identical facts could bring expected damage awards ranging from $10,000 to $2,000,000 depending on the jurisdiction in which they were filed. A study for the New York City government found that the reputation of Bronx juries for handing out high verdicts was not mistaken: the average award in cases against the city there was nearly twice as high as in Brooklyn and Queens and two and a half times that in conservative Staten Island. Often an otherwise valueless claim acquires settlement value if it can be brought in a dangerous court district. In a 1975 New York case, the plaintiff's lawyer confessed with disarming candor that he had made a tactical error by suing in one court and asked permission to refile in a court with higher verdicts.

Disarming candor, however, is the exception rather than the rule. In one of the leading lawsuits over tank-car spills, the lawyers for aggrieved neighbors originally filed suit where the accident took place, in Boone County, Missouri, but after a survey of potential jurors showed resistance to high damage awards they moved the suit across the Mississippi River to the county surrounding East St. Louis, Illinois, one of the most depressed cities in America. It was a good choice: after a four-year trial the jury allowed as how the neighbors had suffered no damage from the spill but tried to award them $16.2 million in punitive damages anyway.

American lawyers have long known how to take a defendant with statewide operations to the right county and city; thus do rural complaints against Illinois railroads get filed in Chicago to avoid the stingy juries often found downstate. Long-arm jurisdiction helped turn this largely local pastime into a big-league national affair. As in any sport, different teams attract different kinds of fans. Litigators with lame, speculative cases love the unpredictable courts where anything can happen; those with solid cases try to avoid the very same courts. Courts with long backlogs repel lawyers who want fast resolution, but attract lawyers whose strategy is to bleed their opponents into submission.

Some states attract shoppers by offering to apply a long statute of limitations to out-of-state transactions. Earl Cowan was hurt in a 1975 highway accident in Texas. Six years later lawyers for his widow had the idea of suing Ford Motor Company for the injury. The time limit for suing had long since expired in Texas, so they sued in Mississippi, a state with no connection whatsoever to the accident but with a longer statute of limitations. Ford was ordered to face the suit.

When Kathy Keeton, an executive with *Penthouse* magazine and wife of its publisher Bob Guccione, decided to sue the rival sex magazine *Hustler* for some scurrilous items it had published about her years before, her lawyers found that the statute of limitations had run out in every state but New Hampshire, so that was where they went. The Supreme Court ruled in 1984 that this was perfectly okay: if *Hustler* had not wanted to be sued in the Granite State, it should not have shipped magazines there. Although Ms. Keeton had no known link to New Hampshire herself, Justice William Rehnquist explained, the state was perfectly free to discipline magazines for libels whether they involved its own citizens or not.

One of the most important consequences of the long-arm revolution in fueling litigation could easily have been predicted. In very many disputes, especially in the business world, both sides have some conceivable grounds to sue. A company orders supplies, claims to find their quality unsatisfactory, and refuses delivery on further shipments; it can sue for a refund of its deposit, or the supplier can sue to enforce the contract. If the two are at a distance, they both have reason to race to the courthouse to get the home-court advantage. Worse, the cycle of suspicion can be self-fulfilling: fear of being struck first can provide reason enough to strike the first blow in a case that should not have led to a lawsuit at all.

Fracases between insurance companies and their bigger corporate customers, a fast-growing category of litigation, have become a virtual Supermarket Sweep of two-way nationwide forum-shopping, with the insurers racing for straightlaced Illinois and the corporate policyholders for loosey-goosey New Jersey. Lawyer Timothy Russell of Drinker, Biddle and Reath says he advises insurance companies to be aggressive: "If forum selection is considered so important, it is probably wise to sue first and talk second."

When Eastern Airlines filed for bankruptcy it was said to have picked the federal court in Manhattan rather than the one near its Miami headquarters at least in part because the late chief judge of the Miami court was known as tough on foot-dragging by debtors and tightfisted with fee awards for their lawyers. The *National Law Journal* reported that "attorneys for ailing companies have routinely filed Chapter 11 petitions in other jurisdictions solely to avoid the judge's reach." Other laws provide more or less openly for forum-shopping. Antitrust suits can be filed in any federal court district where a defendant sells goods, which can mean practically anyplace in the country.

Thus do local lawyering cultures wield national influence. California is popular for air-crash cases and many other kinds of litigation. Philadelphia is a favorite filing site for class actions (although Melvin Belli is reported to have proposed Miami because of the weather). The Texas Gulf Coast, from Beaumont through Houston to Matagorda County, is known for populist juries of oil rig workers and their relatives with a low flash point of anger at deep-pocket defendants. In the *Forbes* list of the nation's richest plaintiff's lawyers, six of the top ten are based in the coastal section of the Lone Star State.

Like other kinds of commerce, forum-shopping has become more international in flavor. Some American courts now listen to cases from around the world filed by litigants who may never have met an American until the tort lawyer flew in to their home town with papers to sign and tales of the high awards to be had across the ocean. If their lawyers can find some defendant vulnerable to suit in an American court, Europeans who get hurt when a helicopter crashes in the North Sea can obtain "mid-Atlantic settlements" much higher than their countrymen can get in similar mishaps where only Europeans can be blamed.

It seems like free money, but of course it is not. For one thing, American companies suffer a distinct disadvantage in bidding for overseas work. In 1985 McDonnell Douglas, trying to sell aircraft to the mainland Chinese, felt obliged to build into its bid a cost factor to cover its inability to avoid being sued in American courts after any crashes that may take place in remote stretches of the Sinkiang desert. (The Chinese reportedly reacted with incredulity at this bit of "American flim-flam.") Perhaps in hopes of correcting the competitive imbalance, some American courts have begun entertaining suits against *foreign* companies for foreign sins against foreign residents when the defendant—in one case, Rolls-Royce—carries on some American operations. The result is to shift the competitive advantage to foreign companies that conduct absolutely no U.S. operations. American trial lawyers like to boast about how they are carrying the valuable goal of deterrence into the world marketplace. Others might say they have pioneered a new form of international commerce, the export of disservices.

Courts can still turn away, on grounds of unfairness or impracticality, disputes that should be heard in other states or countries. (The doctrine is called *forum non conveniens*.) That is what has happened to date with the lawsuits against Union Carbide over the 1984 gas leak at Bhopal, India. But judges don't use that power as often as they might. First, needless to say, they do not turn down cases on the grounds that they are so sympathetic to the kind of suit being put forward that it would be unfair to let them hear it. Second, the defendant who objects to the forum has to shoulder a high burden of proof; if there are doubts, the case stays put.

And convenience is often not what is at stake anyway. The squabbling on this issue can take on a surreal quality: one set of lawyers, living out of suitcases after traveling halfway around the world to find the court with the most favorable verdicts, will insist it is perfectly convenient, while their opponents, so used to being sued in this court that they keep lawyers nearby on permanent payroll, swear it would be vastly easier for them to defend the case in some remote corner of the globe.

Even more to the point, the courts that frown on forum-shopping tend to be the ones where no one wants to shop, because they protect defendants' rights in other ways too. The courts most apt to favor plaintiffs are likewise the ones inclined to open their doors to all comers. Some, like the fabled New Orleans saloons that never close, have practically taken those doors off the hinges.

As states leapfrogged each other with ever wilder, can-you-top-this claims of power, the political environment that shaped the state courts was wholly transformed. No longer did the more ambitious courts have to content themselves with regulating the small share of the nation's grievances that happened to be lodged against their own citizens. They could now boldly project their power to persons, events, and bank accounts around the country and even the world. There was clearly much potential for doing good in this reach-out-and-put-the-touch-on-someone power, especially if one believed that juries and legal cultures in other states were regrettably tolerant of misbehavior or hesitant to hand down big enough verdicts.

Beneath these sweet violin strains of idealism could be heard an insistent drumbeat of old-fashioned political self-interest. State judges are mostly elected or appointed for renewable terms by election-minded governors. Jurisdiction over outsiders gave them a thousand new chances to redistribute money from people who lived in other states to their own constituents. In the days when most defendants were local, both judge and jury might hesitate to approve a crippling judgment against a local employer, magazine, or car dealer; it might hurt real, identifiable neighbors. Now the immediate harm at least would fall on distant and anonymous investors, employees, consumers and taxpayers. Small wonder so many courts were soon observed to dish out "home cooking" to local litigants.

No one ever seriously doubted that shifting the burdens of travel and bias to cut in favor of lawsuit filing, instead of against it, would raise the amount of litigation. Greatly expanding plaintiffs' court options, instead of just replacing one definite court with another, was bound to do the same thing: a smorgasbord calls forth a heartier appetite than a one-dish commissary, especially when "home cooking" is one of the options. But litigation boosters were excited by the promise of making it easier to press meritorious suits, and preferred not to think very much about the costs of making it harder to press meritorious resistances.

The long-established constitutional right not to be sued except at home passed unmourned and unwept by most legal commentators. Like other rights that disappear, it was no longer spoken of as a right at all: first it became a matter of conveniences to weigh and equities to balance, and then it was forgotten entirely. And only later did we learn it had a point after all.

5

⚖

LITIGATION MADE EASY:
Suing Without Explaining

*The procedure [of the Court of Star Chamber, abolished in 1641]
was not as in the common.law courts, by writ, but by bill, as in the
Court of Chancery. The vital difference between the writ and the bill
was that whereas the former specified the entire scope of complaint
against the defendant, the latter summoned him to answer not only
as to matters specified therein, but as to other unspecified matters
as well.*

—*H. G. HANBURY,* English Courts
of Law, *2nd edition*

A young Manhattan urologist
was served one day at his East Side office with the papers in
his first malpractice suit, filed by a middle-aged patient who
had developed complications after prostate surgery.

The document went on for four pages, but in no way
did its allegations add up to a coherent story. Instead they
charged a bewildering variety of generically worded types of
negligence. The doctor had been inadequately trained, it
said. He had negligently hired unsuitable assistants. He had
failed to warn the patient of the hazards of this surgery. And
so on.

"I was stunned," the doctor recalls. "Some of the charges
were inconsistent with each other. Some mentioned compli-

cations that other patients sometimes suffer, but that this patient clearly hadn't. Some were things for which they couldn't have had any evidence, like the attack on my training." On the wall behind him were diplomas from leading universities.

"The lawyers put in everything that can ever go wrong with this kind of surgery, every way a member of my specialty can fall short. If half the things in here were true, I would be drummed out of the profession. What are my other patients and colleagues supposed to think if they hear I have been charged with all this?"

What galled the doctor was that he could not learn what he was supposed to have done wrong. He had no way to know whether the case would be simple or complex, a trivial affair or a headline-grabber that might prove the ruin of his reputation. Nor had he a clue where to turn for vindication. To colleagues who had examined the patient, to vouch for the correctness of his diagnosis? To the professional literature, to confirm his choice of therapy? To an accreditation board, to verify the soundness of his training? To the personnel files, to rerun the references on his assistants?

Some people who get sued are lucky enough, if that is the word, to know what is coming and why. They may have done one of those things that customarily get people in law trouble, like failing to pay their credit card bills or driving into someone's picture window. Others, however, will examine the complaint with much curiosity. What they find there, and what their lawyer can add by way of explanation, is all they may learn for quite a while about the nature and extent of their jeopardy. What are they supposed to have done that was wrong? Which legal norm did they violate? How are they supposed to have hurt the other fellow, and how badly? What happens if they lose?

Unfortunately, it is the nature of trial lawyers—especially those with weak cases—to try to conceal rather than disclose these matters. Even when a complaint seems to be inform- ative at this stage, it is usually trying to imply as much while actually committing to as little as it can get away with.

Suppose you are a divorced mother raising a family. One day your ex-husband hits you with a custody lawsuit. The complaint says you have "failed to supervise the children as to their eating regular and nutritious meals." In fact you have "constantly disrupted" their meal schedules to follow your own selfish social pursuits. The kids are also "embarrassed in associating with their friends and classmates" because you have failed to furnish them with "adequate clothing or cloth- ing appropriate to the changing seasons." You have moreover shocked their sensibilities by entertaining boyfriends at the house. In sum, having "followed a consistent and relentless pattern" of running the house so as to cater merely to your own "personal gratifications," you have "woefully failed to provide a stable environment for the children."

It sounds nasty, but don't take it personally. It's all copied word for word out of *Child Custody & Visitation Law & Practice*, a lawyer's handbook published by the reputable firm of Matthew Bender. The book is full of these sample forms. Some mother across town had the same charges hurled at her last week, verbatim. On closer inspection they are cunningly phrased to make almost any child's existence seem deprived by capturing typical failings of nearly every parent in modern America. What kid nowadays ever gets (or wants) perfectly regular mealtimes? Or has never been tense around Mom's date? Or has not gotten upset when some classmate showed up first with the latest fad in clothing?

But the complaint is almost sure to get your ex into court, because for all the judge can tell you've been sending little Jessica and Michael out in rags to search for bread crumbs in the forest snow while you entertain a party of Hell's Angels. The formbook does make one slip into a self-defeating spec- ificity: it says you have failed to take the children in for dental checkups as regularly as you might. On second thought a shrewd lawyer would probably rephrase this as an unspecified charge that your neglect is endangering their long-term health.

And when you consult your own lawyer you learn another thing. Even if these are the charges your ex uses to get into court, he can throw something completely different (and perhaps much more serious) at you when it comes time for trial. In fact if his lawyer has anything he thinks is really devastating he may well be holding it back deliberately at this point.

Nowadays it is routine for the "pleadings" with which a lawsuit begins to be maximally alarming but minimally informative. They are at most a kind of air raid siren, warning that the enemy is about to attack but not from which direction or how. Yet things were not always so. During most of its history the law, most particularly the common law, tended to give you a much fairer arraignment of charges when first it laid its icy hand on you. Your opponent's pleadings were typically supposed to offer a fairly detailed narrative, based on something more solid than suspicion or guesswork, of what you were alleged to have done wrong, which legal norm you violated, how your misconduct led to injury and what injury that was. Courts often tossed out pleadings for failing to meet these requirements. Once a suit was under way, furthermore, your adversary normally had to win "upon the facts stated in the complaint, or not at all"; it was hard for him to add new and serious charges in mid-course, and almost impossible to change those parts of the story he had already committed to.

The severity of these rules cut both ways. Once a complaint had been sworn out against you in good form, you had to respond in good form too, or lose. Defendants, like plaintiffs, could be held to their pleadings, so you had to frame them with great care: fail to raise a valid defense at this stage and you might lose it for good. You might not be sure on every relevant point—was this person who slipped and fell on your porch an invited visitor, or a trespasser?—and in some situations you could throw up your hands and, as it was called, plead the general issue. But usually the law aimed to extract a candid as well as a prompt response.

These formalities were dictated in part by a sense of what was fair to the opponent. As an English judge wryly observed in 1723, even the very first civil complainant had the grace to offer a bill of particulars to his defendants before dispossessing them of their tenancy in Eden.

But avoiding unfairness to the contestants was not the only reason for strict pleading rules, or even the chief reason. The truth is that the courts did not themselves wish to be trifled with. The world is full of vague discontents, and the king's agents would not commence their majestic operations without something more solid to go on. Nor had they the time or patience to permit one solid grievance to expand into a general venting of all the ways the two sides were dissatisfied with each other. Focused correction, not general recrimination, was the aim.

So the law's first order of business was to contain, delimit, and pin down the quarrel. The respondent might admit a point—and silence was taken as admission—thus sealing off one branch of the inquiry. Or he might flatly deny it, presenting an issue to be resolved by the judge or jury at trial. Finally, he might proffer what was called an affirmative defense, asking, in effect, "So what?": that would cover such defenses as permission in a charge of trespass, or truth in a charge of libel. The onus of response would then fall back in turn on the original complainant.

By the end of these stylized volleys and countervolleys the whole case was supposed to be boiled down to one or more well-formed issues to be decided at trial. This hope was not always quite achieved, in part because some common-law lawyers and judges were better than others at laying bare the essence of the dispute, as the phrase went. And other courts, such as the old chancery courts with their system of "equity," were less insistent on specificity and closure. But on the common-law side, at least, a lawsuit in principle could not get out of the gate unless its possible destinations were known. The pleadings provided a definite road map for the legal journey ahead; admittedly it had some alternate routes, but litigants could not just head out on the open road and see where it took them.

Most judges insisted on sticking to the road map to a degree that now seems persnickety. In an 1859 case a man was trying to collect on a promissory note that he had sworn in the pleadings had a face value of $2,579.00. It emerged that the note's true face value was actually higher than that by 57½ cents. For this piddling error (and in favor of his opponent!) the court overturned the judgment he had won, although it did let him come back to do it right by amending the complaint. "However much courts might regret that a slip in pleading should delay the party in the administration of justice, the rules of law must be observed," the judge wrote in chilly explanation. "If the rule were relaxed in this case, it would be to sanction a looseness in practice that might eventually be productive of more injury than benefit." The fear was that letting the proof vary by so much as a whisker from the original contentions would give lawyers reason to be less careful or honest in framing those contentions.

In the old law, pleadings, among their other functions, served as an immensely important filter in keeping many kinds of litigation out of court entirely. Understanding how things changed calls for a bit of an excursion into legal history.

For six centuries, to sue someone at common law you had to ask a court for a "writ." The different kinds of writs had evolved in the long competition between rival courts that produced the Anglo-American law, and they came in a set number of varieties. You had to figure out which one you wanted, not just ask a judge which one he thought you deserved: judges were terriers who would wait at the hole you brought them to, not pointers who would lead you to prey. If none of the available writs precisely suited your needs, you would seldom have much luck just asking a court to make one up for you based on its sense of what was fair. That sort of thing was jealously guarded against as a power grab—judicial activism, we might call it today.

The differences between writs set many traps for even the well-trained lawyer and generated technicalities that seemed to have so little to do with actual justice that many judges were tempted just to ignore them. David Dudley Field, who became the great American reformer of the system, liked to tell of one of his own close calls. He watched in horror at a trial as the opposing lawyer pointed out what seemed to be the faint traces of a seal on the insurance policy that was at issue. Contracts with seals fell under the writ of covenant, while contracts without seals fell under the writ of assumpsit, which was the one Field had asked for. If the whole case had been assigned to the wrong legal pigeonhole, Field's client was out of court. Fortunately for his cause, the judge squinted indulgently at the document—but without putting his glasses on—declared himself unable to make out a seal, and ordered the trial to continue.

Each of the writs had its own singularities of procedure, which tended to reflect perceived nuances of fairness, practicality, and so forth. This subtlety was bought at the cost of great complication, however, and the whole system of legal procedure tended to repel the understanding of the lay person. (The very names of the writs deepened the sense of mystery, recalling in many instances the far-off days of Norman rule—trover, assumpsit, detinue, replevin.) That legal procedure was close to unfathomable by the lay person did not pose a burning practical problem, because the quaint archaisms seldom confused the standard of actual conduct, but merely the remedies the law provided when standards failed. And laymen were expected to consult lawyers anyway when they needed to know how to sue someone.

By the nineteenth century, however, a great movement for simplification was building. The volume of legal business was growing. Ordinary citizens were encountering more and more loans and mortgages, deeds to land and vehicles, and other legal instruments. More lawyers had to be employed to enforce these documents, and it seemed a good idea to reduce the arcaneness of the training needed to become a lawyer. One promising step was to draw up simpler methods of pleading to replace the old forms of action. The first big venture of that sort was the 1848 Field Code in New York, named after its great advocate, David Dudley Field. For many years, the simplified system of "code pleading" caught on mostly in frontier western states whose rough-and-ready lawyering culture had weaker ties to old English byways. Eventually code pleading spread to all fifty states, but the process took a long time; as recently as 1959 the state of Maine still clung to the forms of action.

Under reformed pleading litigants continued to learn a lot about the charges against them. The complaint no longer spelled out which legal theory it was relying on, but its factual allegations had to be if anything more detailed than before. And the other general rules still held, for a long time at least: pleadings were still thrown out if they were too vague, they were still expected to frame the issues for trial, and litigants were still held to the contentions in them. The revolution was thus more of form than of ultimate content.

Then came a second revolution that truly deserved the name.

Code pleading had not done away with the traps for the unwary. The game of pleading was now less of an obscure ritual, less like bezique or skat and more like gin rummy or canasta. But it still had gamelike features and its outcome could still turn on skill and chance. A clever lawyer might still get his opponent's pleadings thrown out for inadvertent and technical defects, or stymie his proofs because they differed in minor ways from what he had pleaded.

This, it was argued, was not only pointless but unfair. Maybe the opponent had been careless or uninformed or even less than candid and had put forth an inaccurate claim, or omitted to put forth a claim that it later turned out he was

entitled to make. Should he be punished for this mere procedural mistake by losing one of his genuine rights in the
outside world? Worse yet, should the client be punished if
the fault was the lawyer's? Wasn't that letting the rule book
get the better of substantive justice?

The danger of depriving litigants of justice because of
their lawyers' errors sounds compelling to the nonlawyer, but
it was something of a red herring. Any time courts make a
final ruling on anything, lawyers' mistakes and omissions can
deprive their clients of justice. Strict pleading was a way of
bringing finality to certain issues early rather than late, so it
affected the timing of when these fatal mistakes could occur,
but not the opportunity for them. Only experience could tell
whether the slips were worse and more numerous when lawyers had to commit to stories early, thus missing the benefit
of facts that emerged in later stages of litigation, or not so
early, thus missing the benefit of the facts teased forth by
requiring the other lawyer to commit to a story. Against the
abuses of pinning lawyers down when they really don't know
something, in short, must be ranged the abuses of letting
them dodge commitment when they really do know.

Just beneath the surface lurked an even more fundamental controversy. Many lawyers wanted to file suits for
clients but did not know enough to frame them properly, at
least without arduous investigation beforehand. Some hired
private eyes to tail the opponent, interview witnesses or search
through old public records for the information they needed.
Surely forcing them to resort to such measures was undignified
and wasteful. Besides, what if the facts they needed to frame
their complaint were locked away in their opponent's safe?
Did that mean they could never sue at all?

Like so many legal controversies, this one was over the
tension between two kinds of fairness. Requiring lawyers to
line up facts and commit to theories early on will lead to
instances of real unfairness by choking off some valid claims
and making others more expensive to prove. On the other
hand, letting lawyers sue on suspicion and then get around

to lining up their facts and theories is certain to lead to equally genuine instances of unfairness of a different kind by calling forth more suits against people for things they haven't done, leaving everyone who gets sued less sure of how much trouble they are in, and widening the chances for perjury by letting litigants hold back from committing to a story until they see which story seems to have the best chance of success.

The proposed solution was simply to resolve these tensions in favor of those who wish to sue by more or less abolishing pleadings as a separate stage of a lawsuit. Each side could come to court unashamed of not knowing the details of its case. First would come the process of "discovery," in which lawyers force opponents to cough up information, and then there would be plenty of time to get straight whether there was a genuine dispute and what it might be about. The issues would have to be pinned down at *some* point before a jury actually voted on them, but that moment should at least be put off until both sides had been fully educated about their possible claims—though it was not exactly clear how long that educational process would go on. For good measure, courts should stop trying to police amendment and variance no matter how fishy it looked.

Thus argued a group of influential legal scholars in the 1920s and 1930s. The famous Roscoe Pound had provided intellectual ammunition, but the most active in the practical victory was Charles Clark, a dean of Yale Law School from 1929 to 1939 who later served as a federal judge on the powerful Second Circuit Court of Appeals. After Clark departed the cause was carried on at Yale by another highly influential scholar, Fleming James, Jr., who continued to write through the 1970s.

Dean Clark had the good luck to start at the top. The federal courts at the time of the early New Deal were just preparing to adopt their first distinctive code of legal procedure. (Before that they followed the rules of the states in which they were

located.) In the mid-1930s Clark was assigned the chief drafting chores and made the most of the opportunity.

One fateful decision his committee made early on was
to do away with the procedural differences between the various kinds of lawsuits: all would follow a common format.
Instead of trying to maintain nuances of fairness there would
be a great simplification that (it was hoped) would make for
cheaper litigation with less trouble. That common format was
heavily influenced by the perceived needs of antitrust litigation; Clark and others had taken an interest in this area,
consulting with federal officials who were looking for a freer
hand at filing this immensely complicated and expensive variety of lawsuit.

The common format would begin with what came to be
known as "notice" pleading. Pleadings would serve only to
put the parties on notice that they were being sued, and briefly
state the general subject matter of the dispute. Fleming James
and Geoffrey Hazard give as good a definition as any when
they explain that notice pleading lets a lawyer get into court
by "alleg[ing] his claim in very general terms, so that it cannot
clearly be discerned what he thinks the facts might be."

The new rules were greeted with widespread hope and
enthusiasm, but they did not conquer the field without opposition. Among the skeptics were Professor O. L. McCaskill,
who taught at Cornell and Hastings law schools, and federal
judge James Fee of the Ninth Circuit Court of Appeals. Their
arguments were scorned as fuddy-duddyish at the time; later
they came to appear remarkably prescient.

Justice was better served, McCaskill maintained, when
lawyers did their best to investigate claims carefully before
turning them into lawsuits. Once they were allowed to get
away with it, however, many would follow the path of least
resistance by filing the suit first and then checking out its
merits at leisure. Even when they did know the facts and
theory on which they planned to proceed, they would succumb to their natural incentive not to reveal more of their
cases than necessary. The minimum commitment to detail

needed to get their clients into court would soon become the norm. Then would come a rush of weak and ill-considered claims, their defects concealed by evasive pleading, and after that downright abuse, "the bringing of actions for nuisance values and hope of settlement."

The promise of simplification, warned McCaskill and a few colleagues, would prove a mirage: making pleadings a snap would come at the price of making later stages of the dispute more complex. Lawyers would scurry around at great expense preparing elaborate responses to theories that it had never occurred to their opponents to use at trial. Leading California lawyer Moses Lasky called notice pleading "part of a broader tendency of deferring the inevitable necessity of thinking through a case."

Most writers took a blither view. Flimsy claims, it was often asserted, would be well enough discouraged by the prospect of refutation at trial. A few commentators explained that defendants needed no special notice of the charges against them because they had already taken part in the chain of events that led up to the lawsuit, or (to read between the lines) because they had already done the dirty deed.

The Federal Rules of Civil Procedure that Clark and his colleagues drew up were approved by Congress and the Supreme Court and went into effect in 1938. With some changes and extensions, including some important 1983 changes (to be discussed later), they are the rules of procedure we live under today. Slowly but surely the state court systems came around to the new way of doing things, adopting the federal rules as a whole or in major chunks. Several powerful forces pressed toward this conformity. Local lawyers want to learn one set of procedures instead of two; courts with tough pleading rules tend to lose litigants' "business" to other courts through forum-shopping; and, no doubt most important, the same intellectual trends and fashions that had swept elite law circles made it out to the rest of the country. Only a few states still retain what a typical manual dismisses as the "archaic" practice of "pleading formalism."

The federal rules were hailed as the dawn of a new era, which they surely were. Lest any lawyer sleep through that dawn, a wake-up call soon came from the federal appeals court in New York. An immigrant named Dioguardi, acting as his own lawyer, had filed a rambling complaint against the federal collector of customs, a man named Durning. The complaint was in badly broken English, and its meaning was obscure except that it appeared to relate to some "tonics" that Durning had sold at public auction in his official capacity. A trial judge dismissed the complaint, but the plucky Dioguardi chose to appeal. He drew a three-judge panel ornamented by none other than Dean Clark himself, who since the adoption of his rules had been lifted to the bench. In the landmark 1944 decision of *Dioguardi* v. *Durning,* Judge Clark announced that those who wanted to sue were not to be required to allege "facts sufficient to constitute a cause of action." All that should be needed was "a short and plain statement of the claim." Dioguardi's claim was not exactly plain, but it would do. He was back in court. And just as much to the point, so was Durning.

That set the tone. It soon became very hard to get pleadings thrown out on technicalities, or not-so-technicalities. The laxer courts began waving the barest and most fact-free allegations of wrongdoing through the gate. For a while opponents could still pin down contentions at an early stage through certain rights that descended as a sort of wraithlike residue of the old pleading stage. The most venerable of these wandering ghosts was the right to ask for a bill of particulars, which had been carried down from the old branch of jurisprudence known as equity. In 1948, however, reformers managed to exorcise and banish even that "grudging provision" (as Fleming James called it), the problem being, as they frankly explained, that opponents were invoking it too often.

A few federal and state judges tried to fight a rear-guard action against loose pleading. New York judge Samuel Silverman threw out a couple of malpractice suits of this kind. One suit had described a patient's injuries so evasively as to

cover anything (the judge noted dryly) from quadruple am-
putation to "a claim that the cleaning woman wrung out her
mop over a transfusion bottle." In another suit lawyers had
asserted claims against four fictitiously named persons with
no sign that their inclusion represented anything "more than
a hope that in the course of discovery the attorneys will be
able to find somebody else to sue for something." It was
harder to keep wily lawyers from filing "shotgun" or "kitchen-
sink" complaints in which they threw in every charge they
could think of to see if one would stick, like the complaint
that befell the outraged Manhattan doctor met with at the
beginning of this chapter.

Even the modern rules concede in one or two instances
that fairness can call for telling defendants the charges against
them. In a rare exception to their usual indulgence of evasion,
they provide that certain charges with high scandal value,
most notably of civil fraud, still have to be pleaded with
"particularity." "It is a serious matter to charge a person with
fraud," explain two leading commentators, "and hence no
one is permitted to do so unless he is in a position and is
willing to put himself on record as to what the alleged fraud
consists of specifically."

Trial lawyers, and commentators sympathetic to their
cause, have kept up a steady attack on this slender remaining
survival of the due-process tradition. They point out that to
charge a financier with fraud is not necessarily any more invidious than to charge a doctor with malpractice; by now the
charge has been flung at so many respected leaders in both
fields that it is coming to be seen as going with the territory.
If we don't protect doctors, why protect financiers? Of course,
it would be just as cogent to turn the contradiction around
and aim it at the trial lawyers: since we rightly do protect
financiers, isn't it time we protected doctors as well?

The crafty litigator wants to avoid being pinned down to any
one story or having the details of his claim come under an-
noying scrutiny, not just at the start of a case but all the way

through. To do this it is necessary to dodge a couple of other inspection stations that stand along the road to trial, stages that Dean Clark and some other drafters of the federal rules apparently hoped would make up for some of the lost screening and issue-focusing functions of the pleadings.

One is the summary judgment stage, a novelty at the time the federal rules came in. Summary judgment allows the judge, upon motion by a party, to dismiss a weak case, claim, or defense before trial. At first summary judgment looked like a halfway decent method of flushing out lame cases, those that were realistically bound to lose if they ever went to trial. And then came a 1946 court decision in a suit against, of all people, Cole Porter.

An obscure songwriter named Ira Arnstein had sued Porter for plagiarism, charging that several of Porter's most successful songs were knockoffs of his, Arnstein's, work. Both "My Heart Belongs to Daddy" and "Begin the Beguine," he alleged, were based on his own composition "A Mother's Prayer." "You'd Be So Nice To Come Home To," it seemed, had been derived from a lugubrious Arnstein ditty entitled "Sadness Overwhelms My Soul." Other supposedly swiped standards included "Night and Day" and "Don't Fence Me In." The plaintiff asked for an even million dollars.

It required a mighty effort of will to take this suit seriously. Arnstein, who was representing himself without a lawyer, had already filed and lost five similar lawsuits against other leading songwriters. He could offer no direct evidence that Porter had ever heard any of his music or seen it in sheet form, and some of the allegedly stolen-from compositions had never been published or performed in public at all. He could swear, however, that his room had been repeatedly ransacked and that Porter "had stooges right along to follow me, watch me, and live in the same apartment with me."

A New York federal court called the charges "fantastic" and granted Porter's motion for summary judgment against them. Judge Clark himself, one of the three judges on the appeals panel, said amen to that; avoiding trials on this sort

of suit, he thought, was a perfect use of the summary judgment rules. But he was outvoted by his yet-more-broad-
minded colleagues and Arnstein was back in court (where he
went to trial and lost). Judge Jerome Frank, a former Yale
professor and leading figure of the Legal Realism movement,
observed that the charges would stand or fall not on disputes
about the meaning of copyright law, but on questions of fact
and credibility, since if by some miracle Arnstein's charges
turned out to be true the law definitely entitled him to relief.
And the accepted rule—this tradition, it seemed, was not to
be updated—was that although judges could decide questions
of pure law on their own, questions of fact and credibility
had to wait until trials. The ruling became the standard one
down through the 1980s: to survive summary judgment all
you had to do was trump up, assert, or hallucinate a single
factual dispute that would have to be looked into. The let-
'em-sue logic of the modern rules was thus carried to its full
zany extremity.

The second screening device was the "pretrial conference," also a novelty. It allows the judge to call the two sides
together in a discussion to focus and clarify the issues. Unfortunately, it too turned out to be less than a salvation for
the victims of shoddy or ill-thought-out claims. Not all judges
chose to do the arm-twisting often needed to extract cooperation from the lawyers; unlike the pleadings, this device
provided no automatic way to get admissions on the table.
When judges did call the meetings it was usually not until
after people had been tied up in court for long periods on ill-
defined charges.

With the new freedom of amendment and variance, anyway, it was understood that litigants whose original charges
were shown to be grossly unfounded could switch, with little
muss or fuss, to new ones more in line with the current state
of the evidence. A District of Columbia malpractice suit from
early in the history of the rules shows the principle in action.
Dr. Joseph Jordan had been sued for failing to perform a
Caesarean section during the delivery of Alice Ann Robbins's

baby. After the case had gone on for some time the Robbins family lawyer asked to amend their pleadings to add a charge that Dr. Jordan had held himself out as a specialist. To a malpractice lawyer this is a momentous issue, often central to a case: if accepted it means the doctor will be held to a higher standard of care. Any competent lawyer would have probed for the detail in client interviews, and it was hard to imagine why the family could not have remembered it earlier. The trial court refused to allow the amendment. But the federal appeals court in Washington reversed its decision, explaining that the court could handle any possible unfairness to Dr. Jordan by giving him a continuance in which to rethink his defense. There seemed to be no firm deadline on how late damaging new contentions could be pulled from a hat to salvage a losing case or boost the cash value of a winner.

One of the chief uses of shotgun pleadings and easy variance is to tag whole categories of defendants without bothering to sort out who did what. After product mishaps, for example, it has become common for lawyers to sue not only the manufacturer of the product but also the makers of its component parts, on speculation that one of them will turn out to be vulnerable. The charges and theories against the various defendants are often inconsistent with each other.

Rick Sontag, who runs a company called Unison Industries, which makes parts for small aircraft, has had many experiences with pleadings of this type. Sontag's firm makes magnetos, which are part of the ignition system of an aircraft and are a favorite target of lawsuits. After one Hawaiian crash over open water, Unison was sued along with other companies and had to hire a local attorney in the island state to prepare a costly defense. It later developed that Unison's magneto had been replaced with a competitor's one year before the accident, as could have been learned from a glance at engine log books in possession of the plaintiff's lawyer. Similarly, after a mishap on tarmac where a complainant was injured by one of the propellers of a stationary airplane, Unison was sued and spent heavily defending itself although neither the plaintiffs nor their lawyer "had bothered to open the cowling of the airplane to look at the label on the product to see whether or not they were ours."

Another suit followed the crash of a private plane flying from New Jersey to Georgia. All landing runways had been fogged in, and the pilot of the plane had complained of running out of fuel; the National Transportation Safety Board found that fuel exhaustion was the cause of the crash. Unison was sued anyway. After the ABC weekly series *20/20* suggested that the suit was unfounded, the plaintiffs' lawyers— the leading contingency-fee aviation firm of Kreindler and Kreindler—came back with a theory that the fuel exhaustion was really the fault of a magneto malfunction after all; the device had allegedly burned fuel too fast. Later tests confirmed that this theory was equally unfounded: the installed magneto in fact used fuel at a lower rate than when new.

No one feels nostalgic for the technicalities of the old pleadings, but some of their underlying principles are sorely missed. Letting lawyers sue without being sure of their facts and without thinking through the legal issues at the start plainly enabled and encouraged them to file more lawsuits; that much was expected and intended from the start. Some of those suits—from people who know they have a good case but find it genuinely onerous to preassemble its outlines— will command widespread sympathy. But notice pleading also encouraged lawyers to sue without being all that sure that the facts or the law would be on their side when it came time to fill in the blanks. And the habit of suing people without being sure they've done anything wrong to you leads down a steep path.

The pleadings used to form a large, discouraging bump to get over at the very beginning of a suit, a real discontinuity between being in court and out. That reflected a wider truth about the real-life costs that people inflict on each other when they sue, or resist a suit valid on its face. To keep a lawsuit hanging over an opponent is no small matter. It is hurtful on a personal level, clouding reputation and compromising privacy. Litigants soon learn to dread the awkward explanations to neighbors and friends, the need to explain the overhanging risk when applying for a loan or inviting a partner into their business. They are often reluctant to marry or remarry, change their manner of life, take a job in a distant city, for fear of hurting their chances. A lawsuit is an imposition.

The things fought over tend to deteriorate as well. The contested farm or business goes to ruin because none of the feuding heirs or partners will keep it up properly. The divorce or probate home dumped hurriedly on the market tends to fetch a low price. Children have been found to show signs of distress that correlate with how long their custody is fought over. Accident victims who sue get well more slowly than those with similar injuries who don't. The cost structure of litigation should reflect its gravity, and not make the initial step into a lawsuit a tiny and easy one.

But keeping all the options open, at whatever cost, came to seem the most important thing. Notice pleading was indeed litigation made easy, but only for lawyers on the offensive. For lawyers and clients trying to respond to charges, it was litigation made incomparably harder, the terrors of uncertainty multiplying with the knowledge that claims could grow and shift and turn into their opposites as a case went along.

And so the evils of a more rationalist age, born of an inflexible insistence on pinning everything down, were made to give way to the more up-to-date and existential evils of letting everything float free in a roving inquiry into all the folly and mischief to be found in complex human relationships, an inquiry with, as one critic put it, "no apparent origin or discernible direction." Fearful of being accused of pettifogging specificity, the American courts instead made themselves into a place where nothing was secure and anything could happen. What began as a page out of Dickens ended as a page out of Kafka.

♎

THE ASSAULT ON PRIVACY

Here you have the greatest device for generating paper ever thought up by the legal profession: the deposition. All successful inventors know about depositions. They learn to live with them the way one learns to live with arthritis.

—TOM WOLFE, *"Land of Wizards"*
(on patent litigation), Popular Mechanics

If your ex-spouse has sued you over custody of your children, you may open the mail one day to find one of the standard-form information demands ("interrogatories") from the widely used lawyers' handbook *Bender's Forms of Discovery*. It contains 207 questions for you to answer under oath. The actual number is quite a bit higher than 207, however, because many questions are divided into (a), (b), (c), and so forth.

"58: Are there any regular visitors to your home?" begins one series of questions. "59: If so, state: a.) Name and address of each regular visitor; b.) Each person's occupation; c.) The frequency with which each person visits your home; d.) How you met each person." You must then tell what happens when each friend stops by, with separate entries for when their children come along and when they do not.

After a long section exploring your drinking habits and

those of everyone else in your household comes "Social and Political Ideologies. 118. Are you a member of any associations, organizations or clubs?" You must tell how long you have been a member of each group, what you do there, and so forth. (If you are wondering what all this has to do with your fitness to raise a child, wait for the next chapter.) The section probing matters of race and national origin is long and unnerving, but it is outdone by the section on Religious Beliefs: "142. Do you believe in a Supreme Being? 143. How would you describe this Supreme Being?.... 147. How often do you attend church?"

The sheer protraction of litigation, being stuck in it for years while the ruinous legal fees bleed away, is not its only terror. Another is the loss of privacy. Most people have secrets: some off-the-books income, a bad habit that's hard to break, a little ticket fixing, an irregular romance. Even persons with clean records and easy consciences tend to be loath to reveal their bank statements and tax records or repeat the private opinions and behind-the-back utterances they have vented about colleagues and friends. Trade formulas, customer data, and inside knowledge of markets can be a crucial, sometimes the most crucial, asset of a business or organization.

Cross-examination—questioning by a hostile lawyer—has thus long been one of the most feared ordeals in the law. Many a blameless litigant has caved in and settled rather than face such grilling. That is one reason criminal defendants enjoy absolute protection against having to testify against themselves, without adverse inference being drawn.

Those caught up in civil litigation enjoy no such protection, whether as plaintiffs, defendants or bystander witnesses (the latter of which don't even have the option of settling). Fortunately, there is one big safeguard for the target of cross-examination: a judge is sitting there. One of the essential roles of a trial judge is to keep lawyers on the straight and narrow by preventing brutal or overly intrusive questioning. Raising a judicial eyebrow is often enough to curb dubious conduct, but another control is more systematic and reliable: judges enforce rules of evidence.

The exclusion of irrelevant evidence is the great defense of privacy in litigation. Most of us can take comfort in the thought that our most embarrassing secrets aren't very relevant to whatever litigation we might land in. We would feel less comfortable if we stopped to think what a slippery concept relevance is. A good advocate can construct an argument for why aardvarks are relevant to zymurgy, or why your extramarital affair might have been relevant to your auto accident (thinking about it distracted your attention; or maybe you were speeding on the way to the motel?).

The old law had little patience for these games. It demanded a high degree of relevance before permitting lawyers to extract confessions and revelations under oath. In the familiar courtroom drama, the cross-examiner has begun a line of questions of no very obvious relevance. The other lawyer, protecting his client, springs to his feet with an objection, whereupon the cross-examiner approaches the bench and whispers into the judge's ear where the questioning is headed and what he hopes to prove. If the judge is satisfied of the relevance, he can proceed.

If your custody case were at trial, for example, a judge would soon call a halt to lengthy questioning about your religious affiliations, friends, and drinking habits unless it were leading up to a major disclosure. The opposing lawyer would not be allowed to fish around for hours in hopes that an eccentric spiritual belief or ne'er-do-well acquaintance would turn up.

Other rules of evidence protect your privacy as well. The famous old textbook rules against opinion and hearsay, for example, reduce both the time spent on the stand and the painfulness of what is said there. They let you concentrate on telling what you yourself have seen, said, and done, with a minimum of occasions for ratting on your friends or disclosing your personal views of the characters of your in-laws or supervisors.

The power entrusted to lawyers to compel answers to questions under oath is so extraordinary that for nearly all of legal history it was kept under firm judicial control. It was essentially limited to pleadings and trial, the two times when judges supervised lawsuits. Lawyers have all sorts of reasons to want to force their opponents to divulge information at other times and places. But the old system gave them few and meager chances to carry out such advance *discovery* of evidence.

Most notably, they could ask a judge's permission to conduct the sort of interview known as a deposition. The idea here was simple and the limitations revealing. Not all witnesses can be counted on to make it to trial. Some die, some sail over the seas to far places; some go mad, like Miss Flite in *Bleak House,* from the litigation itself or more natural causes. So that the testimony of such witnesses might not be lost, lawyers could request court permission to ask them sworn questions before a notary or other officer.

The deposition was a makeshift, an inferior substitute for live testimony. If the witness on a sickbed did recover by the time of trial, or the emigrant decided not to leave after all, the lawyer had gotten an advance peek at the testimony, but that could not be helped. A clever lawyer might ask to depose a witness who in truth was of sound health and had no plans to leave town. But to do so he would normally have to fool the judge, over the other side's probable objections.

On the rare occasions when lawyers could take depositions, it was under drastic conditions. Of course their questions had to be relevant and admissible under the rules of evidence. Some courts, hewing to the principle that discovery was a last resort, forbade them to compel the admission of facts they could learn elsewhere. (Many of the questions on the custody interrogatory, on such matters as your race and national origin, are meant merely to spare the lawyer the bother of interviewing his own client, who used to be married to you and probably knows the answers.)

Another rule of great importance permitted lawyers to

ask only for evidence that supported their own case, not their opponent's. One reason was that in negotiations people commonly volunteer facts that favor their own side, but often need prodding to disgorge facts that favor their opponent's. But the real point of the own-case-only rule was to foil perjury. To reveal the whole of an opponent's evidence, it was thought, was to teach the dishonest litigant exactly what he could get away with saying. So although legal contentions in the arguable ideal were spelled out with bright clarity, evidence bearing on those contentions was purposely left in some shadow. People have a legitimate interest in knowing which norm they are alleged to have overstepped and how, but much less of a legitimate interest in knowing whether others have seen. Being told the charges against them comforts the innocent; not being told the evidence against them discomfits the guilty. Surprise refutation at trial is the nightmare of the perjurer.

Thus matters stood for a very long time. A few miscellaneous rules aided discovery: for example, lawyers could ask that their opponents be made to present for inspection certain documents of obvious relevance to their case, such as a contract their client had signed. But for the most part they had to rely on what they could glean from friendly witnesses, their own investigations, and whatever the other side revealed in negotiations. In Great Britain, where most of these protections remain in place, the system seems to work well. Neither oral depositions nor written interrogatories are commonly used in British litigation, according to a *National Law Journal* account by Jeremy Epstein. In 1983 an English judge explained why: "Discovery constitutes a very serious invasion of the privacy and confidentiality of a litigant's affairs," he said. It "should not be allowed to place upon the litigant any harder or more oppressive burden than is strictly required for the purpose of seeing that justice is done."

Over in this country, the nineteenth century saw stirrings toward making it easier to impose that burden. New York's Field Code of 1848 allowed lawyers to pose both oral and written questions purely to help prepare their case, and without asking court permission. A few states went even further. In principle, these were startling innovations: the old right to remain silent until one stood before the judge was turning into something like an obligation to pipe up on demand. In practice, the difference was not earth-shaking, mostly because for many years reformers were careful to retain the controls on *what* lawyers could ask.

The more discovery lawyers were allowed to do, the better they seemed to like it, and by the time of the New Deal much was being said of its virtues. It averted the need to draw out laboriously at trial facts that could have been agreed on earlier. Unleashing wider discovery, it was solemnly predicted, would make litigation even more efficient. The sooner lawyers learned the truth, the cheaper they would find it to prepare their cases and the more likely they were to settle. Discovery did add a new stage to the life cycle of lawsuits. But overall, it would lower their cost.

Although the main debate was over *where* truth should be ascertained—in front of a judge or without one—it was also suggested that more and better truth would be found if it could be gathered outside supervised channels. As for the old admiration for surprise revelations at trial as a vehicle for truth, it was turning into a pronounced dislike. Surprise testimony, it was pointed out, could confound the innocent as well as the guilty; it might be false itself. Discovery might help curb perjury by "freezing" a story early on before a witness had thought up elaborations or been coached.

The most important driving force behind the broadening of discovery, however, was the sue-first-and-verify-later spirit of the new federal rules. Under the modern rules, to quote the James and Hazard treatise, "persons who may not know *whether* or how they were wronged" can sue anyway [emphasis added]. No one wanted to send all those suits-on-suspicion to trial. Which inevitably meant some way would have to be provided for eager litigants who hoped they would turn out to have a valid claim to "use discovery to find out—the 'fishing expedition.' "

The Clark committee that came up with the 1938 federal rules assigned the drafting of the discovery provisions to Professor Edson Sunderland of the University of Michigan. His new rules appeared only to extend earlier principles in a modest way, but again the changes made for a revolution in the practical law.

The logistics were not all that different from those of the earlier codes. Lawyers could demand oral and written disclosures without a court's say-so for purposes of frank discovery. The great difference was in what they could ask. The own-case-only rule was tossed out. The questions no longer had to be relevant to the issues actually in dispute so long as they related somehow to the litigation's *subject matter*, whatever that might mean. This allowed no end of probing on matters that were not being raised as a legal issue or had already been fully conceded. More astounding, lawyers could demand hearsay, opinion, or other information that was concededly *not* admissible at trial so long as they could argue that it might lead them to other facts that they could use at trial. Before 1938 a few questions were clearly permitted and most others were out of bounds; afterward, the litigators were in virtually full mastery, save for a few shrinking areas of privacy protection that were ominously labeled "privilege."

The simultaneous changes in pleading rules of course greatly unfettered the discovery process. Now that venturing into a lawsuit was to be less like solving a crossword puzzle and more like exploring a trackless wilderness, who knew what the subject matter of a case might turn out to be, and thus what was too irrelevant to ask for? "Anything goes," complained California's Moses Lasky. "Attorneys must inquire into everything and prepare for everything, because no court will tell them where to stop or permit them to stop an adversary. The waste of time and money is immense."

As the federal rules spread among the fifty states, so did

the new modes of discovery. That is why a child custody lawsuit filed in state courts under state laws will follow basically the same discovery format as a billion-dollar federal antitrust or oil-spill case.

It soon became apparent that discovery was not turning out to be as short and simple a process as had been hoped. By 1949 an author in the *Yale Law Journal* was already proposing to require court approval for depositions that lasted longer than one business week. (The idea went nowhere.) In another early case federal judge Robert Gibson ordered the plaintiffs in a Pittsburgh business squabble to stop their "oppressive" badgering of Margaret Bultman, secretary to the president of a railway company, after her deposition had already reached one thousand transcript pages. The judge said that in perusing the transcripts, with their "constant repetitions of matters incompetent for admission in evidence," he had "progressed from interest to boredom, and thence to a certain amount of shock. . . . Granting that [the discovery rule] has a tendency somewhat to encourage fishing expeditions, still the fishing is subject to some license and limit, and should not be continued day after day when the catch is composed of minnows."

As it was realized that the point of the rules was to put a minimum of constraints on the inquisitive lawyer, however, judges tended to let discovery go forward in all but the most flagrant cases. They are not privy to lawyers' private views about what the evolving subject matter of the case will turn out to be, and trying to block requests that are probably abusive risks keeping out a few that are sincere or legitimate. There are bothersome logistical problems anyway in interrupting a deposition to appeal to the absent judge, and one's own lawyer tends to advise a teeth-clenched compliance.

Nowadays a thousand-page transcript is nothing special. Former California bar president Dale E. Hanst of Santa Barbara's Schramm & Raddue recalls a construction contract case where the deposition of one side dragged on for twenty days.

In the now-common lawsuits with multiple parties, the targets may have to go through the process for one set of lawyers after another, which of course in no way relieves them from going over the same ground again at trial. Of course, not just litigants but bystanders face these ordeals too; deposing third-party celebrities has become a regular tactic, especially when publicity-seeking is part of one side's strategy.

In antitrust cases lawyers will often conduct hundreds of depositions probing a defendant business's entire course of behavior over decades. Nicholas deB. Katzenbach, who was house lawyer at IBM during many of the years that it spent fending off antitrust suits, has said the company's chief executive officer was deposed by private and governmental adversaries for a total of forty-five days. "In one of the last depositions, which was 11 years into the case, and two or three years after the government rested, the questions asked clearly indicated that the attorneys involved had never read any of the earlier depositions." Among the questions were: "When did you become chairman?" "Where is the corporate office of IBM?" "What is the approximate size and square feet of the facility in Poughkeepsie?" with much more along the same lines.

When ordered to a deposition you had better hop to it, or you risk very real sanctions. A Texas lawyer pressing a slip-and-fall case against Wal-Mart Stores had the bright idea of demanding a deposition from its billionaire chairman, Sam Walton, the immensely successful retail magnate whose time is arguably as valuable as any businessman's in America. Walton dragged his heels in making it to scheduled appointments, and a state judge in Fort Worth proceeded to order his company to pay a fine of $11,550,000 for this insult to the law's majesty—as well as the $36,000 that a jury had awarded for the slip-and-fall injury itself.

A widely cited survey of lawyers revealed that the most common objectives in depositions include ensnaring the witness in contradictions, getting him to agree to phrasings that hurt his side's case, and drawing out weaknesses in his char-

acter and demeanor for later attack. A key objective is to show
that the lawyer is the one in control: one leading handbook
advises that a simple way to get this message across is for the
lawyer to ignore any questions the witness may try to ask.
James Jeans, Sr., a former board member of the Association
of Trial Lawyers of America, has put the point ever so delicately in his handbook on litigation: "There is no judicial
officer in attendance so the ground rules are often established
by the more forceful personality." Judge Richard Posner of
the Seventh Circuit U.S. Court of Appeals is blunter: "The
transcripts of depositions are often very ugly documents."

The hostility is not always open: calmer tones may work
better at lulling a witness into a misstep or reinforcing damaging memories that might otherwise fade (and of course sly
suggestion can refresh memories that weren't originally
there). Whichever tack they take, good lawyers tend to keep
a poker face when they succeed in getting the reactions they
want, lest they educate the witness as to what he is doing
wrong or reveal their later line of attack at trial.

Written interrogatories, by contrast, might seem like a relatively calm and civilized mode of confession. The propounder
gets to ask questions that cannot be answered from memory.
The target has time to draft a considered response (in practice
his lawyer does it), so there is less danger that a careless
phrasing will do mischief. And where depositions call for the
coordinated presence of set-aside meeting space, lawyers with
their ticking meters, stenographers or video cameras, notaries,
and what not, not to mention advance coaching sessions, the
medium of the interrogatory is as seemingly cheap as paper.

As with some street drugs, however, the yours-for-the-
asking cheapness of procurement brings its own distinctive
risks of abuse. These questionnaires can take minutes to draft
and weeks to answer. On one side a fifteen-dollar-an-hour
paralegal downloads the questions from a disk of standardized
"pattern interrogatories"; on the other a team of top lawyers
is scrambling to draft a response after an exhaustive file search

and discussions with engineers, hospital administrators, or actuaries. Richard Field of Los Angeles's Adams, Duque & Hazeltine observes that a discovery litigator is "perfectly content to ask General Motors if it has ever received a claim pertaining to a faulty headlight before and if so, to answer twelve subquestions as to each such claim."

The requesting lawyer may have to pay minor copying costs, but otherwise there is not much reason to go easy on the adversary; an extra hundred pages of responses, thumbed through in an idle moment, might yield a welcome nugget. In one big securities case a set of interrogatories 381 pages long was served; 150,000 pages of deposition and testimony transcripts were prepared in the same case. Formbooks and -disks bring this kind of imposition within the reach of the humblest lawyer: one of today's compendiums of "pattern interrogatories" for filing in medical malpractice cases goes on for 955 densely packed pages.

Some requesters do not even bother to put their cut-and-paste questions in consecutive numerical order, let alone make sure all of them are pertinent. Atlanta lawyer Edward Savell, representing a taxi company after an accident, recalls being asked where the company learned to drive, whether it had a driver's license, whether it was married or divorced, and whether it had any children. In a Maryland case the form questions asked whether it had snowed on the day of an accident in July.

The protection of private papers and correspondence from arbitrary search and seizure has had a long and honorable history in this country, and before that in England. So it is not surprising that even the 1938 rules provided a good deal of protection for this dimension of privacy. Lawyers who wanted to demand documents from their opponents had to designate what they wanted with clarity; they had to show a judge good cause beforehand; and the relevance and admissibility of the matter had to be plain.

The litigation lobby devoted years of effort to battering

away at this remaining protection. Why, they asked, should no-doubt-incriminating documents sit untouched in files forever simply because a lawyer could not request their contents precisely enough or demonstrate their relevance in advance to a judge? The key to nailing the world's malefactors, they fervently maintained, was to lay open the secret memos in which they plotted their nefarious designs. Cracking these file cabinets, they insisted, would be like getting Moriarty to talk: a thousand crimes long shrouded in obscurity would be cleared up. Mantra-like they repeated their soothing assurances that the innocent had nothing to fear; nor were they above hinting that businesses and persons who wished to avoid releasing their papers must have something to hide.

In 1970 they got their way. The federal rules of civil procedure were amended to allow litigators to demand any private papers they had a mind to. The onus was now on the opponent to trouble the judge with an objection. And to cut down on those pesky objections, the revisers dropped the rule that a demand had to be backed by good cause.

Document requests soon became a major hub of litigation in themselves. In the first five years of the IBM antitrust litigation 64 million pages were obtained. Ronald Olson of the Los Angeles firm of Munger, Tolles & Rickenbacker recalls a case where one of his clients spent nearly $2.5 million responding to discovery demands as a third party, not a litigant. Then began the format wars. A lawyer in a liability suit against Sears, Roebuck demanded to see all customer complaints relating to a particular product. Sears kept its immense files of consumer correspondence organized not by product but alphabetically by individual, which made obvious sense in providing quick turnaround in customer service, but also made it crushingly expensive to search every file. In desperation Sears offered to fly the lawyer to Chicago, plop him down amid the file cabinets, and let him browse at will. No cigar: he wanted Sears to do the compiling. A Massachusetts federal judge agreed with him. The judge did not deny that Sears had good reason to arrange its filing system the way it did, but declared that allowing it to plead impracticality would encourage other companies to set up their files deliberately to repel discovery.

The next step, reported in a 1978 case, was to require the target to create a computerized data bank for the convenience of the lawyers suing it. In 1987, vaccine maker Wyeth Labs was ordered to establish a special research library for the more than two hundred lawyers who were suing it over the alleged side effects of vaccine formulations fully approved and endorsed by federal authorities. The judge explained that Wyeth need not fear the disclosure of its internal operations to competitors because it had already (under litigation pressure, not from lack of support in the medical community) pulled the vaccine in question off the market.

The hope that discovery would cut the cost of litigation was abandoned early on. It had been promoted as a way to dispose of unfounded suits and arguments; it quickly emerged as a way to prospect for more and wider legal claims. Cases settle before trial at no higher a rate here than in Britain, with its protections for pretrial privacy. A major 1960s study by academics highly sympathetic to the new order conceded that it "does not appear to save substantial court time. On the evidence we obtained discovery cannot be called an efficiency-promoting device."

One reason discovery is so expensive is that garnering data relevant to a client's case is only one of its objects, and often a minor one at that. A favorite catch is data on the opponent's fiscal situation. A Legal Services Corporation internal manual for litigators explains that the chance to obtain "information about a person's financial resources and ability to withstand certain sorts of losses" may be "one of the most important reasons you want to go to court." How well a defendant is insured is seldom relevant to the merits of a case against him, but highly relevant in extracting top dollar in settlement. Formerly lawyers had to angle for these disclosures by pretending that they were somehow relevant to one or another aspect of the case; a 1970 amendment ended the little sub-terfuges by making insurance data routinely discoverable.

Competitors, unions, and pressure groups are happy to rummage among the accounts, customer lists, engineering memos, and board minutes of the companies they sue. "Executives who keep little notebooks with scribbles in them are asking for trouble," says Miami lawyer Lawrence Bemis. "One of the first things a good litigator does is ask to see them." In 1985 the Coca-Cola Company had its corporate mind focused on the importance of settling a contract dispute with some bottlers when a court said it would have to yield access to its famed secret formula. In some cases the secrets sought are more important than the relief, and an odd negotiating posture is observed: the defendant is seemingly offering to pay the full value of the claim, but the cagey plaintiff refuses to hear of it.

Injury lawyers also benefited from the demise of the own-case-only rule, which left them free to scoop up any adverse medical reports and observation films that their opponents may have made. When defense lawyers in accident cases sniff fraud they sometimes hire cameramen to catch supposedly paralyzed or bedridden plaintiffs taking out the trash or slipping off to the new hit movie. Of course, filing a demand to see any such tapes is the perfect way to find out whether they exist. In this case the honest claimant has little to fear from surprise at trial; the not-so-honest has much to gain from its passing.

Along with the rest of its bounteous harvest, the fine-meshed discovery net hauls to the surface a great many curious and wriggling creatures from the lower depths. It's standard to probe in discovery for intimate or embarrassing revelations that a target would not want to come out at trial. Divorce and custody lawyers now routinely demand that their opponents submit to examination by a hostile psychiatrist and to hair, blood, and urine tests that might turn up signs of drug abuse or the AIDS virus. Such physically invasive measures still require advance court permission, but in line with the spirit of the rules judges seem to resolve doubts in favor of more inquiry. The late Supreme Court Justice William Douglas warned of the dangers of leaving people at the mercy of medics hired by their adversaries, with no one present "to stop the doctor from probing this organ or that one, to halt a further inquiry, to object to a line of questioning." But those libertarian scruples were expressed in a dissent. The Court majority declared it perfectly proper to turn a litigant over to examiners who would search on a clinic table for physical or mental frailties that might have led him to be negligent.

The shadier sorts of lawyers have long fed pretrial tidbits to scandal sheets or reserved them for outright blackmail. If the accounts in *Hollywood Babylon* are to be relied on, unsavory tactics of this sort helped treat a panting nation to the details of Charlie Chaplin's pillow talk and Mary Astor's racy diary. They continue today as a staple of the gutter and even the uptown press. Such abuses may be inevitable on the tortured fields of family law, where courts regularly probe the most wrenchingly personal issues. But with the discarding of the old discovery controls they have blossomed forth in many other types of litigation as well.

One half-protection remains for the privacy of tax returns, trade secrets, and love letters: the disclosing party can ask the judge to order the opposing lawyers not to release them to outsiders. Obtaining one of these "protective orders" is not much comfort, of course, if the opponents' real goal is to get their hands on the material for their own future use. And unsatisfactory as it is, even this degree of protection has been hard to achieve in practice. Where many lawyers in a suit get to see the same documents, as is common these days, the cheater who leaks the material to a tabloid or business competitor may leave no fingerprints. "If you are not bound by the oath of confidentiality and get hold of the materials, you cannot be held civilly or criminally liable for releasing the materials," the Legal Services manual notes helpfully. It explains that any "juicy tidbits" from discovery "can be plastered on flyers or posters" later on. "Discovery items need not be used in total; they can be excerpted for dramatic effect." Incidentally, if the target successfully resists coming across with his tax returns, the manual for these federally funded lawyers says the thing to do is "cultivate relationships" with "divorced or estranged spouses" who "have greater access to this information than any other person."

Legal Services Corporation internal literature, to judge by the sampling turned up by researcher Rael Jean Isaac, is unusually indiscreet about tactics. Another LSC training program puts it this way: "The opposition may seek a protective order to tone down your aggressiveness in using discovery. You may be barred from giving information thus gathered to the [advocacy organization with which you are working]. You cannot be barred from giving information to your clients. What your clients do with the information (i.e., give it to their organization) is their business."

For whatever reason, confidentiality breaches routinely go unpunished, and many a target organization that summarily wins the underlying lawsuit loses the war for its privacy. And inevitably it has begun to be argued that this is really a good thing, that pretrial data should be routinely released to the general public even when the case never gets to a trial. Why make other lawyers go to the trouble of requesting the same items—perhaps in their ignorance overlooking some of the most titillating—when the litigation community could share the findings at once so much more efficiently? Why not treat the public to any details unearthed through allegations of private misconduct, whether those allegations prove well-founded or grossly unfounded? A few judges, in line with these views, are predisposed against granting protective orders at all. And the Association of Trial Lawyers of America, the plaintiff-lawyers' lobby, has launched a public campaign against protective orders; the Texas courts in 1989 cooperated by making it far harder for the victims of discovery in that state to preserve confidentiality.

Every discovery excess is in the end based on the same rationale: the search for the totemic, grail-like "smoking gun." But it's a funny thing about smoking guns. Given a big enough file cabinet to search in, or a long enough list of questions to ask a single parent, a lawyer willing to spend some time at it can quite often find something portrayable as the fabled firearm. Were there harsh words in the dismissed worker's personnel folder? That shows the managers were prejudiced against him. Kind words? Then they couldn't have been displeased with his job performance. Had others been fired in the same circumstances? Then this employer has made a habit of trampling workers' rights, and a large punitive award is needed to mend its ways. Had others been let off with warnings? Then this victim was singled out for arbitrary treatment and deserves to win.

Any experienced advocate can play these games. Among the favorite smoking-gun generators are memo debates or unheeded suggestions within an organization. The sought-after memo will advise the hotel to dismantle the diving board, the brokerage to go easy on the risky investment, the magazine to kill the hard-hitting investigative story, the hospital to close down the vaccination program that has attracted malpractice suits. (They knew it was wrong to go ahead!) New York City injury king Harry Lipsig's law firm got a $1.8 million settlement for forty-six-year-old postal worker Freddie Brown, mugged and badly hurt in a housing project lobby, after they found a security specialist whose recommendations to upgrade security at the project had gone unheeded. "We couldn't lose," jubilated lawyer Thomas Stickel. "With that witness, we had the city by the throat." Actually, it would be a wonder if the files of a city as intensively governed as New York did not contain unheeded recommendations by the bushelful on countless subjects.

The great advantage for discovery litigators, at least until the system adjusts to the loss of privacy, is that they get to browse among letters and memos written long before, with no thought of litigation. These are far more likely to mortify in retrospect than the considered words of persons who know what they say will be held against them. No long-forgotten scratch-pad doodle or marginal comment on a while-you-were-out slip is now too obscure or insignificant to be seized on and triumphantly decoded as evidence of bad faith. Especially dangerous are the banter, devil's advocacy, and striking of attitudes that seem inseparable from professional camaraderie. The trap for the unwary, the source of surprise in litigation, has now become life itself, and the everyday instinct to record and comment on its events. Discovery was said to be calmer and more rational than the "ambush" of revelations at trial. It emerged as a source of mingled dread and ennui, a reign of terror combined with a rain of paper.

The power to extract confessions and inspect private correspondence has long appealed to a certain type of ambition. Were it used with complete unconstraint, a certain type of justice might be very well served for a time. Every diary, dossier, and archive would be thrown open to inspection. Each of us could be made to answer questions about our past deeds and thoughts and whereabouts, with our answers cross-checked against those of our boon companions and partners in mischief, with a new round of questioning to follow, as in a well-run prisoner-of-war camp, boys' boarding school, or ecclesiastical body for the suppression of heresy. Many long-suspected sins and scandals, and others not even suspected, would at last be brought to light, and the reign of the saints be complete. The human race would walk around with a perpetual blush on its face, as perhaps it ought.

Few of us would want to live in such a world for long (though we might consent to hang around for the first thrilling revelations). We value our privacy, although we wish we could change the guilty habits it shields; we respect the privacy of others, although we know it sometimes conceals real wrongdoing. Then, too, we fear that no one could be safely entrusted with the power of the inquisitor. We would never in this country entrust such a power to the public magistrate, even in a time of emergency and civil disorder. It would too obviously be a weapon of tyranny.

And yet somehow we have been led to entrust it to private lawyers who use it for private profit.

The litigation lobby often congratulates itself on its unrivaled devotion to Truth, a commodity said to have been less esteemed under older procedures more protective of privacy. But this devotion is highly selective. American lawyers now pry into the papers, conversations, and thoughts of citizens as they have never before dared. But they themselves are permitted an unprecedented degree of concealment. The law brusquely demands disclosures in torrents on matters that do *not* advance the requester's legitimate case. But it draws a modest veil over the contentions that the lawyers intend to put forward. It extracts discovery under a bare light bulb in the back of the police station. It countenances pleadings that stonewall the most basic issues.

So let none accuse our law of going to extremes in demanding the disrobing of souls. From its general rule that revelation is everything and privacy nothing, it is always careful to carve out an exception for lawyers themselves.

In the landmark 1947 case of *Hickman* v. *Taylor*, Hickman had the impertinence to ask not for the list of prescription drugs his opponents took, not for the telephone logs of their private residences, not for the diaries they had kept since childhood, but for some of the output of their *lawyers*—specifically, memoranda and deposition transcripts. All the well-worn arguments about making sure both sides have early access to information, about saving on redundant expense, about avoiding surprise at trial, would seem to have been at their very strongest here. But the Supreme Court rebuffed his request. It proclaimed a well-nigh bulletproof privilege against the discovery of lawyers' "work product."

The reasoning of the Court's *Hickman* opinion repays careful study. "[I]t is essential that a lawyer work with a certain degree of privacy, free from unnecessary intrusion by opposing parties and their counsel," the Court pointed out. "Were such materials open to opposing counsel on mere demand," it added, "much of what is now put down in writing would remain unwritten. An attorney's thoughts, heretofore inviolate, would not be his own." The consequences of this loss of privacy would soon follow. "Inefficiency, unfairness and sharp practice would inevitably develop" in lawyers' everyday work. "The effect on the legal profession would be demoralizing."

The breaching of the "heretofore inviolate," the dangers of proceeding on "mere demand," the risks that frank opinion would no longer be set to paper, are compelling concerns, no mistake about it. Too bad they did not loom equally large when it came to the professional confidentiality of accountants, university tenure committees, adoption workers, and consulting psychiatrists. The demoralization of the legal profession was avoided, and a narrow escape it was. The demoralization of everyone else was allowed to proceed apace.

· THE ·
L A W

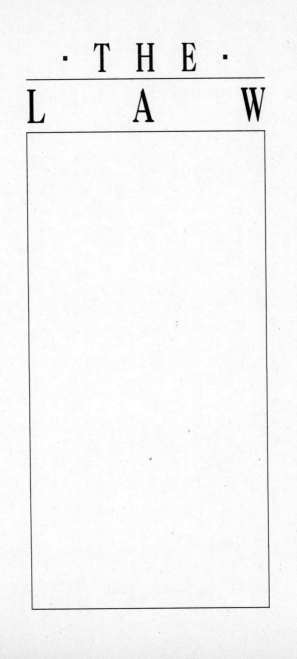

⚖

UP FOR GRABS:
How Everything Became Litigable

That system of law is best which confides as little as possible to the discretion of the judge.

—Latin proverb

Marie and Anthony B. of New Orleans were divorced in 1978 after a ten-year marriage. Marie was awarded custody of their two-year-old son Terry; she later moved upstate to Shreveport, where she practiced dentistry.

Within a year of the divorce decree, Anthony sued her to win custody of the boy, but did not get it. He sued again in 1980, and yet again the next year, each time without success.

In 1983 the child, then eight, visited his father for Christmas. Rather than send him back Anthony enrolled him in a local school for the coming semester. Anthony later claimed this was done with Marie's consent, but a court credited her story that it had happened against her will; she explained that she had not gone to court because the child had been disturbed by the prolonged litigation and she had not wanted to put him through more of it. In any event, when the school year ended in June Terry returned to his mother. On his next visit to his father, however, in August, Anthony filed suit once more to have himself declared legal custodian of the child—his fourth try, not counting the original divorce.

The suit ground its way forward and finally came up for trial. The court found that Marie was highly fit as a parent, and that the boy had flourished under her care. End of case? Just the beginning. Under Louisiana's 1977 child custody law, the court explained, it mattered not how fine a home Marie had provided; the only question was whether Anthony might perhaps provide one that was even better. The court confessed that it saw a "dilemma" on this point, since Anthony also appeared to be an excellent parent and the boy had done well under his care, too. Apparently swayed by a wish to avoid another change of schools, and by the boy's expressed inclination to go on living with his father, the court ruled for Anthony. Marie appealed, but the next court let the ruling stand. She appealed to the state's supreme court, and this time she won—at least in a sense. The court overturned the decision for Anthony, but only to send the case back to the trial court for still further litigation. Thus, after a half-dozen rounds of courtroom fighting stretching over eight years, no end was in sight for this wretched family.

Custody disputes are as old as Solomon, but the fight between Marie and Anthony was in its own way at ground zero of America's litigation explosion. It shows the effects of distinctive changes in what our courts try to do when they hear lawsuits.

What might be called the standard, traditional sort of custody fight begins when one parent accuses the other of being so gravely troubled—constantly drunk or physically abusive, say—that the child would be at risk of serious harm under his or her care. Cases like those are still litigated as much as ever, of course. The new wave is of fights between good parents. Some of these fights take place at the time of the original divorce, but a large number arise later, when one side challenges an original court decree or out-of-court agreement that had settled the custody issue. In one oft-found pattern, the father gets his life organized, does well in his career, and perhaps remarries, while the mother struggles on in some disarray as a single parent. He then comes back to argue plausibly that he can now provide the children with a better home life than she can. Not surprisingly the mother is prone to differ with him. After a thorough venting of all the bad habits and character flaws on each side that were discussed the first time around, and any new ones that have emerged in the meantime, he may win or (more commonly) lose. Either way, whichever side loses this second bout can gather strength and then return to the mat a year or two later. Some contests continue round after round until the child finally grows up, or starts making so much trouble that one parent stops wanting custody.

One authority has concluded, astonishingly, that American couples spend more time in custody squabbles after their divorces are final than while they are in progress. Challenges to existing custody decrees have become what a *Yale Law Journal* commentator calls "a hotbed of litigation." For a closer look at why we must wade into some deeper waters of legal philosophy.

Until not long ago, most American courts resolved custody disputes through "mechanical" rules or presumptions. If the parents had agreed on custody at the time they separated, the agreement stuck. Otherwise, the mother beat the father, at least where the children were of "tender years." Both mother and father beat third parties. Once custody was awarded, it tended to stay put.

These rules of thumb were not the last word, and sometimes the calculations got more complex. The firm preferences of an older child were hard to ignore. And a losing parent might regain custody by proving there had been a "significant" change of circumstances since the divorce, although that hurdle was usually not an easy one to jump. In general, the various exceptions and deviations were hard to invoke in the ordinary case. Judges could dispose of most of the cases most of the time in a fairly rigid way, with an air of looking up the answers as from a cookbook or logarithm table. They ran their courts as a sort of answer machine.

The drawbacks were obvious. Some children who went to their mother might on more careful individual consideration have done better with their father. Others stayed with the parent who won initial custody although a later switch might have benefited them to some degree. By disposing of cases wholesale, in other words, the law deliberately turned its gaze from individual equities. Some fathers felt the gnaw of injustice: wasn't it unfair to lock the courthouse doors against someone because of his gender? Joining them in their discontent were many mothers who had been in no position to contest custody at the time of their divorces: didn't they deserve their day in court to prove they could be the better parent? And what of the children? Surely, it was urged, each and every one deserved a searching look at his own personal situation, with as much warmth and personal attention as a court could muster, and no presuppositions or bounds on the questions that could be asked. Yet many judges seemed more concerned with following abstract rules than with understanding the particular life stories before them.

Through the 1970s and 1980s the mechanical presumptions were softened and weakened and diluted, state by state and issue by issue, usually with little fanfare. A 1982 case came to symbolize the new approach.

A separation agreement with her husband Elliot gave Sharon F. custody of their daughters, Lisa and Nicole. Less than a year later Elliot sued to overturn the agreement. His charges, as accepted by New York's highest court, ran as follows. Sharon had "frequently left her then 11- and 8-year-old girls alone in the apartment until late at night when she went out for the evening even though the children informed her that they were afraid to stay alone." Though professing to raise the children in the tenets of Orthodox Judaism, in which both she and Elliot had been reared, she was "flagrantly violating those tenets by permitting a male friend to share her bed to the knowledge of the children, by failing, except rarely, to take the children to Sabbath services, and by permitting the male friend to violate the Sabbath by turning on the television, all of which confused the children and was contrary to their religious beliefs and detrimental to their religious feeling."

Amid the manners and mores of Manhattan circa 1980, it was hard to make the case that simple cohabitation, let alone Sabbath-breaking, made a woman unfit to raise a child, and in fact the New York court conceded that Sharon was not at all unfit. It merely observed that Elliot now appeared more fit, and awarded him the children. It dismissed the arguments of Sharon's lawyers that Elliot should have to show "extraordinary circumstances." The sole criterion for a custody switch, it said, should be the "best interests of the child when all applicable factors are considered."

The formula sounded so reasonable that it spread rapidly around the country: courts should order a custody shift between parents whenever it promised to make a child better off. The "best interests of the child" standard, it soon became apparent, has three interlocking features. First, it provides what might be called hair-trigger litigability. To get into court, you need not assert that a switch would make the child better off by a mile; a millimeter will do. And in many states besides Louisiana, you don't have to show that the child's home life with the other parent has deteriorated in any way since the original decree; an improvement in the home situation you can offer is just as valid.

The second feature of the standard is subjectivity: no two parents, judges, or hired experts ever quite agree on the precise content of a child's best interests. Is it better off with a parent who hews to higher moral standards, or one who is more affectionate? With a parent who will spend more time looking after it, or with one who will arrange for it to get superior schooling? With a brilliant achiever subject to emotional extremes, or a parent of mediocre wits but rock-solid temperament? There is no real answer to these questions, at least none we can all agree on. So a lot depends on which judge you draw, and what mood the judge is in this morning.

The third feature of the standard is that everything comes to be relevant and nothing, as the lawyers say, dispositive. Does your ex swear? Smoke? Gamble? Watch too many soap operas? Has he been known to roam the beach gathering driftwood? Do the neighbors find her standoffish? Perhaps none of these peccadillos *significantly* endangers a child, but all can have some effect on its welfare, and you never know what will tip the balance. So it can't hurt to bring them all up.

As the courts left off trying to be like answer machines, they inevitably started to become more like hot-tub discussion groups. ("Tell us *all* about the relationship.") The recriminations grew ever more numerous and petty. Does the child resent the mother's disciplinary efforts? Fair game. Does the father hang out with riffraffy associates? Certainly grounds for concern. The boasts multiplied too, since each of a parent's own virtues and achievements will be worth mentioning.

Civil libertarians were soon expressing unease about custody litigation: parents were feeling pressured toward conformity, and privacy was getting lost in the trample. Elsewhere in the world of the law the right to hold eccentric ideas, mingle with friends of one's own choosing, or quit one's job at will, without answering to the authorities, are jealously guarded. Yet so long as custody remains unsettleable, no parent will feel entirely free to do things that might draw opposing fire. Take your religion too lightly, and you could end up like Sharon F. Take it too seriously, and you could lose the kids just the same, for consorting with what a court deems a "cult"; that happens in plenty of cases too. Under the best-interests regime, as in the town of Middlemarch,

sane people did what their neighbors did, so that if any lu-
natics were at large, one might know and avoid them.

Louisiana joined the best-interests trend in 1977, one
year before the beginning of Marie and Anthony's eight-year-
plus bout of litigation. By now most states have followed.
The Virginia high court's 1983 opinion was typical in its optimism. A "settled environment may have its benefits," it
allowed airily, but "is simply another factor to be considered
in determining the best interests of the children." It dismissed
the concerns of a lower-court judge that switching children
too freely might lead to a "yo-yo" back-and-forth syndrome,
since "to date, there has never been a change in the custody
of the two children whose interests are here under review."

The good-parent wars turn out to have made surprisingly
little difference in actual custody outcomes. Most children
still go to the mother, and the exceptions tend to come in
the same old areas: when she is gravely troubled, or the two
sides have agreed otherwise, or an older child prefers the
father's custody. Most custody decrees that are challenged
are still not overturned. Rather as in World War I, the vast
bloodletting has brought little change in the location of the
trenches.

And yet the effects have been profound just the same.
To avoid custody battles many mothers will make major
concessions on financial issues. Knowing this, many lawyers
for fathers deploy the custody weapon even if their client is
not really all that keen to take the kids; some even feel that
not to do so would violate their ethical obligation to get their
clients the best possible deal. Relatively few mothers lose
their children, but many lose the means of supporting them
comfortably.

As for the children themselves, a distinguished battery
of psychologists, social workers, and sadder-but-wiser judges
themselves have by now concluded that the sheer experience
of being fought over for years can endanger the emotional
health even of a normal child with good parents. Joan Wexler

of Brooklyn Law School sums it up: "It is repose, according to all the social science data, that all the parties concerned truly need after a divorce."

The maternal-preference rule may or may not embody any timeless wisdom about the special bond between mother and child. Actually, as a rule, it is of relatively recent vintage: for a long time, strange as it now may seem, it was the father who got presumptive custody. What is important, almost more than which rule prevails, is that there *be* a rule, and one as clear, knowable, and universal—as mechanical, in short—as can be. A good rule is comprehensive, disposing of run-of-the-mill cases so courts can concentrate on the unusual. It is objective, so different judges can hope to rule the same way, and the parties themselves have some hope of agreeing on how the law will treat their case. And it is clearly spelled out in advance, so everyone can know where they must toe the line and where they are free to behave as they choose. When the law takes the form of clear, comprehensive, objective, and preannounced rules, litigation is mostly a waste of time.
Lawyers speak of these as *bright-line* rules; few cases fall into their gray zone. The age of a child is usually known to the exact day, and seldom is there much doubt about just which woman is the mother, the tale of Solomon notwithstanding. The "significant change in circumstances" test for custody-switching is not quite so sharp, since there is always room for some difference on what is truly significant, but its line is plenty bright compared with what came after.

For a very long time the law in this country, and in England before that, showed an overwhelming preference for fixed rules over fuzzy standards at almost every opportunity. Some of these rules have survived more or less intact to our own day. Take the idea of an age of majority. When is someone old enough to get married, or sign a binding contract, or order a drink in a bar? If the answer depends on maturity, it will always be in dispute; some of us are ready for independence at fourteen, others lamentably unready at forty. If the law were fully alive to human realities, it would entertain much litigation on this subject. Instead it plays dead, and promulgates a no-thinking-required rule—count the birthdays—lest it cast perennial suspense over the eligibility of a million bachelors, the validity of a million credit cards, and the retention of a million liquor licenses.

How should we behave on the highway? Presumably we owe our fellow motorists some general duty not to endanger them unreasonably. Fortunately, most accidents are handled under rules of the road that are much more cut and dried than that. One familiar rule holds that if you bump into the driver ahead of you, you pay for the damage, even if he slammed on his brakes for no obvious reason. If courts tried to work out responsibility on a case-by-case basis they'd find it hard to distinguish the occasional innocent rear-car driver from all the tailgaters who'd be clamoring to be let off for the damage they had done. Many more full-blown trials would be held, yet injustice would hardly be avoided. And the simple rule of thumb provides a generally sound maxim for driving: pay more attention to the car in front of you than to the car behind. As a group, drivers benefit.

Why rely on breathalyzer tests to define drunk driving, when some drivers who flunk are less of a menace on the road than others who pass? For that matter, why ban drunk driving as such at all, when what we want to ban is incompetent driving by anyone, drunk or sober? Again, one reason is that we distrust subjectivity on both sides; if every case pits the policeman's bare word against the driver's, there will be much strife but by no means a perfect winnowing of innocent from guilty. So we give the officer a device we hope is simple to use and the motorist a rule we hope is simple to follow (one-drink-an-hour, or whatever).

When does a binding contract come into existence when you are negotiating by mail? In principle, perhaps, when there's a "meeting of the minds." But minds are annoyingly inscrutable. It might seem the minds meet when you resolve to accept the offer, or later when the other guy opens and reads your letter of acceptance. The problem is that afterward you alone know exactly when you made up your mind and he alone knows when he opened the envelope. Relying on either trigger would leave too much room for mistakes or fibs in comparing stories afterward. Hence the law's "mailbox rule," which provides a fairly objective trigger: you're both locked in when you drop your letter of acceptance into a mailbox.

The sheer formality of formal rules, as we keep seeing, invariably leaves them open to objection. No preannounced rule of thumb ever quite fits the perceived merits of all the cases that come in. To follow a formal rule is thus to sacrifice some measure of the law's underlying policy.

When the immensely influential group of thinkers known as the Legal Realists came along early in this century, they launched a devastating attack on the effort to maintain clear, knowable-in-advance legal rules, an effort they came to call legal formalism. Roscoe Pound, Karl Llewellyn of Columbia, Jerome Frank of Yale, and others attacked formalism at its strongest point: its claim to provide a way of deducing what a court would or should do in a given situation from a combination of precedent and abiding legal principle. In fact, they said, judges were strongly tugged by their sense of the equities of a case, the policy of society as a whole, and other factors outside the letter of the law; and they had a dozen ways to manipulate cases to make them come out according to these lights.

Language itself, for starters, was slippery: the town elders might think they were being plain enough when they banned vehicles in the park, but did that mean a court had to apply the law to bicycles? Wheelchairs? A child's wagon? A statue of the general in his Jeep? Something other than the letter of the law would decide these issues. There was a malleable quality as well in the way a case's facts were "characterized" among legal categories. Most devastating of all, there were so many different precedents, maxims, and canons of interpretation, and they overlapped and contradicted each other so comprehensively, that by picking and choosing among them a judge could seemingly steer cases to any desired destination point.

Uncertainty, then, or at least future mutability, seemed to be around every corner in the law. And yet judges announced each decision as if they had worked it out with mathematical inevitability by applying the rules to the facts. Why not be candid and admit what was going on—this was the "realism" that became the rallying cry—and turn judges' seat-of-the-pants or seat-of-the-robe instinct into a virtue? Why not drop the answer-machine pose, and announce openly that the reasons for decisions were not easily pinned down?

Even the traditionalists, if it came to that, had resigned themselves to a considerable tincture of indeterminacy in at least a few areas of the law where it seemed hard to avoid. The whole concept of "negligence" in injury cases was sadly amorphous, with many outcomes unguessable until a jury came back with a verdict. A dispute over whether someone named in a will exerted "undue influence" over its maker requires a study, by circumstantial evidence, of what commentators have called the psychological world of the dead person, with results that often turn on how sympathetic a case each side can put forth. The antitrust laws from early on were vague and open-ended in their commands.

This was not exactly an encouraging sign, since negligence, will-contest, and antitrust disputes were all notorious for their expense, vexation, and scope for litigious zeal. But the Realists carried the day against all dispute. Certainty and predictability of outcomes, formerly seen as the virtue of virtues in legal craftsmanship, came to seem less achievable and then somehow less important. A closer fit with good "policy," even if it meant phrasing the law's orders in sonorous generalities, loomed ever larger. From the courts' undeniable failure to provide perfect guidance or apply wholly neutral tools of analysis, it was deduced not that they should try harder but that they should stop trying so hard.

The basis of the custody-challenge explosion thus turns out, with appropriate substitution of subject matter, to be the basis of most of the rest of the litigation explosion. The history of the law in the last generation or two—and the pre-history of the litigation explosion—has been one of the replacement of crisp old rules with fuzzy new standards.

Vagueness creeps into the law on the padded feet of words and phrases like *fairness, equitableness, good cause, good faith, reasonableness under all the circumstances*—pillowy expressions that tend to soften the blow of what is in fact a grant of wide judicial discretion over some area. Consider the splitting up of the property that a divorcing couple acquired during their marriage. Until recently most states applied either the common-law rule (keep what is in your name, subject to alimony) or the community-property rule (income goes in a common pot). The edges of these rules were ragged and the exceptions many, so there was a lot of fighting, but the underlying principles were not wholly inscrutable. Now most states have embraced the "equitable distribution" of property, a nice-sounding phrase that means nothing in particular but calls for a long fight on everything of conceivable relevance. "Equitable distribution has dramatically changed the practice of family law," writes Lawrence J. Golden in his manual for practitioners in this area. "Advocacy and litigation skills are required to a far greater degree than before; extensive discovery, use of expert witnesses, and lengthy hearings now characterize many equitable distribution proceedings. All of this has increased the cost of divorce." *Forbes* has estimated that a single new-style divorce case, that of the Texas couple Sid and Anne Bass, could wind up costing as much as $10 million in legal fees and related expenses.

The equitable-distribution property standard is especially potent in conjunction with the best-interests-of-the-child custody standard, putting more or less everything up for grabs when a marriage fails. Hence the central paradox of today's divorce courts: the law congratulates itself endlessly for doing away with "fault," yet divorcing couples keep descending into all-out warfare.

Legal indeterminacy, although often inflicted by way of frank generality, is just as compatible with useless specificity. A favorite device in today's law is the "balancing test" that instructs future judges to weigh ten, twenty, or thirty factors and considerations against each other. No method is provided for figuring out which factors should trump which others, or what to do when six factors cut one way and eight the other. Some equitable-distribution states, for example, are squeamish about giving the judge open discretion to carve up a divorcing couple's property as he sees fit. Instead they lay out a long list of factors for him to consider: the marriage's duration, each spouse's economic situation, forgone education or career, services as homemaker or adviser on family investments, and so on.

On the child-custody front, one survey found that judges had invoked 299 distinct criteria in determining children's disposition. Some states thoughtfully add a provision allowing the judicial balancer to take into account any other factor he may deem relevant, which serves much the same purpose as the fifth "reason" in the old English drinking song:

> *If all be true that I do think,*
> *There are five reasons we should drink:*
> *Good wine—a friend—or being dry,*
> *Or lest we should be by and by—*
> *Or any other reason why.*

But such a wild card is scarcely needed in this game. Except in the uninteresting cases where all the factors cut in the same direction, the ordinary balancing test already gives the court all the discretion it could want.

Lawsuits against manufacturers over injuries in the use

of products, one of the biggest growth areas in litigation, is handled through one of the most amorphous balancing tests yet invented. Someone hurts himself using a caustic drain cleaner, or playing with fireworks, or trying to pull a carving knife out of its original holder. Should the product maker have to pay? The most widely used set of modern guidelines invites the jury to consult at least a dozen factors in answering this question. They include the likelihood that users will hurt themselves with the product; the probable seriousness of those injuries; the danger signals, if any, communicated by the "obvious condition of the product"; the ability of users to avoid danger by being careful; the user's likely awareness of the dangers and how avoidable they are; and the general public's knowledge of the same thing.

Got that figured out? There is much more. The bewildered jury must then consider the product's usefulness; whether it could have been made safer without making it less useful or "too expensive to maintain its utility"; whether other products on the market might serve the same need and not be as unsafe; and on and on. This meandering list of things to keep in mind might be useful as an agenda for a talk-show discussion of product safety. What it is not is law. Not surprisingly, many companies have decided to flee the uncertainty by declining to market useful products frequently found on the scene in injuries, from football helmets to life-saving drugs. Businesses will forgo quite a bit of short-term profit rather than roll the dice on a standard that they can never know for sure whether they are complying with.

Indeterminacy is also on the march, or slither, in business-versus-business commercial litigation, with equally baleful implications for American enterprise. Benjamin Cardozo spoke of "the overmastering need of certainty in the transactions of commercial life"; the law formerly cooperated in strengthening that certainty. It encouraged dealmakers to find an unmistakable signal of agreement, document what they were agreeing on, and approach the signing with a certain solemnity. One sharp dividing line between obligation and no obligation was the handshake or its equivalent; until then you were merely negotiating and could pull back with no liability. Another momentous step was the act of reducing an agreement to writing, and affixing signatures. The very old rule known as the statute of frauds provides that many important promises, like those to sell land or commit to a long-term obligation, have to be given on paper or not at all. Under the equally venerable "parol evidence" rule, the plain meaning of a written agreement is supposed to take precedence over anything the two sides might have said verbally.

The language of commerce still conveys a flavor of the sought-after certainty and finality behind these rules: "shake hands on it," "get it in writing," "signed, sealed and delivered," and so forth. But courts in recent years have begun blurring the old lines. Some have accepted suits seeking damages for bad faith in negotiation, even when no handshake or other agreement was ever reached. Others have been finding ways to get around the statute of frauds to enforce alleged oral promises even where the subject matter is so momentous that misremembering is a grave temptation and drawn-out uncertainty hard to bear. Yet others have been chipping away at the parol-evidence rule to enforce alleged verbal representations even when a written agreement had seemed to settle the matter otherwise.

There is something to be said for all this attaching of penalties to loose talk. It puts a fear into some people who say careless or unscrupulous things, or toy with their opposite numbers by dragging out talks on purpose. Unfortunately, it also sets off endless squabbling over who said what when. Are you dissatisfied with a course of business dealings? You may find nothing to object to in the standard-form contract you signed and have used to your satisfaction a hundred times before. And your partner may have *done* nothing to violate that contract. But very likely someone in your partner's organization has *said* something to which you can take exception. Organizations desperately need to know what their obligations are, and it is hard enough for them to keep track of a web of duties committed to paper. Once the obligations can hinge on the idle chat of some long-since-departed salesman, ordinary people's bets are off, and lawyers' bets start going on.

Elected legislators might be expected to help in the quest for objective law. One of the textbook arguments for making law in legislatures rather than working it out through the common-law process used to be that legislators can be as specific as they wish: they can write an age limit into a law directly, for example, whereas judges in the common-law tradition may have to converge on a number such as eighteen or twenty-one over a series of cases. As recently as 1950 a commentator in the *American Bar Association Journal* summed up the ideal of legislative precision that still held sway in a former age. He explained that the perfectly written law would leave "no contingency unprovided for" and be "clear and unambiguous in its direction as to each and every conceivable fact situation which may take place in the world of affairs."

Instead, today's legislators are making things far worse. Federal appeals judge Alex Kozinski writes that it "seems as if legislators now pass statutes because of, not despite, their lack of clarity. Indeed, imprecise or ambiguous language has become a tool of political compromise. . . . By using vague language, legislators can avoid making the difficult political choices that they have to confront when drafting a statute precisely."

Space, even ten times our space, is too limited for a proper survey of every link between vagueness in law and resulting litigation; as well try to enumerate every link between tinder and flame. Whole books could be written on the impossibility of getting clear answers to single questions like "Is this a legally adequate environmental impact statement?" or "Is this a lawful way to draw the bounds of city council districts?" or "Does this firefighting exam unlawfully discriminate against the handicapped?" Bias laws are more commonly vague than not. Hundreds of thousands of potential lawsuits are generated each year, for example, by what are known as "mixed-motive" firings: an employer had independent reasons to let a worker go, but somewhere along the line a manager or supervisor committed some infraction such as writing an arguably sexist comment in a personnel file. The improper remark will be enough to get the dismissed worker to a trial, while the independent reasons will be enough to keep the employer's defense alive. Who wins is anyone's guess.

Likewise, Congress has prohibited employers from imposing mandatory retirement at any age, but left them free to dismiss workers for "good cause." The hopelessly subjective nature of the good-cause standard can only result in an unending series of face-offs in which employers tell workers they are being terminated because they personally aren't up to the job (a particularly unpleasant form of individualized scrutiny) and then get taken to court for a second opinion, always with the chance of losing a verdict for a few years' worth of back pay. Employers know full well, of course, that an arbitrary cutoff deprives them of the services of many capable workers; but they fear that litigation will otherwise become the normal and expected cap to a career.

Supreme Court decisions in the last generation have brought balancing tests to many constitutional issues as well. Does an official action count as a "search" or "seizure" for which a warrant is needed? Is there probable cause for it? Does the First Amendment give a government-run broadcaster the right to editorialize against the wishes of those who foot its bills? Does a land-use regulation count as a "taking" of property for which the owner must be compensated under the Fifth Amendment? The Court shows unsettling pride in its refusal to offer guidance through any set formula, insisting instead on "ad hoc, factual inquiries into the circumstances of each particular case."

One result has been a litigation explosion on the constitutional side of the law to go with the one on the civil side.

The unclearness of the standards for permissible search and seizure, for example, gives countless criminals the chance to appeal their convictions, yet it does not give law-abiding citizens a reliable sense of what we may expect to keep private should the police take an unwarranted interest in our affairs.

Many thinkers in the law schools have pushed to erase just about all the remaining bright lines in the law, both in matters of procedure—where, as we have seen in earlier chapters, the fog has already gotten up to pea-souper levels—and on the substantive side. The momentous married-versus-not-married line has come under assault from ideas of palimony and other case-by-case creations of rights and responsibilities for unmarried relationships in such a way as to make it impossible to guess who qualifies and who does not, as well as from the rise of liability between spouses for such things as emotional injury. The age-of-majority concept is still with us for the moment. But it is worth noting the suggestion of influential Harvard professor Laurence Tribe, in a 1975 law review article, that youths be given many more chances to attempt to rebut their presumptions of incapacity after disputes have arisen—which could make for considerable turmoil as teenagers began trying to enter transactions whose validity could be determined only after the fact.

Theory often follows practice, and now some members of the leftish Critical Legal Studies movement have come along to proclaim that indeterminacy is not just a tolerable evil in the discipline of the citizenry but a downright good. Leading C.L.S. light Duncan Kennedy of Harvard, in a well-known article, has suggested that vague standards are preferable to definite rules precisely because they give citizens the sense that the totality of their behavior is under scrutiny by the tribunes of society.

Formalism in the law was born of a profound sense of fairness and a humane desire to spare citizens the misery of litigation. Fairness demanded that people be given notice when their rights were in peril; humanity recognized that life has enough wrenching uncertainty without having to fight constantly over whether what you have is your own.

Simple, formal rules lie well within our reach in most areas of the law. Perhaps it is hard to retain an explicit preference for mothers in a day when many consider it improper to hinge any legal entitlements on gender. But the old maternal preference rule has a natural successor called the *primary caretaker rule.* It gives a presumption of custody to whichever parent has spent more time tending to the child's direct personal needs—feeding, diapering, and the like. Occasionally a father will qualify, but seldom will there have to be much real dispute as to who fits the bill.

The West Virginia Supreme Court adopted the primary caretaker rule in 1981, in an opinion by Justice Richard Neely, author of a number of well-received books about divorce and other legal topics. Neely observed that "it is no more reprehensible for judges to admit that they cannot measure minute gradations of psychological capacity between two fit parents than it is for a physicist to concede that it is impossible for him to measure the speed of an electron." What is needed instead is to "provide a reliable framework within which the divorcing couple can bargain intelligently."

The right to be given notice of whether conduct is legally hazardous or not is an intimate part of that nowadays-more-praised-than-analyzed precondition of liberty known as the rule of law. Friedrich Hayek, the economics Nobelist and penetrating social thinker, put it this way nearly fifty years ago in his classic *The Road to Serfdom:*

> Nothing distinguishes more clearly conditions in a free country from those in a country under arbitrary government. . . . Stripped of all technicalities, [the rule of law] means that government in all its actions is bound by rules fixed and announced beforehand—rules which make it possible to foresee with fair certainty how the authority will use its coercive pow-

ers in given circumstances and to plan one's individual affairs on the basis of this knowledge.

Lofty ideals of jurisprudence can sometimes seem remote
from the needs of everyday life, but legal determinacy and
predictability have the homely as well as the transcendent
virtues. They allow us to plan our dealings in times of legal
peace. They take on new importance at the first signs of a
quarrel, when we want to know whether we have fallen short
of our duties, so we can make amends, or stand on firm
ground, so we can frame demands. If the quarrel goes to
litigation, reliable law encourages a prompt settlement or, if
worst comes to worst, cabins the bounds of what is at stake
in a trial. Afterward it provides reassurance that the verdict
hung on objective factors rather than bias or luck, and quells
the nagging suggestion that fighting just a bit harder might
have turned the outcome.

The Realists had a point when they exposed the many
ways actual judicial practice fell short of this ideal. If rules
are sweeping, blunt, numerous, and unthinkingly applied,
there will be much danger of overlap and contradiction. But
so long as certainty remains the aim, there is at least the hope
of convergence over time: when rough surfaces are rubbed
together for long enough, the interface eventually becomes
smooth. Big rules give way to smaller, finer rules. And the
virtues of exhortation and aspiration should not be dismissed
lightly. We want judges to resist the impulse to behave law-
lessly, although we know they will sometimes yield. Jurisprudence may fall short of determinacy even when it makes
a concerted effort to provide it; but it becomes certain to fail
the moment it ceases to try.

The surest way to destroy predictability is to tell citizens
and judges alike to decide what to do when interests clash
by looking into their consciences. Until that happy day on
Canaan's shore when all consciences converge, the only result
can be a Babel of disagreement. Today's voluminous case
reports are filled with lawsuits between respectable citizens

whose sense of fairness inevitably differs but who would not for that reason, in an era of clearer law, have had to come to legal blows. Where people of honest intention are suing each other in large numbers, it is because they have been baffled in their efforts to learn in any other way what the law expects of them. "No profound social theory is needed to explain why people are more litigious today than ever before," as Richard Epstein of the University of Chicago puts it. Legal uncertainty "breeds litigation. . . . It's that simple."

8

⚖

GUESSING FOR VERDICTS

Man's most valuable trait
Is a judicious sense of what not to believe.

—*EURIPIDES*

Judith Haimes, being treated for a brain tumor, underwent a CAT scan at Temple University Hospital in Philadelphia. She sued the hospital and Dr. Judith Hart, a neuroradiologist, claiming she had suffered an allergic reaction to a dye used in the scan. It felt "as if my head was going to explode," she said.

Pain and suffering were only part of the claim. Formerly Ms. Haimes had conducted séances at which such eminences as the poet Milton had spoken through her. Now she said the dye had interfered with the psychic powers that had enabled her to divine persons' past and future. She could no longer make a living at this trade.

Judge Leon Katz ordered the jury to disregard the psychic-damage claims, but after 45 minutes of deliberation it came back with an award of $986,000. Over the strenuous objections of Ms. Haimes's lawyer, Judge Katz ordered a new trial, declaring the verdict "grossly excessive." Four years later the litigation was still dragging on.

The trouble with subjective law is that it keeps everyone guessing: guessing about what the law means, about whether a suit is meritorious enough to file, about how the court will or should rule this time. The old courts had an intense dislike of guesswork, or "speculation," up and down the line. Their caution lent a deeply conservative tone to the complex body of procedure known as the law of evidence.

Evidence rules, as we have seen, protect litigants' privacy. But of course their larger purpose is to protect the court itself from influences that over long experience have been shown to make its fact-finding less accurate, to throw it off the right scent more often than on. Rules of evidence had to be strong (it was thought) because distracting comments, misleading factoids, and red-herring visual displays don't just appear in the courtroom by chance. They are hyped. They are thrust forward. They allow the lawyer with the weaker case to change the subject; to play on emotion, prejudice, and awe of the fine-sounding; to sow doubt where there should be certainty, or the reverse. "Irrelevant evidence by definition," as the authors of the *Federal Rules of Evidence Manual* put it, "cannot help" the judge or jury. "It can only hurt. . . . Whatever the advantage that is sought, it is an edge to which the proponent cannot properly lay claim."

Especially dangerous in the classical view is secondhand evidence, the two main kinds being hearsay and opinion. Filtering data through intermediaries allows more chances for mistakes to creep in and more scope for manipulation by the lawyer who can make a feeble assertion seem strong through a clever choice of witnesses or the mere din of repetition through many mouths. And secondhand testimony, opinion especially, tends to repel scrutiny on cross-examination. The mistaken or dishonest witness may flinch at being asked "Are you sure you saw that happen?" but is unlikely to flinch at being asked "Are you sure that's your opinion?" Everyone is entitled to his opinion.

But some matters are too technical to be resolved by firsthand accounts alone. And so the major exception to the opinion rule allows opinion when it comes from an expert: courts would be hard-pressed to resolve mining squabbles without geologists, art world wrangles without appraisers, or immigration controversies without translators. Experts in a field can agree on propositions that lay opinion would have to guess at, and the genuine expert has some credibility at stake when he gives an opinion.

The big problem is when to label a witness an expert. In the 1665 case of *Rex* v. *Culander & Duny* the court admitted the testimony of Dr. Browne of Norwich, a "person of great knowledge"

> who after the evidence given, and upon view of the three persons in Court, was desired to give his opinion, what he did conceive of them; and he was clearly of opinion, that the persons were bewitched; and said that in Denmark there had been lately a great discovery of witches, who used the very same way of afflicting persons, by conveying pins into them, and crooked as these pins were, with needles and nails. And his opinion was, that the devil in such cases did work upon the bodies of men and women.

The courts took a long time to live down the witch trials. And from an intermittent history of embarrassment along these lines they grew nervously inhibited about what they said. They hoarded their credibility. Presumptions and downright fictions might be all very well in setting out the law's categories, which were artificial anyway. ("Twenty-year-olds can't take care of themselves. Twenty-one-year-olds can.") But when it came down to individualized findings—was John the one who hit Mary?—they let many a plausible truth go

unendorsed rather than risk falling into an error. They tried
to exclude all but the strongest evidence.

The makers of the latter-day legal system, as we have
seen, were impatient with long-accreted formal rules that
seemed to cramp courts' discretion in litigation. Keeping options alive seemed more appealing than ruling anything out
for sure; sensitivity and openness to new experience had it
all over timid adherence to a rule book. Inevitably, the rules
of evidence—artificial-looking and mechanical as they were,
born more of long experience than of a fashionable theoretical
construct—began to look like yet another dispensable legacy.

These days many law school commentators no longer fret
so much about the dangers of letting in testimony in civil
litigation that might taint the atmosphere or mislead the court,
and instead tend to fret a good deal about the dangers of
keeping out testimony that might in some way be helpful.
They express high confidence in the courts' power to thread
the maze of trial amid ever-more-highly-orchestrated distrac-
tions; or, put differently, low confidence in the legendary
power of a good lawyer to make crows appear swans and swans
crows. Maybe (they seem to suggest) evidence rules are just
a holdover from an era when things were kept from the judge
or jury as the uglier side of life used to be kept from the eyes
of small children.

The trend has thus been to let more and more evidence
into civil lawsuits. A milestone came in 1975 when Congress
enacted new Federal Rules of Evidence to replace older,
uncodified rules. (Most states followed suit.) Federal judge
and leading commentator Jack Weinstein describes the rules
as "generally biased in favor of admissibility." They take a
relaxed approach, for example, on the central issue of relevance, providing that a piece of evidence is irrelevant only if
it has no tendency, however slight, to make any material
proposition in the case look more or less probable than otherwise. Most of the old exclusions are still carried forward in
the textbooks, but their application has decayed. Bit by bit
and court by court, for instance, more hearsay and opinion is

being admitted these days. Cornell law professor Faust Rossi has gone so far as to say that the hearsay rule "is now almost a fiction" and "faces extinction."

All this had profound effects in widening the scope of pretrial discovery. But it was even more significant for what happened later at trial, above all in the realm of expert testimony.

Formal legal rules had tended to keep the need for experts to a minimum by sidestepping the knottiest factual inquiries and hinging entitlements on factors that are relatively easy to ascertain. Back when divorce was mostly handled through a few relatively sweeping presumptions, for example, likely custody and property outcomes could often be worked out on the back of an envelope from a few simple factors: the ages of the children, the balance in the joint checking account, and so forth. A home appraiser might have to be called in now and then, but other expert testimony was not very common. Once everything was put up for equitable grabs, the courtrooms were bound to fill with child psychologists, social workers, value-of-a-professional-degree appraisers, and forensic accountants.

Similar trends have been seen in other areas of law dominated by vague standards and balancing tests: any thoroughgoing effort to consider the totality of someone's circumstances calls for a ton of factual input, not all of which lay persons can readily provide. Lawsuits charging that a product was defective used to be handled by asking the sorts of unpretentious questions that courts could hope to resolve without specialized help: was the product delivered in its intended form? Where had the two sides agreed the risk of accident should fall? Now the prevailing "risk-utility test" calls on the jury to carry on a global cost-benefit balancing of all the pluses and minuses of the company's decision to put a given product on the market. Trials soon demanded a traveling caravan of engineers, statisticians, consumer psychologists, economists, and more.

As experts piled and tumbled into the courtrooms in such disconcerting numbers, some rational way might have been found to elicit their massed opinions. One old idea is to combine the experts with the judges or juries by assigning tariff, patent, and suchlike recondite matters to special courts or boards, or empaneling a body of merchants or doctors to decide whether one of their peers has breached a professional standard of competence or ethics. More practical for the run of ordinary lawsuits where a new kind of expertise is needed every day is for the judge to pick an outside expert or a panel of them to testify on a technical matter, as is commonly done in European courts.

Visiting European lawyers are often dumbfounded to learn that in this country most experts are recruited, sent into courtroom battle, and paid by the contending litigants themselves. Credentials are nice, but partisan reliability usually has to come first. "I would go into a lawsuit with an objective, uncommitted, independent expert about as willingly as I would occupy a foxhole with a couple of noncombatant soldiers," former American Bar Association president John Shepherd has said. Frequently the lawyer writes the testimony for the expert to deliver on the stand.

This elite technical corps in the ranks of the partisan armies, like some other high-tech military establishments, does not come cheap. Medical experts are reported to charge around $15,000 to $20,000 a case for malpractice testimony. A leading witness who testifies for plaintiffs in pollution-illness suits has reportedly charged a flat $20,000 per complainant, and the number of complainants in those cases can run into the dozens or hundreds.

This kind of weaponry can be worth every penny. If one side resorts to it, the other side must respond in kind or fear the worst: dueling experts may cancel each other out, but the expert who advances uncontradicted can wreak devastation. That lesson was brought home in the famous 1985 case of *Pennzoil* v. *Texaco*. Texaco was accused of snatching Getty Oil away from a binding commitment to merge with Pennzoil.

Confident it would win by showing the commitment was never binding, it did not deign to dignify Pennzoil's case by calling economists or geologists to testify on how much the collapse of the deal might have cost its rival. Pennzoil proceeded to call experts who testified that by not getting to buy Getty their client had lost a business opportunity worth $7.5 billion—a number later dismissed as absurd by a number of outside economists and financial analysts who noted that since oil prices went down after the deal Pennzoil may actually have saved money by not having to go through with it. But that number was all the jury was given to go on, and when it came back with a verdict for Pennzoil it attached the $11 billion price tag (counting punitive damages) that forced the sixth largest American corporation into bankruptcy.

The old rules, mindful of experts' enormous power, kept them under strict limitations. First and crucially, they could not be deployed unless they were truly needed, unless the jury could not expect to get at the truth of a matter on its own. Once let in, they could speak only to the area of their expertise, and not start sounding off about other issues in a case.

A further and somewhat artificial set of rules governed what they could say even within the scope of their expertise. They could base their remarks only on data that had been admitted as evidence (and was thus subject to cross-examination or impeachment by the opponent). If they wanted to reason from a disputed proposition they had to frame their remarks in response to a sometimes-elaborate hypothetical question ("Assuming that Mary repeatedly confined the child to its room without good reason, would you describe her as a possible candidate for mental disturbance?"). Finally, they could not speak in the language of legal conclusions ("In my professional opinion, it would be in the best interests of the children to change custody"); that would be impermissibly to "invade the province" of the judge or jury, as the case might be.

Most important, the courts tried to keep up a sort of quality control, by actively excluding testimony from experts whose views were fringy or speculative. The *Frye* rule, as it was named after a 1923 case, held that courts should admit testimony only if its underlying precepts had "gained general acceptance in the particular field."

This rule was not ideally objective in operation; the boundaries of a "particular field" were not always obvious, for example. A more practical problem was that the courts in their caution were slow to jump on scientific bandwagons that turned out to be genuine. Often they did not recognize a consensus among the knowing until years after one had co-agulated. A Florida judge, chiding his colleagues for their hesitance in accepting new criminal forensic tests, complained that society should not be forced to tolerate murder while waiting for some "body of medical literature."

By the 1960s, the courts' application of the *Frye* rule was coming under quite an opposite kind of criticism, not for trailing behind the scientific consensus but for paying it too much attention. Wasn't it elitist to embrace some views as mainstream science and dismiss others as not worth hearing? Why risk keeping the next Galileo out of court because of a misplaced faith in Establishment credentials?

Fatefully, the 1975 Federal Rules of Evidence declared that courts should admit expert testimony whenever it might prove "helpful" to a jury. The old *Frye* rule fell rapidly into disuse: it was hard to deny that the testimony of an offbeat practitioner of "accidentology" or "human factor engineering" might at least be helpful, if not exactly necessary. So it also went with testimony that although shrouded in scientific trappings spoke to issues of common-sense observation. No doubt it could prove helpful to call a specialist in warning-label psychology to help decide whether someone should have dived head first into an above-ground swimming pool, or a post-horrible-catastrophe-syndromist to shed light on whether the family of the deceased could be expected to be distraught afterward.

Before long all it took to be an expert in many courts was a call from a lawyer. The controls on what experts could say on the stand began coming off as well. Tired of the word games, many courts started letting witnesses baldly announce their ultimate opinion, not fooling around with hypotheticals; testify directly to the legal issue of a case; and base their opinion on hearsay and other data not before the jury, such as off-the-record interviews with the client. Each change fed the sense that these people had to be taken seriously because they knew something the rest of us didn't, and heightened the impression they could make on novice listeners.

The purveying of expert opinion soon became a busy hub of the litigation industry. The back pages of *Trial*, the magazine for injury lawyers, set forth a vast bazaar of testimony that can be had for a price on everything from aerobic dance injury to exploding bottles ("100% success to date"). Other experts will help you sue people after weather disasters, medical mishaps ("Two of our recent cases settled for $1.45 million and $990,000.00!"), water-ski calamities, "sport surface failures and related slip-fall." The headline over a nearby article begins: "Expert Medical Witnesses: They Need Careful Coaching . . ."

Matchmaking outfits have sprung up to bring these dignitaries to market, and they are eager to please. One of the larger ones, Medical-Legal Consulting Service of Bethesda, Maryland, has promised that if the first doctor it refers doesn't agree with your lawyer's theory of the case, it will send over a second at no extra charge. The impressively named Medical Quality Foundation takes a leaf from the prevailing code of legal ethics by charging contingency fees: it pockets a share of the winnings if its expert convinces the jury but takes nothing if his performance leaves them unmoved.

The contingency fee would seem to be the coming thing in the rent-an-accuser business, if the apparent success of the MQF is any indication. "Our statistics top the charts," its ads have boasted. "If experts have stated that they find no liability in a medical malpractice claim with catastrophic injuries . . .

let us analyze the case for you." The group also provides lawyers with forensic artwork, "day-in-the-life" films showing the sad daily routine of injury victims, and seminars on how to run suits for top dollar payout. "Learn to effectively maximize recovery in all your Medical Malpractice and other Personal Injury cases," runs its capitalization-infatuated full-page ad in *Trial*. "Our Senior Medical Director will discuss the winning tactics."

MQF director Dr. H. Barry Jacobs has also written how-to books for lawyer clients, at least one of which sports an introduction by Melvin Belli. "Since big cases get big damages," Jacobs has written, "be sure the courtroom is full of people watching this trial." He advises renting a bus or van and rounding up retirement-home residents by promising the chance to observe a very important real court case. "Bring in friends, relatives, associates, and neighbors who should not, of course, in the presence of the jury, show familiarity with the plaintiff or the plaintiff's attorney or staff." Dr. Jacobs's experience in the courtroom is not just on the civil plaintiff's side: according to a 1983 *New York Times Magazine* article by John Jenkins, he served ten months of a two-year term in prison for Medicare and Medicaid fraud and lost his medical licenses for a time.

Most experts say they are chagrined at the doings of what they call the hired guns. Many struggle bravely to keep up their objectivity and cringe at the thought of being paid on contingency. (Court rules usually prohibit a direct contingency payment to the expert himself, while allowing such a fee to be paid to the expert's handlers. Courts have no effective way, however, to monitor later transactions between the handlers and the expert.) But mainstream scientists who venture into the courtroom often come away disgusted and unwilling to return. Some are put off by cross-examinations that strike them as aimed more at making them look foolish than at engaging the issues. Others lack the stage presence and knack for simplicity needed in a good witness; more than one genuinely eminent physician or engineer has blown a client's case by seeming like a know-it-all or drawing so many careful distinctions that the jury's eyes glazed over.

The expert who does enjoy the courtroom and scores a few victories is likely to be asked back again, picking up what you might call frequent-testifier bonus points. The Association of Trial Lawyers of America's *ATLA Law Reporter,* which keeps injury lawyers apprised of major new victories, lists the name not only of winning lawyers but also of winning experts, who get new business that way. Hence the rise of the professional witness who works closely with lawyers and knows what they want. Some travel around the country and have testified at more than a thousand trials. "An expert can be found to testify to the truth of almost any factual theory, no matter how frivolous," notes Judge Jack Weinstein.

Of course, opponents counter the more eccentric claims by calling their own scientists to give the mainstream side of the story—leading to the "battle of the experts." All too often the bewildered jury concludes that even the pros can't agree on the science and proceeds to decide the case on sympathetic or other grounds.

A curious group of expert witnesses has emerged in the sympathetic sort of case where neighbors charge that pollution from a chemical factory or dump has made them ill. Lawyers for the neighbors can usually show that the defendants released at least minute quantities of hazardous substances into the local air, water, or soil. The experts then come along to testify that even very low-level exposure to chemicals can ravage people's immune systems—the dramatically effective catch-phrase is "chemical AIDS." The pollution is thus said to be responsible for an enormously wide range of common maladies among the neighbors, from colds to cancer, measles to gallstones. The experts do their own battery of tests on the complainants and come up with immune system abnormalities that tests by other scientists fail to reveal.

The "chemical AIDS" idea has been emphatically rejected by leading medical authorities as without foundation.

But a Missouri court awarded $49 million after claims of this sort—later remanded for retrial—and complainants from Tennessee to California have been winning verdicts ranging up to $13 million, although many get thrown out on post-trial motions or appeal. In a Philadelphia case now on appeal, various neighbors came to court with a grab bag of miscellaneous symptoms that included arthritis, heart problems, and insomnia that they blamed on a nearby Conrail repair yard that had been leaking polychlorinated biphenyls (PCBs) from rail-car transformers. A federal study found no evidence that neighborhood residents had any more PCB in their systems than average Americans. This time the claims ran into skepticism from federal judge R. F. Kelly, who tossed the case out summarily with a swipe at the plaintiffs' experts, one of whom he said had blamed the chemical exposures for asthma and hypertension in patients with family histories of those ailments.

The other expert for the plaintiffs in the Philadelphia lawsuit, Dr. Arthur Zahalsky, has turned up in many interesting cases. According to the *ATLA Law Reporter* for February 1988, he was the plaintiff's expert in a successful Texas lawsuit brought on the theory that an auto accident had caused or contributed to cancer. $248,600 reportedly changed hands in settlement of that case, an outcome that might surprise workaday cancer specialists who long ago abandoned trauma-cancer theories.

It can hardly be a coincidence that exotic scientific theories have cropped up with special frequency in the sort of injury cases where an intractable factual barrier is all that stands between a contingency-fee lawyer and a vast reservoir of jury sympathy. Exhibit A are the so-called bad-baby cases. Few hearts can resist the plight of a deformed, paralyzed, or brain-damaged infant, or of the family that faces great expense trying to care for it. When someone can be blamed to a jury's satisfaction, million-dollar verdicts are routine.

Under older evidence rules, not many bad-baby lawsuits would get very far. Mainstream science is still dubious about the cause of most birth defects (which seem to be equally prevalent in countries with widely differing cultures, levels of technological development, and legal systems). When causes are known or suspected, they are often causes that are hard to turn into lawsuits, such as genetic inheritance or the mother's alcohol or drug abuse. Still less can scientists move from statistical correlations among millions of births to a reasonable certainty about what caused a particular baby's retardation or cerebral palsy.

When the evidence rules crumbled, the search went out. Ambitious lawyers soon discovered at least a few experts willing to blame almost every solvent party on the scene of a new human being's appearance in the world. Some blamed contraceptives taken in the weeks before pregnancy became apparent or medicines commonly taken during pregnancy itself. Others blamed fetal asphyxiation during labor, which they said obstetricians should have detected by the use of electronic fetal monitoring and relieved by performing a Caesarean section on the mother. Yet others blamed vaccines that are widely administered in an infant's first months before many handicaps manifest themselves. John Jenkins's *New York Times* article reported that an outfit called the American Palsy Society was run out of the same offices as the Medical-Legal Consulting Service, the Maryland-based clearinghouse for expert referrals.

Most bad-baby cases that go to actual trial appear to lose. Most juries have agreed that the drug Bendectin, prescribed safely for decades against morning sickness in pregnancy, does not cause birth defects. By far the majority of doctors who go to trial on malpractice charges win their cases, and there is scant reason to think obstetricians are an exception.

But every so often trial lawyers get lucky. One angry Bendectin jury voted $95 million, reversed on appeal after years of fighting. The drug's manufacturer offered $100 million to settle a thousand-case consolidated action. Lawyers greedily turned it down and went to trial, where they lost outright and got nothing. A federal judge in Georgia, ruling in a rare case without a jury, decided that a commonly used spermicidal contraceptive caused birth defects and awarded $5 million to the parents.

The sheer volume of cases against obstetricians and vaccine providers means that even with a low victory rate many million-dollar verdicts can get through. Three respected Washington, D.C., practitioners lost a $10 million verdict, later settled for $4 million, in a case where their professional peers, as quoted in the local magazine *Regardie's*, viewed them as clearly innocent. "We feel as if we've lost the right to a fair trial," said one colleague. "If there's any case that could have been won, it was this one."

Later research, as it scurried to keep up with the court activity, exploded the underlying scientific basis for most of the bad-baby claims. "Whooping Cough Vaccine Found Not to Be Linked to Brain Damage," ran the headline over a March 1990 *New York Times* news report, after uncounted trial lawyers had become millionaires claiming that it was. The federal Food and Drug Administration and virtually all researchers continue to reject the idea that Bendectin or spermicides cause birth defects; after the Georgia contraceptive decision the *New England Journal of Medicine* complained editorially that "courts will not be bound by reasonable standards of proof." Most dramatic of all, extensive research has concluded that obstetrical errors are not in fact responsible for most cases of cerebral palsy; that the much-demanded use of electronic fetal monitoring does not reduce the incidence of that affliction; and that Caesarean sections, far from being underprescribed as trial lawyers had gotten rich claiming, are disastrously overprescribed by doctors terrified of being sued.

The bad-baby litigation industry was eventually exposed as resting on a foundation of gross, systematic untruths. But in the meantime the world of obstetrics and newborn care was devastated. Thousands of doctors, especially family doctors in rural areas, stopped delivering babies; by common estimates one-fifth of those in the field departed over a span of a few years. Bendectin, although fully vindicated, was pulled off the market by its maker and kept off, as have been other valuable drugs, vaccines, and medical devices. Of those still available, many have skyrocketed in price; the litigation costs are often very much higher than the underlying cost of manufacturing the product. After American trial lawyers stoked a worldwide panic over the whooping cough (pertussis) component of the diphtheria/pertussis/tetanus (DPT) vaccine, vaccination rates against whooping cough declined in Japan and parts of Europe and many children died from the disease itself.

And still, incredible as it may seem, the cases will not go away; they are simply too profitable for the lawyers. The usual targets continue to be sued, and new ones are constantly being lined up; the latest twist, in a bid for a jury-sympathy double-header, are suits claiming that air pollution from local factories causes birth defects. No doubt most such claims will lose in the end. But as the Irish Republican Army said after its Brighton hotel bombing failed to assassinate Margaret Thatcher: "We only have to be lucky once. You have to be lucky every time."

The influx of marginal experts and low-grade evidence helped make possible another great outbreak of guesswork in the legal system. This one came in the law of damages.

One of the running complaints against the old courts was their stinginess in awarding damages. Verdicts were so low that they often seemed very poor recompense for having been injured. Yet the courts were not miserly on principle. Their bias, as usual, was in favor of outcomes that were particular and determinate. They were quite prepared to squeeze someone till the pips squeaked to get him to pay for a certain sunk boat, support a named child, make good on a given promissory note. What they shunned was the open-ended claim whose blanks could be filled in only through guesswork. Two recurring themes were that damages to be recoverable had to be direct and certain.

Consider the vast and now more or less wound-up annals of lawsuits over bungled telegrams. Telegraph companies, because of their monopoly status, came under unusually rigorous liability by the standards of their heyday. When they delayed or garbled or failed to deliver a message and someone's affairs came a cropper, they were frequently called on to pay. But when had the harm proceeded directly and certainly enough from the mix-up to make liability appropriate?

The neatest case for an award was when an error had sufficed to make or break a "done deal." A merchant wired an offer to sell certain apples at $1.75 a barrel; the price was mistakenly sent as $1.55 and the apples were snapped up; the telegraph company had to make good the difference. Damages one step more remote might not be obtainable. A man sent on an unnecessary journey recovered for the out-of-pocket costs of his trip, but not the fatigue and exposure involved, or the cost of leaving his affairs unattended in the meantime.

Almost any intervening factor, especially a human factor, could cut short one of these cause-and-effect chains. One telegram that went astray had suggested but not commanded a purchase that would have proved highly profitable; the sender could recover only his transmission fee, because who knew whether his agent would have followed his advice? An error that caused a company to wire too much money to its agent, who promptly absconded, was again not actionable because the agent's guilty act had intervened.

The epithet that comes up again and again in these cases is "speculative": those were the claims the courts tried to disallow. Just as the law ruled out evidence that was too shaky, so it ruled out whole categories of claims that, while by no means always imaginary, could rest only on shaky evidence. Because a message went astray, a horse was not sent to a prize sweepstakes race; but who is to say it would have won? Might-well-haves and could-easily-haves would inch courts into dangerous territory. Or a man did not hear from his stockbrokers; but who knew whether he would have picked the right time to sell the stock being bought? The only testimony would be unhelpfully self-serving.

The principles that governed most other businesses and professions were if anything more lenient to defendants. The law was full of formal, sometimes artificial lines between reliable and speculative damages. The case of lost business profits is a typical example. A renovator leaves a job half-finished and a guest house has to turn away customers at the height of the season; can its owners recover the profits they had expected to earn? The traditional answer was yes, but only if they had a track record of past profits for comparison. If their venture was new, they would have to content themselves with some other relief—maybe getting back their deposit or the money to finish the job. Most start-ups never turn a profit at all, and how much to award would be a mere exercise in (that word again) speculation.

It hardly seemed ideally fair for the law to insure the full-grown bird in the commercial hand for its cash value while allowing the two fledglings in the bush to be slaughtered with impunity. Yet the old courts applied the track-record rule rigidly. In fact they had an exactly parallel rule for individuals. You could recover for disruption of your professional work if you had launched an actual practice, but not if you were still at the student stage. Which is why Gloria Grayson's case raised so many eyebrows back in 1959.

Gloria, twenty-one years old, was walking by a sidewalk work site one day when she caught her foot in a hole, fell, and broke her leg. She sued the owners and contractors for failing to put up better lighting, and asked for compensation for her leg injury; nothing unusual there. But Gloria had also been studying to be an opera singer, and after her mishap it seemed she had trouble staying on pitch. She blamed a blow to her head in the fall, and began to despair of ever becoming a famous diva. And for this loss of a lucrative potential career she deserved added, sizable compensation. So at least her lawyer argued.

Gloria's voice teacher testified that she had talent and might have gone far, though of course she hadn't yet. Other evidence was put forward, however, that she had had ear trouble before the accident, and an "eminent physician" from a court-designated medical panel offered what the appeals court called "highly credible proof" that any hearing loss she might be suffering arose from an ailment that predated her fall. But a Bronx jury did not go along with this less-than-generous appraisal. It chose to award her $50,000 damages, an enormous sum at the time (in 1960 the median American family earned $5,620). The defendants appealed.

The appeals court was a bit skittish about approving the award: sure, big-name opera stars make a lot of money, but hardly any young hopefuls, talented or not, get to the top. Yet a probably-never-to-pay-off ticket in the lottery of fame was something worth having, for all that, and its economic value could even be guessed at, "although, obviously, without any precision." So the court, over dissents from two of its justices, uneasily allowed the award's reasoning and precedent to stand, while cutting its actual amount down to $20,000. It added a wistful hope that every "gleam in a doting parent's eye and every self-delusion as to one's potentialities" might not in future come to manifest itself in the form of a lawsuit.

In the years that followed, one formalist damage limitation after another collapsed in similar fashion. One of the old rules in negligence cases provided that you could not collect money for intangible harms—fright, emotional distress, humiliation, and so forth—unless you had also been physically hit or touched. (Deliberate injuries were another matter.) Even bodily symptoms brought on by mental disturbance alone—nausea, sleeplessness, angina, or worse—didn't count.

Like all simple rules, this one generated a few extremely harsh results at the edges. The most spectacular case came at the turn of the century, when runaway horses stopped within inches of a terrified woman who then suffered a miscarriage. Because the horses hadn't actually touched her, the Massachusetts courts denied recovery. A pinched interpretation of this sort could never inspire much affection for the courts, but as one writer noted it did make getting around town less of a legal hazard: you may be quite sure you haven't hit anyone in your driving recently, but are you positive you haven't frightened anyone to the point of showing physical symptoms?

Lawyers and commentators began to batter away at the rule as artificial, however, and by the middle of this century it was collapsing court by court. The landmark case in a state usually came after someone had had a close brush with fearsome injury. New York joined the trend in 1961 after little Carmen Battalla, improperly strapped to a ski-lift chair, dangled amid mounting hysteria before being pulled to safety. Soon it was possible to sue airlines not only for crashes but also for worrisome safe landings. After the landing gear failed on a Trump Shuttle flight, the pilot managed to bring the plane in so smoothly that the only injury was one passenger's cut finger; the inevitable claims would focus on the emotional trauma of having had such a close call. An especially harrowing Aloha Airlines mid-air blowout was reported to have brought unhurt but badly shaken passengers settlements ranging from $65,000 to $400,000. Lawsuits over fear of developing future illness from chemical exposure, by persons apparently unharmed otherwise, have been accepted by courts in California, New Jersey, Ohio, and elsewhere.

Before long the courts were leaving behind the context of physical jeopardy as well. The Hawaii courts decided that the Dold family, tourists from the mainland who had been overbooked by their hotel and bumped to less desirable lodgings, deserved money for their "emotional distress and disappointment" on top of the actual economic costs of the inconvenience. Doris Barnett filed suit after she was told she had not won the jackpot in the California lottery (a literal lottery this time) even though her ball had momentarily entered the winning slot before popping out again. Her lawyer convinced a jury that although the official rule book was against her, lottery officials had ignored their rules before and should have done so again. The jury awarded $400,000 as recompense for her emotional trauma, on top of $3 million for the jackpot itself.

As usual, these trends have their fast-growing equivalents in financial and commercial litigation. Until recently, accounting firms could not be sued for negligence (as opposed to knowing wrongdoing) by outside investors and creditors who might have lost money dealing with companies whose books the accountants had helped prepare. Benjamin Cardozo, who wrote the landmark decision, explained that it would be wrong to saddle the accounting profession with "a liability in an indeterminate amount for an indeterminate time to an indeterminate class." Now California, New Jersey, and other states have thrown their courtrooms open to exactly this kind of triply open-ended liability, and accountants' insurance rates have skyrocketed as they try to figure out which total strangers will sue them next and for how much.

As the courts got more ambitious about compensating all of people's injuries rather than just the highly knowable and reliable components thereof, it sometimes seemed no new damage theories were too indeterminate to be taken seriously. Trial lawyers have long been vexed by their inability to claim pain and suffering in cases where an accident victim is killed instantly or rendered comatose. Hence the new theory of "hedonic damages," supposed to represent the lost value of the victim's "enjoyment of life." David S. Evans of National Economic Research Associates, Inc., explains that there is a bit of disagreement on how much in the way of hedonic damages would be owing in a sample case: "Total estimates range from $450,000 to $13,400,000 in 1989 dollars."

One thinks of trials as places where right and wrong are decided, but nowadays blame is often a side issue and the grand-scale fighting goes on over the damage figures. After Kodak lost a patent-infringement suit to Polaroid, a second and separate trial was scheduled to calculate damages. Kodak, applying a conservative "lost-royalty" theory, conceded that it owed $150 million. Polaroid, using a speculative and highly optimistic "lost-profits" theory, countered that it deserved $12 billion, not counting interest. "In most cases, I can come up with five different theories of damages and they're all fair," says Miami lawyer Joseph Klock. This of course means that many disputes go to prolonged litigation that would have been settled promptly if there were a reliable way to estimate damages.

Of course, not every ambitious damage claim succeeds. Ruth Johnson encountered a setback in her "wrongful pregnancy" suit against University Hospitals of Cleveland when, in a fit of conservatism, the Ohio courts ruled that the hospital whose sterilization attempt had fallen short could be made to pay only for the cost of her unwanted pregnancy, and not, as her lawyer had argued, for the cost of raising the boy through adulthood. Perhaps thinking of such cases, many writers in law reviews kept gravely assuring each other, as they had done for decades, that awards still fell far short of full compensation.

Even so, the idea of an adequate award had swollen and metastasized and sent out runners to an extent that would have left yesterday's legal profession reeling. Not without reason did Melvin Belli name his yacht the *Adequate Award*. The news clips continued to pile up: this lucky litigant made more money suing than he had in a lifetime of steady work; that business had become the most prosperous in town by suing its competitors. A curious thing was happening: some of the hapless plaintiffs were beginning to attract not sympathy but downright envy; their injuries were the best thing that had ever happened to them. Evelyn Waugh said that when funds were tight he used to pick up the newspapers each day in hope he had been libeled. Here in America, too, for a fortunate few though definitely not a majority, victimization was becoming something to look forward to.

The boost of damages into hyperspace did not tend to increase people's respect for the court system. In the first place, people kept comparing lawsuits to crapshoots, roulette wheels, keno lounges, and fan tan parlors. Most workers who became ill after many years of on-the-job exposure to asbestos, in cases where smoking was involved, obtained smallish settlements; Michael Coyne and Albert McCoubray, Jr., were offered a combined total of less than $3,000. They held out for trial and a jury voted them $152 million, including $150 million in punitive damages, the case later being settled for an undisclosed sum. Most workers suing their former employers over libel and slander would get either nothing or a few thousand dollars; then a lawyer convinced a Florida jury that former John Hancock insurance salesman Clifford Zalay deserved $26 million, nearly all of that in punitive damages.

As the variability of awards went up, their credibility began to go down. Broken hearts are easier to fake than broken bones. Gone was any hope of what has been called horizontal equity between cases, since we can't all hire the hot lawyers or draw the loose juries. Pick-a-number damage awards say a lot about the emotions lawyers succeed in evoking within the courtroom, but they can hardly reflect anything durable or objective about the world outside.

Guesswork on science and damages can combine with guesswork on the meaning of balancing-test legal standards to produce wildly disparate results from case to case. The closest thing to a controlled experiment are lawsuits over product liability, where the same allegedly defective drug or automotive design is put on trial again and again with results that vary wildly all over the map. The Sabin polio vaccine, strongly endorsed by public health authorities, had a string of victories, scattered defeats, and then in June 1984 ran into a $10 million verdict, $8 million of it in punitive damages. The Searle company, which used to make the Copper-7 IUD contraceptive, won eight trials and lost two small ones. Then it was hit with an $8.75 million verdict, including $7 million in punitive damages; the stock market value of its parent company dropped $750 million in a single day. At each stage public health and Planned Parenthood officials reiterated their view that the device was a good one that deserved to be on the market.

All major makers of compact cars have lost lawsuits on theories that their vehicles should have withstood crashes better, with several staggering jury verdicts ($120 million against Ford, $59 million against Toyota) that have then mostly been reduced or thrown out on appeal. But no make or model, not even the much-vilified Ford Pinto, has lost at all consistently. In suits over supposed "sudden acceleration," the makers of the Audi 5000 won once on summary judgment and once at jury trial, and lost twice on quite different theories of what might be defective about the car. Elaborate studies by the governments of the United States, Japan, and Canada confirmed that the car was not, in fact, defective.

Guesswork in the jury room is usually not the last round of guesswork. Trial and appellate judges are gravely embarrassed by randomness in verdicts and commonly strike down or reduce the awards that (they guess) are truly outrageous. Even the A.B.A., not the world's leading critic of runaway litigation, has recommended that judges use these powers more vigorously. Because of the expectation that this will happen, cases with joltingly high verdicts are often settled before appeal for a small fraction of what the trial jury actually voted.

Plaintiffs' lawyers, who play the first round of guesswork for all it is worth, often feel cheated when their hard-confiscated money dribbles away in these later rounds. (Isn't it disgraceful, they ask each other, that judges can cut awards just by picking a number out of a hat?) They get especially indignant when public discussion focuses on outlandish jury outcomes, like the psychic-injury case, without giving equal time to their sad tale of how judges later threw out or reduced these verdicts.

These lawyers should have the courage of their (attempted) confiscations. If (as they always do) plaintiffs' lawyers feverishly oppose reduction of jury verdicts at the time it is being considered, they should be willing to defend those original verdicts in public discussion later. For them to turn around and treat judges' reduction of verdicts as the saving, neglected virtue of the whole system—making it needless to seek any more systematic reform—is rather like for an auto-maker to defend its production quality by pointing out that its models are constantly recalled to the factory for repairs.

When jury verdicts are routinely slashed or overturned it is a sign of distress in the legal system, not health. Jurors themselves (who in the overwhelming main are shrewd and rational folks) frequently put their finger on the reason why when they complain after trials that they were given "nothing to go on" in turning the complex mass of observations and assertions into a verdict. This is an accurate summary of the predicament of the fact-finder in a system that welcomes and invites guesswork at every turn.

Like everyone else in the court system, juries need and deserve objective rules for decision. Deprived of any fixed landmarks and guideposts, any of us can be distracted, played on, and befuddled to the point where our best guess is far from reliable. Inevitably, the sentiment has grown that juries have somehow outlived their usefulness and that judges, who as repeat players can bring a second-best sort of uniformity to the output of their courtrooms, should decide civil lawsuits all by themselves.

Yet over the centuries juries have shown themselves to be a superb brake against tyranny (they were never intended to be an accelerator of anything). It would be a shame to give up on them when it is within our power to give them the strong evidence rules, no-guesswork damage principles, and bright-line legal standards that would bring their findings re-newed respect. A jury system with believably objective rules would be the best of all legal worlds.

The randomness of courtroom outcomes is not a new concern. Some of the Elizabethans thought that by carrying around a piece of hyena gut a man might "foreknow the success and event of his petitions and sutes in Law." Earlier generations, by and large, have seen the battle of wits in court as a way to put to rest particular tangible disputes that would not go away otherwise, but not as an especially potent engine of wider truth. Older courts had few pretensions to lead the advance parties at the frontiers of human knowledge, and were pleased if they could avoid falling into gross error.

The invisible-fist school took a far more utopian view. Litigation, they argued, precisely because of its painful sharpness, is a fine way to drill beneath the surface of human affairs to the wellsprings of limpid truth. Where else under our system of government, short perhaps of the legislative investigating power, can investigators demand access to private correspondence and compel persons to testify against their own interests under threat of penalty? Surely with such resources lawyers could turn courts into a supreme tribunal of disinterested inquiry. They could uncover social evils of tremendous importance and take the lead in alerting the public to the dangerous aircraft design or unhealthy day-care-center practice, the unethical homebuilder or cheeseparing tradesperson, the irresponsible ex-spouse or neglectful parent.

The irony is that when the law was more modest about its ambitions it actually fulfilled a bit of this promise. Back when malpractice verdicts were a highly unusual blot on a doctor's record they were a real signal for patients to watch out. Now that 70 percent of obstetricians have been sued and many very fine ones have lost, the sensible mother-to-be hardly bothers to inspect her doctor's rap sheet unless it is yards long. Nor would the prudent consumer today hesitate to buy a car just because it has been adjudged defectively unsafe by some court somewhere, or open an investment account just because the brokerage has recently gone on trial on charges of civil fraud. And the targets of the accusations, slowly but surely, are ceasing to attach much value to the advice they get from the courts. Rand Corporation researchers studying the internal decision-making process in manufacturing firms found that all firms surveyed saw product-liability litigation as essentially a random matter that offered no clear signals on how products should be designed.

As the courts have gotten more ambitious about their role as oracles of truth, their credibility has sunk. They have boldly followed the hired experts into unsettled border zones of human knowledge, only to fall into growing disrepute among mainstream technologists. They have begun casually second-guessing established techniques of surgery, swimming pool design, and pension fund management, only to find their advice being taken less seriously by professionals in those fields. They have declared the goal of considering all relevant factors, each time anew, in deciding immensely complicated social questions, only to generate a randomness of outcome that is forever being compared to a lottery. Aspiring to attain perfect truth, they are taking us back to the days of the hyena gut.

⚖

HAVE LAWSUIT, WILL TRAVEL

Where am I, or what? . . . Whose favor shall I court, and whose
anger must I dread? . . . I am confounded with all these questions,
and begin to fancy myself in the most deplorable condition imaginable,
inviron'd with the deepest darkness.

—*DAVID HUME*, Treatise
of Human Nature

For many years Massachusetts law protected doctors and hospitals from lawsuits in cases arising from less than gross negligence. The state kept these laws on its books long after many other states had done away with theirs. One result was that as of roughly the end of the 1960s Massachusetts surgeons were paying only one sixth as much for liability insurance as their more lawsuit-exposed colleagues in New York.

The invisible-fist theory would lead you to expect that by "underdeterring" ordinary negligence the Bay State would have attracted an especially bumbling and incompetent medical profession. Somehow that didn't happen. Boston's hospitals won world renown for state-of-the-art medical practice. Patients flocked there from all over the country.

But even good doctors lose patients. That happened in 1969 to Dr. Kenneth Warren, the nationally recognized chief of surgery at the New England Baptist Hospital. Before long Dr. Warren found he was being sued in New York; the patient was from that state, and the lawyers for his family had invoked the innovative long-arm doctrine by which New York courts could pull in complete outsiders whose liability insurance companies did business in the state. The suit also named the hospital as a defendant. It asked for $1,250,000, a very high figure in those days.

There was one obvious problem. Massachusetts law limited damage awards in cases of this sort to a fraction of that figure, and also required that such awards "be assessed with reference to the degree of . . . culpability," further reducing what the doctor might be made to pay. And the state's "charitable immunity" law exempted the philanthropic Baptist hospital from being sued at all for ordinary negligence.

No problem, said the court. Just because the whole episode from start to finish had taken place in Massachusetts was no reason to apply the liability limits of that state's law. New York and its courts strongly disapproved of such limits, and as the home of the patient and his family would apply its law rather than the "anachronistic" alternative on the books in its sister state. And so Dr. Warren and his hospital could both be sued for as much as if the surgery had taken place in midtown Manhattan. The ruling was upheld on appeal.

For centuries, judges have spent a fair bit of time applying in their courtrooms the laws of other states and even other countries. This is not as strange as it may sound. If you sell someone a car in Tennessee and his lawyers catch up with you in Alabama after it breaks down the next week, neither of you should have to worry about what Alabama law says about car sales. Whether you owe him anything should depend on the law of Tennessee, where you made the deal. And that is the law Alabama's (or for that matter Zambia's) courts are supposed to apply when they hear his case.

That the first court is out of sympathy with the second's law need make no difference. When Dalip Singh Bir came to this country from India he left behind two wives, both lawfully married to him in the Punjab. He never did go back and died in 1945 an old man, having reached not just one but a pair of golden anniversaries. Should California recognize both wives for purposes of distributing his estate?

A court decided that it would. Of course, it did not suddenly decree the legalization of bigamy in California. In fact, the state might not have deferred to Indian customs so far as to let Singh Bir cohabit with both women on its soil had they come over to join him. But on the less scandalous issue of succession rights, what India had joined California would not put asunder.

Most legal authorities agree that the California court did the right thing. So far as is practical the law should judge people's actions by the rule they acted under at the time, which in this case was "the law and manner of the Jat community," where bigamous marriages "are lawful and valid." Paradoxical as it may sound, judges can often advance the rule of law by applying someone else's law instead of their own—even when the foreign law strikes them personally as bizarre or mistaken.

Over the centuries an enormous and sophisticated branch of legal thinking, variously called choice of law or conflict of laws, grew up to help courts settle on a single standard to judge people's actions. Notice that the question of choice of law—which law can a court apply to your actions or situation?—is quite distinct from the question of jurisdiction—which court can force you to stand trial? As we shall see, however, courts that get rambunctious about grabbing power on the one front do not usually remain shy or retiring on the other.

When conflicts law breaks down and states end up applying different rules to the same affair, the results for the individuals on the scene can be thoroughly disastrous. A New York court calls into question whether it will recognize an old Rhode Island marriage, and six children are suddenly menaced with illegitimacy. Illinois decides it cannot tolerate Kentucky's law permitting cousins to marry, and a widow is done out of her husband's death benefits. North Carolina disagrees with Nevada on the proper terms of divorce and vents its opinion by prosecuting a remarried spouse for bigamy.

The widely reported case of Baby Lenore arose when a New York mother gave her newborn daughter up for adoption and then changed her mind five days later. New York law apparently supported her position, but on advice of counsel the adopting couple moved to Florida, which takes a different view. The woman pursued them. After years of expense and disruption of lives the U.S. Supreme Court in 1972 finally refused to review a ruling that Florida was free to apply its own law instead of New York's, allowing Baby Lenore to stay with her adoptive parents.

Interstate divorces are a perennial chamber of horrors in this branch of the law. When husband and wife live apart, each can usually get his home state to assert its own law over the relationship and any children or property on hand. The race can thus be to get the objects of dispute, human or otherwise, into the favorable state. Mom might be sure of winning custody in West Virginia where the family had made its home, but if Dad could get the kids into Ohio he could open the fray under a much more favorable legal standard. The problem of interstate child-snatching got so completely out of hand that it had to be made the subject of federal law. But similar games are still played over property. High-earning husbands from pro-homemaker states stow assets away on the sly in pro-breadwinner states, in preparation for a break.

Family breakup aside, fortunately, these tales of woe have been the exception and not the rule. With their customary dread of indeterminacy, the older courts and legal scholars saw certainty of result as more important than getting their own way. The old law was thus fond of simple, sweeping rules intended to provide instant preresolutions of potential conflicts of law. A marriage (the general rule arose) was valid everywhere if it was valid where performed. A will would stand up if it conformed to the law of the place where the signer regularly lived. A question of real estate would be handled under the law of the site of the land. The internal affairs of an association could be contested only under the laws of its state of chartering, no matter where it happened to hold its convention this year.

Ideally, these rules were supposed to allocate each event of life automatically to its proper law slot. The more mechanical the process, the less chance lawyers would have to shop around for favorable laws and perhaps play on judges' natural inclination toward their own citizens and laws. Courts were supposed to make the choice of law without peeking in the envelope, so to speak, to see whether it was their law or someone else's, let alone whether they liked the results. "It would be as unjust to apply a different law as it would be to determine the rights of the parties by a different transaction," wrote Joseph Story, the Supreme Court justice who was long the chief American authority in the field.

The rules of choice of law, like those of jurisdiction, were sometimes thought to follow from abstract ideas about sovereignty. Just as Tennessee could not tread on Alabama's majesty by sending its sheriffs to arrest persons in Alabama, so Alabama could not insult Tennessee by applying its own law to transactions that arose on the soil of, or in some other way belonged to, its sister state. Some dealings might not obviously belong more to one state than the other, as when a Tennesseean and an Alabaman strike a deal over the telephone, or the blasting from an Alabama quarry keeps neighbors awake across the state line. But if the two states are to live in peace, or "comity," they should find a way for one to defer to the other's law, rather than risk having both try to grab the wheel at the same time.

For the ordinary citizen, once again, the frigid formalities had some surprisingly favorable implications for individual liberty. The rules of choice of law, like those of jurisdiction, promised to shield the citizen from the wrath of any more than one sovereign on a given matter. The benefits were shrewdly practical as well. If you were arranging a home sale or corporate merger or child's adoption across state lines, you could hope to fit your actions into one set of consistent laws, not two or more potentially contradictory sets.

The right not to be sued civilly under the law of an inappropriate state was understood to be an important part of that right to due process of law guaranteed by the U.S. Constitution. Down through the 1930s the U.S. Supreme Court upheld those rights, as it did the parallel right to be free of the jurisdiction of an inappropriate state.

It's not as if courts owe absolute deference to all foreign law: they wouldn't enforce the order of a cannibal kingdom that its recalcitrant subjects come back to be eaten. Once in a blue moon local "policy" would be invoked in this way as a reason for a court not to take positive steps to enforce a sister state's law on a sensitive matter such as the enforcement of gambling debts run up in a place where gambling was lawful. But "policy" was hardly ever used as a ground for asserting *affirmative* judicial power: it was too obvious that that way lay chaos. For the most part states showed an amiable modesty about pushing their own policies to the point of collision with those of other states.

This of course did not mean that cases always came out the same way no matter which court they were taken to. Lawyers could still shop around for favorable procedural rules, jury climates, and legal cultures, as we saw in Chapter 4. And they could exploit, or try to exploit, the occasional overlaps between the sweepingly worded choice-of-law maxims. A lawsuit over a property sale might try to invoke whichever was more favorable of the rules for sales (place of signature) or real estate matters (place of the land). Injury suits against product manufacturers might be couched as matters of negligence (place of the wrongful act) or breach of an implied promise of safety (place of sale).

For a while courts and scholars seemed to be making progress toward developing finer sub-rules to handle the borderline cases. But as the long-arm revolution combined with the decay of formalism in the 1950s and 1960s, pressure began building for changes in quite a different direction. Lawyers could now shop around for forums as never before, but it was far harder for them to shop around for laws. And what stood in their way? An artificial system of formal rules.

The initial pressure for change came in one-car auto accident cases where allegedly negligent drivers were sued by their own injured passengers, who often were their own family members. The various states and Canadian provinces followed very different rules on these cases. Many essentially shut such claims out of the legal system. They were afraid of both sincere suits, which might poison relationships between intimates, and insincere suits, where the claimed negligence or even the fact of the accident or injury were essentially means of getting at an insurance policy with the connivance of the nominal defendant ("Yes, your Honor, I sure was negligent. No doubt about that. No sirree.") These states barred lawsuits between husband and wife, parent and child, and by a sort of analogy guest-passenger and host-driver. The argument was that people should provide against these accident risks by buying direct health and disability insurance, which is vastly more efficient than liability insurance, since it pays off without lawsuits.

Other states took a diametrically opposed view of these suits. They were less fearful of fraud or acrimony, and they saw guest-versus-driver lawsuits as a way of getting money to crash victims who as a practical matter had very often not bothered to stock up on direct insurance. So they not only allowed such lawsuits but virtually welcomed them. Between these extreme positions were states that tried to split the difference by putting a dollar ceiling on the amount that could be recovered in guest cases or requiring proof of gross rather than simple negligence.

The geographical differences created a problem for residents of the high-liability states. They were paying the higher insurance rates that inevitably went along with more lawsuit exposure, the hope being that the added rights to sue now available to their friends and family would be worth it. Yet

having given up the quid, they were not entirely sure of
getting the quo: their guests might be out of luck if hurt in
a crash while the family was driving out of state. Wouldn't it
be nice if the law on these suits, in line with the typical terms
of auto insurance itself, tracked the place a car was normally
used rather than the place it happened to crash? Thus ran
the line of academic speculation when Georgia Babcock's case
came along.

One autumn Friday in 1960 the Jackson family of Rochester,
New York set off for a weekend trip to Canada with their
friend Georgia Babcock. They had crossed into the province
of Ontario when William Jackson, at the wheel, apparently
lost control of the car and went off the highway into a stone
wall. Georgia was hurt and sued William in a New York court,
which was no problem under old rules of jurisdiction or new
since that was where he lived.

   No one denied that under the age-old principle of *lex loci
delictus* (the law of the place of wrong governs injury lawsuits),
Ontario law was to govern the case on such matters as whether
William had followed proper rules of the road. But did New
York have to recognize and apply Ontario's law against guest
lawsuits? The state's highest court announced in the landmark
1963 case of *Babcock* v. *Jackson* that it would not. It observed
that New York had by far the most significant "grouping of
contacts" with the dispute: it was where the car was registered, where both parties lived, and where their outing was
to begin and end. Yes, the actual crash happened to have
taken place in another country. But that was in the nature of
a technicality.

The 1963 *Babcock* decision was widely hailed as epoch-
making, and other states soon climbed on board with similar
rulings. Of course the moment word got out that New York
was offering to apply its law to out-of-state accidents, lawyers
for plaintiffs from points north and south, east and west began
lining up to ask for it. They plausibly declared that their

crashes in Michigan, Colorado, and elsewhere had a very compelling grouping of New York contacts: the car was from New York, or the driver, or the guest, or maybe the trip was to begin or end there. The feeling was that a single such contact might not do, but two or three made a promising case.

Forward as along a darkened corridor the New York judges groped their way. First they said they would apply their law only if a guest and driver both from New York had actually struck up their acquaintance in the Empire State, the apparent idea being that a friendship formed in New York, like a marriage, was a distinctive legal entity that persisted whithersoever the principals might wander. Before long, however, they had agreed to apply their law even when the two had met elsewhere. The next step, which arrived in 1970, was for a court to apply New York law where only the driver was from New York, and guest, car, starting point, accident, and destination were all from other states. For a moment the idea seemed to be that New York legal obligations to guests should follow the state's motorists wherever they might drive, around the globe. Then the New York high court retreated from that notion in a 1972 case, though Rhode Island picked it up the next year.

Meanwhile confusion was developing in the cases with the reverse pattern, where a crash happened to take place in New York but its most significant contacts plainly lay elsewhere. Logically you would have expected New York to start applying other states' or countries' law in these cases. Three years after Georgia Babcock's case, its exact mirror image came up. Albert Henderson and Stephanie Kell of Ontario set off in a car registered in that province on a short pleasure trip to New York. Albert drove off the highway and into a bridge, and Stephanie sued him in New York. Would the New York courts apply the Ontario guest statute against her? No chance, a state appeals court announced; *Babcock* had brought New York law to Ontario accidents, but no one had said anything about doing the reverse.

By now the explorers found themselves entirely in the

dark; the last flicker of intellectual coherence had given out. It was quite clear that within some band of cases where the courts thought they could get away with it, they would simply give the plaintiff the more favorable law. (At least one bar review course in the early 1980s taught students to *learn* the New York rule that way but never ever dare *state* it that way on the essay question.) But no one could predict what the state's courts thought they could get away with, and the line kept shifting from year to year. "A New York lawyer with a guest statute case," wrote one leading commentator, "has more need of a ouija board . . . than a copy of Shepard's Citations."

Many theorists in the law schools volunteered to guide the séance. And just as the apparitions conjured up by canny mediums tend to voice sentiments their listeners are eager to hear, so the theories of new-wave conflicts writers tended to give courts an excuse to apply their own favorite laws. The most popular theory was called "interest analysis," and centered on the idea that states with laws discouraging litigation did not always have a strong interest in enforcing those laws. A typical technique was to observe that the sister state did not have a really intense commitment to its law; perhaps it had recently shown the feebleness of its attachment by cutting back the scope of its rule, or nearly but not quite passing a bill to repeal it. Thus Rhode Island could assert with confidence that Massachusetts "does not appear to have a strong interest in having its [liability limit] applied even in its own state."

"Interest analysis" offered a powerful way to exorcise not only guest statutes but also a wide range of other unwanted curbs in litigation. And in fact the loudest table-rappings now began to be heard in two-car crashes between strangers, as distinct from one-car crashes among friends. In one landmark case, an Oregon resident had collided with a local car while driving in the state of Washington. The injured Washingtonian sued him back in Oregon, which had a stricter liability law. The Oregon court agreed to apply its law to the Washington accident. It explained that Oregon had an interest in disciplining its errant citizens wherever they might roam. Washington for its part had no real interest in having its milder law applied to help an outsider when the result would just be to keep one of its own citizens from collecting heaps of money. Both states really shared an interest in applying Oregon's law, so Oregon's law it would be.

Observe what was going on here. As the focus of litigation shifted from one-car to two-car crashes, it could no longer be argued that the people filing the suits had in any way expected to come under the more remunerative law of the other state; its application was a pure delicious windfall. And to reach this result the Oregon court had to ascribe to its neighboring state of Washington a grab-what-you-can, look-out-for-number-one philosophy of always wanting its own plaintiff-citizens to win and win big in their disputes with citizens of other states. It had to ignore any possible interest Washington might have in discouraging litigation; in making legal jeopardy more regular and predictable; or in attributing responsibility correctly even when (or especially when) the result was to attribute responsibility to one of its own citizens.

The interest-analysis theory became immensely popular. It helped accustom states to the heady idea of applying their law in cases that to all appearances had squarely arisen in other states or countries. And about half the time, when a defendant's home law would impose stricter liability than a plaintiff's, it virtually guaranteed that plaintiffs who would have lost under earlier rules would breeze away with the law they wanted, with no need for further inquiry.

But what about the other half of the cases, where the defendant had acted in his own state under a law that exonerated him or limited his liability? What if the defendant's state had recently reaffirmed its antilitigation policy in unmistakable terms, or even strengthened its provisions? Here, the law school theorists explained, the clash of sovereignties was real, and the interests of one state or the other would have to yield. But not to worry: the tie had to be broken somehow, and more than one influential scholar argued that the way to break it was simply for each court to go ahead and pick its own law. After all, its own law was the law with whose application it was most familiar and adept; besides, it owed a sort of loyalty to its own law, simply because it was its own. If the court wanted another reason, it could declare (as the judge did in Dr. Warren's malpractice suit) that its own rule was objectively "better" in content, as presumably the other state would some day come to see. The whole process called to mind the way Gilbert and Sullivan's Lord Chancellor persuaded himself to grant his own suit for the hand of the ward-of-the-court heroine:

> At first I wouldn't hear of it—it was out of the question. But I took heart. I pointed out to myself that I was no stranger to myself; that, in point of fact, I had been personally acquainted with myself for some years. This had its effect. I admitted that I had watched my professional advancement with considerable interest, and I handsomely added that I yielded to no one in admiration for my private and professional virtues. Conceive my joy when I distinctly perceived a tear glistening in my own eye! Eventually, after a severe struggle with myself, I reluctantly—most reluctantly—consented.

And so began a second War Between the States, in which states began casually to denounce each other's laws as unjust and wrongheaded, and seize on excuses not to enforce them. New York said it had every intention of "protecting its own residents" against "unfair or anachronistic" laws that they might encounter in their travels elsewhere in the United States. Kentucky announced that it would stamp its law onto each and every traffic accident on its own roads, and also onto out-of-state accidents where "there are significant contacts—not necessarily the most significant contacts"—with Kentuckians. All thoughts of symmetry, let alone displays of Alphonse-and-Gaston deference, were forgotten. Some courts began to count, for purposes of getting to apply their own law, contacts that arose by happy coincidence *after* the event being litigated, such as a plaintiff's move into their territory.

It was boasted in the palmy days of the British Empire that an Englishman's rights clung to him wherever he might venture around the world. A similar privilege now seemed to attend plaintiffs from the states with the most aggressive court systems. The same year that New York law was accompanying Dr. Warren's patient onto his Boston operating table, it was clinging, aura-like, to an unfortunate New York resident who was struck and killed by a local car while on a visit to the state of Missouri. His survivors got a New York court to take jurisdiction over the local Missouri driver under its insurance-policy ploy, and then apply New York law to dispose of Missouri's limit on court awards. Another court used Illinois law to knock out the liability limits of the country of Mozambique in a case where American tourist Rosemary Pancotto had been struck by an attendant's swamp buggy while on safari in the African bush. By the end of the 1970s legal commentators were inching their way toward a general theory that would allow every court, once it found enough contacts with its territory to take jurisdiction over a case, to trump all opposing laws with its own. Choice of law would disappear as an independent subject and an independent barrier to the ambitions of litigators; it would be exactly as easy to shop for laws as for forums.

A whole mall's-worth of shopping choices now loomed before some kinds of plaintiffs' lawyers. Lawyers sue airline companies after midair mishaps in the state of the airline's offices or maintenance facilities, the ticket sale or takeoff or crash, the passenger's residence. After one helicopter crash, a court noted the involvement in the case of Alabama where the craft went down, California where it was designed, Virginia where it was manufactured, New York and Delaware where the manufacturers were headquartered, and Iowa and

Texas where the crash victims had lived. Prescription-drug makers get sued over alleged side effects in states where the pills were manufactured or prescribed or dispensed or consumed, where the effects showed themselves, or where the drug company has its headquarters or research labs. So long as each state can apply its own law, plaintiffs can win by finding even one bullet among the six or ten chambers.

Defendants are peculiarly at risk in cases where an alleged libel or slander has been circulated nationally. A court agreed in 1986, for example, that California law could properly be applied to a New York press conference that had allegedly defamed a California complainant. In fact, it appears on current precedent that a libel plaintiff can pick among any of the fifty states' laws; no less than the U.S. Supreme Court has endorsed the idea that a plaintiff's reputation within each individual state is a distinct subject of suit that can be the proper concern of that state's government, whether or not either side of the dispute happens to live there.

Once again, formalism had fallen and guesswork reigned. The potential defendant could indeed hardly guess, as he went about his daily routine, whose laws he might be accused of violating. To drive down a Missouri road, or tend to a round of Boston hospital patients, or lead an assortment of American tourists on a safari through the African bush, was to wade through a thicket of amorphous legal obligation, exposed to one unfamiliar code of law and then another as to a succession of viruses; apt at any instant to be abducted to some distant state and made to undergo its hostile law. Having first lost their right to entrust their fate to the courts they hung out around, defendants had now lost their right to entrust their fate to the laws they hung out around. As Professor Aaron Twerski of Brooklyn Law School has observed, the courts had managed to induce by artificial means the confused sense of multiple realities that the malignity of Nature inflicts on schizophrenics. "The essence of a normal human existence is the ability to integrate one's experience," Twerski has written. "Delaware drivers driving in Delaware deserve Delaware law—for better or for worse."

Some commentators explained reassuringly that the clash and overlap of laws were all for the best: defendants were merely being obliged to seek out and obey the highest standards of conduct—and who could object to keeping up high standards? Trouble is, the zenith of one person's responsibility always coincides with the nadir of someone else's. If South Carolina law cuts off "crashworthiness" lawsuits by drunk drivers against the makers of their automobiles, but the Charleston drunk can get Michigan law applied instead, you might as easily say a standard of conduct has been lowered as raised. In the many cases where both sides can sue, who will be held to the most demanding standard and who will get off with the least demanding will depend merely on who wins the race to the courthouse.

Where was the U.S. Supreme Court during all this? Mostly hoping the problem would go away, it would seem. In the years after 1936 it declined to provide any real content to the constitutional due process protection to which it had long acknowledged defendants to be entitled. Its major recent pronouncement, in a 1981 case, offered another count-the-contacts test for permissible choice of law that was as hopelessly vague as its *International Shoe* rule on jurisdiction. The Court noted without apparent discomfort that the same set of facts could justify the application of more than one state's law. The one welcome exception to this drift came in 1985 when the Court kept Kansas from applying its own pro-plaintiff law to a nationwide class action mostly arising out of transactions in other states.

Plaintiffs' lawyers now faced a new dilemma born of their own good fortune. They were enjoying unprecedented success in getting courts to apply their own pro-plaintiff law, in defiance of long-accepted principles as to which law it was proper to apply. But to get that favorable law the lawyers frequently had to travel to some other state; and that meant giving up the long-fought-for advantages, in travel cost and local sympathy, of being able to sue in their own home court. Wasn't there some way of combining the two advantages, of suing at home but getting the court to apply the other state's stricter law?

This required some delicate maneuvers. Up to now appeals to local chauvinism had worked well for plaintiffs' lawyers, simply because the more courts applied their own laws the wider the shopping choices for them would be. Now they needed a way to convince a home court *not* to select its own law when that would be unwelcome. Sometimes the answer was to reverse field and resuscitate some traditional rule that pointed toward invoking the other state's law. But sometimes the old rules instructed the home court to apply its own (inconvenient) law.

Before long a few of the more creative judges were being prevailed on to help local plaintiffs by picking the pro-plaintiff law of some *other* state over their own legislature's duly enacted statute on the subject, simply on the grounds that it was "better." And some legal scholars were happy to cheer on this approach too. They explained that courts should resolve conflicts in line with the "underlying policy" in a field of law—getting money to plaintiffs in accident cases was said to be one of these underlying policies—even when their own state's legislators had been benighted enough not to join the trend.

A 1972 *California Law Review* article on product liability, declaring that " 'neutrality' is nothing but a euphemism for arbitrariness," unveiled the ultimate answer: "the law most favorable to the plaintiff ought to be applied." R. J. Weintraub's standard 1980 commentary on the conflict of laws seems to agree: if it would be "reasonable" to apply any of several states' injury laws in a case, none being "anachronistic" or "aberrational," Weintraub says the answer is to "apply the law that will favor the plaintiff."

Similar principles, if that is the right word for them, have been adapted to commercial disputes, "invasion of privacy" suits over bad job references, and more. Not everyone feels comfortable stating the rule as one of explicit favoritism for the plaintiff's side, but nothing else can explain what has happened across wide areas of the law in many courts.

And so, for at least some courts and commentators, conflicts law had become what for centuries it had been hoped legal process would not become: a way of manipulating rules to make cases come out however the authorities wanted. The law's policy was one of helping plaintiffs win (which sounds much nicer than making defendants lose), and it would select from the shelf whichever rule was needed for that to happen.

Most judges recoiled from that extreme, and some stoutly resisted the academic fads. But in the long run, short of intervention by the Supreme Court or Congress, this was a race only one side could win. States that favored a right to sue could export that right quite effectively; those that preferred a right not to be sued could only watch the action from the sidelines. If California threw its doors open to a new kind of suit by gardeners against seed companies, it would hear the grievances of both Wisconsin gardeners against California seed companies and California gardeners against Wisconsin seed companies, and Wisconsin could do nothing in either case. In effect it was a scheme of nullification, in which the laws of states that wished to discourage litigation could be denied effect aside from the smallish class of transactions where no link to one of the pro-litigation states could conceivably be argued even after the fact.

The collapse of the intellectual integrity of this obscure branch of the law made few headlines, but it signaled some trends of wide-ranging significance. For starters, the idea that courts should manipulate rules to pursue a "policy" of helping plaintiffs win is obviously applicable to countless other areas of legal procedure and interpretation. It has in fact been applied to countless other areas, whether openly or covertly, too often confirming defendants' suspicion that the system is stacked against them.

The acceptance of outright multiplicity and contradiction among legal standards also marked a new stage in the ongoing decline of formalism. The trouble with vagueness and guess-work in legal rules is that they bring with them a submerged, latent multiplicity based on the courts' inability to come up with consistent answers from given facts. Now the proliferation of clashing obligations was to be accepted openly. Not surprisingly, the law has steadily moved away from its once-intense aversion to "squeeze plays" that impose possible liability on someone either for taking an act or for not taking it. An employer now faces a lawsuit from victims if it lets a suspected-but-not-proven drug abuser stay in a safety-related position, and a lawsuit from the worker if it does not. A clinic counselor fears an invasion-of-privacy lawsuit if he warns a client's wife that her husband is infected with the AIDS virus, and a failure-to-warn lawsuit if he does not. Athletic doctors have been sued alike for ordering their patients not to take part in big games (interference with contractual opportunity) and for letting them play in cases where they then collapse on the playing field.

The ultimate effects of the choice-of-law revolution were felt again in the political dynamics of the state courts. Once opportunities multiplied to hand out local law to local complainants in long-distance controversies, expanding liability became more than ever a way for states to siphon money mostly to their own citizens mostly from people in other states, leaving the other states scrambling to keep up or lose out. The game is one of beggar-thy-neighbor, rather like the development of local prosperity by dumping smokestack emissions on the residents of distant states. States have responded by making their laws more and more favorable to plaintiffs and their lawyers over the past three decades, a trend that has not really reversed itself despite modest recent efforts at liability reform.

And *that* has the most momentous implications even for lawsuits that never cross a state line. Vast tracts of the litigation landscape have by now been blighted by suits against distant moneyed defendants, and the lay of the land remains much the same even if the defendant happens to be local and of limited means. If you're in charge of a local park or swimming pool where a child hurts himself, the legal issues that will determine whether you must pay—issues like adequacy of warning, the definition of defectiveness, and the assignment of the burden of proof—will have emerged from years of lawsuits aimed at Fortune 500 corporations. If you are a motel owner sued for negligent security after a customer's room is burglarized, you will encounter laws of innkeeper's liability crafted in large part to raid the distant treasuries of Hyatt, Ramada, and Holiday Inns. If you are paying the bill to defend your own suit, you will encounter levels of expense and complication designed on the assumption that an out-of-state insurance company is around to pay. For neither the first time nor the last, rules designed to hit Wall Street have hit Main Street on the ricochet.

10

⚖

NO EXIT:
The Death of Contract

Better a bad agreement than a good lawyer.

—*Italian proverb*

The Bartell Drug Company gave its film-processing customers a receipt with a clearly printed disclaimer: "We assume no responsibility beyond retail cost of film unless otherwise agreed to in writing." All its competitors used disclaimers with similar language. Film processors are invariably reluctant to accept more than nominal liability for lost or spoiled film; if you ask, they will say that there's no way to know how valuable someone's pictures are to them, and who wants to argue over that?

Virginia Mieske took her home movies in to Bartell's camera department to have them spliced onto a smaller number of reels so they could be shown more easily. Bartell gave her the ticket with its disclaimer, and sent the film on in paper bags to the processing lab of the GAF Corporation. By the next morning the bags had disappeared, probably thrown in the trash by a janitor.

Virginia and her husband Edwin sued Bartell and GAF, asking to be compensated not just for the cost of the film but for the personal value of the never-to-be-recaptured family scenes. In this case it happened to be plain that the movies were dear to Mrs. Mieske's heart, and a jury set an award of $7,500. Bartell protested: what about the disclaimer? No matter, said the supreme court of the state of Washington; it was "unconscionable" and would not be enforced.

The great principle of freedom of contract was very dear to the heart of the historic Anglo-American law. It was felt that people had a right to choose obligations for themselves, and that in holding people to those freely undertaken obligations courts were not imposing legal rules on the parties, but—to quote Oxford's Patrick Atiyah—"merely working out the implications of what the parties had themselves chosen to do." The spirit was one not of coercion but of empowerment: people were encouraged to write their own ticket, to choose the rules they would live by.

It wasn't just that the common-law tradition saw freedom of contract as a good in itself, although it did. Free contract was an essential preventive against endless litigation, a way to settle disputes before they arose while heads were clear and tempers cool. "Partnerships often finish in quarrels," observed Benjamin Franklin in his *Autobiography*, "but I was happy in this, that mine were all carried on and ended amicably, owing, I think, a good deal to the precaution of having very explicitly settled, in our articles, every thing to be done by or expected from each partner, so that there was nothing to dispute." Thus were averted, said Franklin, "lawsuits and other disagreeable consequences."

Over most of economic life—purchases and sales of goods, hirings and firings, landlord-tenant relations, trading in stocks and bonds, and so forth—explicit agreement tended to avert exactly those disagreeable consequences. So seriously was freedom of contract taken that you could contract around

large sectors of the law itself, up to and including the definition of what was a contract. Suppose you were putting in
a bid on a construction job. The law employed some rather
technical rules of "offer and acceptance" to determine when
it would deem your bid to have been accepted by the other
side, thus binding both of you. But if you disliked these rules
you could label your bid "not a firm offer," preserving the
right to snatch it back. Or you could make the bid firmer than
the law required by couching it as, say, a thirty-day option.

Similarly, another venerable old rule provided that a
promise was binding only if it had been given for "consideration"—that is, if something of value had been conceded
on both sides. But if you wanted to conspire with your deal
partner to get around that condition, you could arrange for
some purely token object to change hands; that is why so
many promises of gifts and other one-way transactions were
carried out for a token dollar. Even a lone peppercorn might
do the trick. As Chicago's Richard Epstein puts it, the law
allowed persons to contract out of most of the law student's
first-year course in contracts.

Significantly, you could opt your way around much of
the procedural machinery of the courts themselves. Were you
worried about finding your partner in some distant place if
you ever had to sue him? You could get him to sign a note
submitting to the jurisdiction of a certain court. Were you
fearful that it would cost a lot to prove he owed you the agreed-
on sum of money? You might prevail on him to "confess
judgment" in advance, waiving his right to contest the issue.
Were you nervous, as Bartell was, about how open-ended
your own exposure might be should your partner take you to
court? You could stipulate to limit liability to a stated sum,
perhaps a money-back guarantee or the repair or replacement
of what you were selling.

In many cases you could even choose which state's law
would govern your dealings with someone, by arranging to
sign the papers in the right place, or simply by declaring in

the document which law was intended to apply. This in practice gave people a certain amount of wiggle room to slip out from under their own state's ideas of how they should behave. Arkansas might maintain drastically low ceilings on interest rates for consumer loans, but borrowers could head just over the river to Tennessee or Mississippi to where lenders had set up thriving offices. Pennsylvania might try to impose a waiting period for marriage licenses, but Maryland was more indulgent of matrimonial impatience and attracted many an eloping couple.

This room for interstate maneuver posed something of an insult to the sensibilities of lawmakers, and always did have its limits: Iowa gamblers have never been free to phone in bets to Nevada casinos on the theory that they are just electing to place their dealings under the more liberal law. But for the most part the courts not only accepted the dodges but even connived at them, by stretching when several laws were in contention to find the one that would uphold the validity of a will or a business deal or the legitimacy of a child's parentage. Whatever the loss to abstract principles of sovereignty, it was thought, was more than made up for by the benefits in making citizens surer of getting the legal rights they thought they were getting. As so often, the law was dominated by its horror of vagueness and indeterminacy, its dread of a state of suspended half-legality. For similar reasons, one of the important exceptions to complete contractual freedom was that agreements with overly vague terms could not be enforced; but here again, of course, to cure the defect all you had to add was specificity.

Free contract, then, served as the balance wheel in the vast legal machinery, the ecological feature that kept society and its relationships from veering into litigious disequilibrium. The random or not-so-random drift of judicial mutation would constantly produce errors, uncertainties, occasions for guesswork in the law; that much was inevitable. The trick was to get the citizenry to cooperate in correcting these mistakes.

In 1901 Queen Victoria died and her son Edward VII succeeded to the British throne. After a suitable period of mourning it was decided that the gala coronation rites would take place on June 26 and June 27 of the following year. A lively rental market sprang up for rooms overlooking the scheduled path of the royal procession through the center of London. Then a surprise: the new King was struck down by an attack of appendicitis, and the ceremonies were postponed for a month and a half.

Those who had taken out leases on rooms along the parade route tended to feel that if there was no pageant to see, they should not have to pay. The other side countered that a deal was a deal; for many it had no doubt been a bother to have arranged to vacate the rooms, and who knew whether the same rooms would be in equal demand for a rescheduled procession, if indeed it took place at all? Besides which (they pointed out), some renters had taken out rooms on speculation expecting to rerent them at a higher rate, and those who angle for profit should not be shocked to find a risk of loss. The lease terms themselves typically made no direct mention of the coronation or what would happen if it did not come off as planned. They merely named the relevant calendar days.

A spate of lawsuits followed, in which the English courts—in what might seem to be defiance of the contract principle—wound up letting most of the renters out of the leases. Since then generations of law students on both sides of the Atlantic have puzzled over the coronation cases and the countless other instances where the same basic issue crops up under such headings as "omitted terms," "frustration," and "mistake." If a music hall burns down, is its owner relieved from a bargain to lease it for a later performance? If Mideast tensions suddenly close the Suez Canal, can a shipping line collect an extra charge, above the agreed-on rate, for hauling the goods the long way around the Cape of Good Hope?

Although these conundrums have spawned a huge legal literature, their importance in a world of free contract is less than may at first appear. The first time the coronation is postponed or the Suez Canal shuts down, bickering may prevail; but by the next time the situation is likely to have calmed down, no matter which way courts ruled on the first wave of cases. If they assigned the loss to the "wrong" side, people can write agreements that shift the risk explicitly. If no such contracting-out is observed, it will be a sign that the courts got it right, or at least that the issue is not important enough to the losers to be worth pressing. At any rate, the next crop of leases or shipping agreements will no longer present so blank an aspect on the matter of canal closures and royal maladies, silence now being something closer to consent than it was the first time. Guesswork on the "omitted terms" of contracts is perhaps not quite so dangerous as other guesswork in the courtroom, because its ills can be put right by more contract.

The various switches that go into making a contract thus came preset in certain positions; but as with the factory settings on an appliance, most were suggestive rather than conclusive. If the toaster is shipped from the factory at the "medium brown" setting, many users will never get around to dialing in one direction or the other in search of a more perfect match for their tastes. Judges, like toaster makers, knew that the factory settings they furnished for society were influential; and the more farsighted ones found chances to educate and persuade the market, tugging it gently toward new ways of doing business, not too sharply at odds with the interests of one side or the other, that might catch on once familiar. But toaster makers have no desire to meet with the near-universal rejection of knowledgeable users by shipping their appliances set to, say, the "burned-to-a-crisp" spot on the dial. In much the same way the courts were loath to risk the embarrassment of being vigorously contracted around by everyone in sight.

If the idea was to minimize later contracting-out, the best settings to pick were typically the customary "terms of the trade" understood by most of those in a field to govern their dealings. Those, at any rate, were the settings older courts tended to adopt. At center stage was the expressed will of the two sides; the customs of the marketplace furnished the background of unexpressed conditions and understandings to fill in the inevitable chinks and gaps in the explicit understanding. Only where both visible intent and visible custom failed, as in the coronation cases, was there any troublesome need to fill in terms according to a court's own guess as to what the two sides might have agreed on had they been forced to consider the matter explicitly.

Contract has its uglier side. Courts were not unacquainted with the high-pressure tactics by which the door-to-door salesman plied his trade, the shoddy tenement leases foisted on hard-pressed immigrants, the one-sided arrangements that let the boss dock the miner's or lumberjack's pay down to zero when he quit, and the infinity of schemes by which spendthrift heirs and sailors in port could be parted from their money.

Then as now the instinct of a judge faced with a hard case was to look for some escape route for the sympathetic side. Easier looked for than found: none of the more obvious legal hatches would open very wide. To begin with, the law would not listen to someone complain that he had signed a contract without troubling to read or understand it; in those stern days of individual responsibility people were expected not to put their names to something until they felt willing to commit themselves to what was in it. Children and the mentally unsound could be let out of contracts for lack of "capacity," but that was a rather insulting ground on which to excuse a grown-up.

Claims that an agreement had been made under "duress" were no more likely to succeed, unless there had been threats of actual violence. Some writers came up with a theory of "economic duress," arguing that since everyone needs to find work, get food, keep warm, and so forth, agreements to further these needs are not truly voluntary. But they didn't get very far with that one: for one thing, too many of the market abuses that smell worst involve transactions beyond the bare basics. People may be tricked into buying a lame horse, a penny stock, a tract of undeveloped swampland, or a here-today-gone-tomorrow health-spa membership, but they are not forced to buy them.

There was such a thing as an "unconscionable" deal that a court could strike down, and a slightly broader class of deals that courts did not have to go out of their way to enforce by the ordering of "specific performance." But the formulas were astoundingly stringent. To be struck down a deal had to be such as no one in his right mind would knowingly have entered. In one hoary English example, a sharpster had prevailed on a rural innocent to promise that, in exchange for a stated sum, he would hand over two grains of rye on a certain day, four the next week, eight the week after, and so on doubling each week for a year. Belatedly the countryman discovered that by the end of fifty-two weeks he would have to furnish more grain than grew on the planet.

Such half-comic cases aside, the one thing the courts insisted they would not do, right down through the mid-1960s, was strike down a freely and knowingly entered deal just because they disapproved of its terms. It was not as if freedom of contract were inviolate. Even before the New Deal enormous holes had been punched in it, in the form of legislation setting maximum hours and minimum wages, regulating banking, utilities and railroads, and much more. Many more lines of business had come under government supervision by the time of World War II, and the war itself brought price and wage controls, rationing and requisitions that curtailed market freedom in every walk of life. But whatever the merits of such regulation, and whatever its peacetime constitutionality (which was itself much disputed during this period), the courts would not launch new incursions on their own initiative. If the right of free contract were to be abridged, it would have to be with due notice after fair public debate, and by the sort of deliberative or executive body that could arrange to deal with the inevitable side effects. A judge's say-so was simply not enough.

But although contract officially ruled the roost, judges had a number of indirect ways to rescue the inexperienced or just plain unlucky from being pecked to death. By reading an agreement's terms broadly or narrowly enough, like Shakespeare's Portia, judges could sometimes make an unwanted clause disappear without disputing the sanctity of contract. They could look for some ambiguity in the contract's language to construe against the schemer, or seize on some trifling circumstance to treat as a case of frustration, mistake, or omitted terms.

These methods of letting people out of contracts, however, had all the discomforts of a furtive makeshift. In particular, they promised no durable solution to the problem of human gullibility. The result of identifying a new ambiguity or omitted term was typically to make offerers of deals spell out their deals more clearly. But not all customers will respond by doing a better job of choosing. Some will listen to the sales pitch, complete with mumbled ritual boilerplate, and then cheerfully initial each questionable clause in the salesman's agreement. Hard cases, if not perhaps quite so many of them, keep coming back to court.

Along came the Legal Realists to propose another huge new assertion of judicial power, as usual under the guise of being "candid" about the exercise of existing judicial power. The problem, they explained, was that the courts pretended to object only to the way a deal had been negotiated or worded when they really objected to its content. The "difficulty with these techniques of ours," Columbia's Karl Llewellyn wrote in 1939, is that because "they all rest on the admission that the clauses in question are permissible in purpose and content" they "invite the draftsman to recur to the attack. Give him time, and he will make the grade." Eventually terms would be spelled out so clearly and brought to the customer's attention so forcefully that even the most tenderhearted judge would have to admit consent had been real. And in the meantime, by fiddling with their treatment of language and the negotiating process, the courts cast doubt on whether they would enforce even aboveboard deals as written. "Covert tools," wrote Llewellyn in an oft-quoted line, "are never reliable tools."

The obvious way out, the Realists concluded, was for courts to assume a direct power to strike down contract terms that seemed to them unfair, putting the world on notice that any attempt to recast and reinsert those terms would be struck down too. This was such a drastic departure from the accepted tradition that for the next couple of decades courts could not work up the nerve to try it on their own. By the mid-1960s a chorus of legal commentators was urging them to go ahead.

Meanwhile, a second, converging line of thinking was making its way in the law schools. It had long been noted that many lopsided contracts followed a pattern: they had been drawn up by a legally sophisticated party and handed to a naive party to be signed. In 1873 the chief justice of New Hampshire described an insurance policy of this sort as being, to an ordinary buyer, "an inexplicable riddle, a mere flood of darkness and confusion . . . [I]t was printed in such small type, and in lines so long and so crowded, that the perusal of it was made physically difficult, painful, and injurious. Seldom has the art of typography been so successfully diverted from the diffusion of knowledge to the suppression of it."

By the early years of this century, it seemed as if this old problem might be getting worse instead of better. Ordinary citizens were now buying and selling real estate and cars, taking out mortgages and loans and several kinds of insurance, maybe even dabbling in the stock market. Large enterprises had begun using preprinted contracts by the million in their dealings with all comers. Some influential law professors of that day believed that capitalism had an irresistible tendency toward monopoly: eventually the citizen would have no real choice but to deal with the emergent trusts on whatever terms they offered, and the terms of these contracts "of adhesion" (you stuck to them, like a bird to a limed twig) were bound to be as unfair as the finest drafting talent of the legal profession could make them. Their conclusion was that courts should at least lean extra-hard toward letting customers out of this kind of contract, if not follow Llewellyn's indicated route by striking down the worst clauses directly and inserting replacements.

What was truly odd about this logic was not so much its fear of impending universal monopoly, which was typical of its day, as its flying leap to the idea that standard off-the-rack contracts are more dangerous to a monopoly's customers than contracts dickered one by one. The most fearsome monopoly would be precisely the one that dickered with each of its customers, because it could then skin each one to the exact limit of endurance. Even where monopoly as such is not a problem, markets where haggling is the norm—rug bazaars, antique shows, Tijuana novelty shops, used car lots—are hardly known for consistency of customer satisfaction. Most of us are edgy, or ought to be, if we sense that the terms a merchant is quoting us have no necessary relation to those he quoted the last customer: leeway to negotiate is what allows him to start with a truly bad offer in hopes of catching the novice buyer.

Years ago, for this very reason, the rise of supermarkets and chain stores with one price and policy for all was hailed as a great advance in fair dealing. A merchant's willingness to treat each customer alike is of special benefit to unsophisticated buyers, who can piggyback on the wariness of their more experienced neighbors; that is why most of us don't agonize over the terms of airline tickets or credit card applications that millions of people have filled out before us. The ultimate in offerers of take-it-or-leave-it contracts is the homely vending machine, which is completely unwilling to haggle. But most of us have better sense than to kick these impassive monoliths, so long as they do not breach our contract by swallowing the coin without dispensing the product.

Whole books have been written about the supposed unfairness of "fine print" as such. Actually, the purpose of most fine print in mass market contracts is not to alter the primary transaction in sneaky ways but to avoid litigation by specifying how contingencies will be handled. So long as this language is upheld it tends to avert litigation quite effectively. And so the theoretical attack on standardized contracts was an indispensable step if the litigation industry was to visit its unwanted attentions on the world of everyday commerce: sales, employment, financial services, and much more.

The attack also subtly shifted the focus of desired judicial correction. Formerly judges had been tempted to bend the rules to outwit the sharpster or confidence operator who fell grossly short of customary commercial ethics. The new theory, by concentrating on the evils of the mass-produced and impersonal, suggested that the most successful and reputable national marketers were if anything more deserving of scrutiny than the fly-by-nighters.

By 1947 the academic critique of standard-form contracts was beginning to make itself felt in the courts. The H. & M. Parcel Room was located on the West Side of Manhattan at what are now known as the PATH trains to New Jersey. It charged ten cents to check a parcel and gave customers a ticket with a printed disclaimer limiting claims for loss or damage to twenty-five dollars an item. A man named Ellis dropped off a plain parcel tied up in brown paper. When one of his business associates showed up to claim it, he was told it had been given to another customer by mistake. Consternation followed; it seemed the nondescript bundle had contained furs worth a thousand dollars. (Unlikely as the customer's story might sound, it may have been true. New York furriers who send out work to nonunion shops on the sly have been reported to stash pelts in public lockers, the trunks of parked cars, and other unlikely depositories.)

A New York court threw out the disclaimer and allowed recovery of the furs' full value. In the customer's mind "the little piece of cardboard . . . did not arise to the dignity of a contract," it explained. "If the [checkroom] wishes to limit its liability for negligence, it must at least show that it has given adequate notice of the special contract and that it has received the assent thereto of those with whom it transacts business."

The parcel room case was not the stuff of headlines, but it was a milestone in its way. The courts were beginning to lose the sense, still very much present in the coronation cases, that they were filling in contract terms as the two sides themselves would have done if the matter had been "brought to their minds," as the saying went. It could hardly be doubted that if the matter had risen to the level of an outright negotiation, the checkroom would have stood by its disclaimer, or at least insisted that Ellis disclose the unusual value of his package so someone could keep an eye on it. And it would have charged him more than a dime.

Still, the implications hardly seemed serious. Startled checkroom operators around town might be on the phone with their lawyers, but no doubt they were being advised just to print their ticket disclaimers in larger type or in ink of a bolder color, or maybe to post an eye-catching sign over the counter. At some point courts would have to find they had given adequate notice of their policy. And then everyone would be happy. Or would they?

Mrs. Ora Williams supported herself and seven children on a $218 monthly check from the government. Between 1957 and 1962 the Walker-Thomas Furniture Company of Washington, D.C., sold her sixteen household items on an easy-credit plan, culminating in a stereo set ticketed at a hefty $514. Soon after buying the stereo she defaulted on the payments.

There was a reason why the credit was so easy at Walker-Thomas. Its installment loan had a "dragnet" provision: if the borrower defaulted on his payments the store could repossess not just the most recent items but everything it had sold him for as long as there had been a positive balance on his account. Over the years Mrs. Williams had paid enough to have bought most of the items outright if not for the dragnet provision. As it was, her only established legal right was to get back any money that might be left over after the store resold the items and paid off her loan. And since secondhand household goods sell at a steep discount, that was almost sure to be nothing at all.

Mrs. Williams lost in the local D.C. courts, but her Legal Aid lawyers had the luck to draw a federal appeals panel on which sat Skelly Wright, one of the most famous liberal jurists of his day. In a ruling that was to be cited countless times in later years, Wright pronounced the contract "unconscionable" and said it should simply "not be enforced."

Now it can hardly be said, per the old definition of unconscionability, that no loan applicant in his right mind would ever knowingly agree to a dragnet provision. Borrowers who are confident about repaying their loans often volunteer to put up a lot of collateral. For someone with a poor credit rating, the alternative may be a higher interest rate or no loan at all. So Judge Wright was plainly not defining unconscionability in the old way. But what exactly was his new way? That was hard to say; in fact, it was a real stumper. "The test is not simple, nor can it be mechanically applied." It had something to do with whether a deal's terms were in some way "unreasonable," and also with whether there was an "absence of meaningful choice" on one side. A "gross inequality of bargaining power" might be fatal, or again might not; it all seemed to depend: the way the contract was negotiated, the level of education of both sides, and the customs of the trade seemed relevant too, although of course in no way dispositive. To figure out whether any particular contract should stand up in the future, Wright concluded, a court should look at "all the circumstances surrounding the transaction."

One of the three judges on the panel dissented. He said Mrs. Williams "seems to have known exactly where she stood," and warned that if stringent repossession policies were outlawed some poorer clients who would have used credit responsibly would never be offered it at all. (Later reports indicate that this is exactly what happened after *Williams* and similar cases. The point of the case, said Arthur Allen Leff of Washington University, seemed to be that "the poor should be discouraged from frill-buying"; and yet "no legislature in America could be persuaded openly to pass such a statute, nor should any be permitted to do so sneakily" by empowering judges to undo such transactions.)

Most reactions in the law reviews, however, were greatly admiring. Nearly everyone seemed to agree that the whole idea of liberty of contract should be sent off to the intellectual landfills as hopelessly obsolete and incoherent. The "will of the parties," declared one article after another, was a mere fiction. Consumers seldom bother to read standard-form contracts, let alone mull over their terms. Even if they feel some sort of subjective sensation of having consented to the obligations recited in such agreements, that sensation was illusory, a mere artifact of their deficiency in bargaining power, whether they knew it or not. Most everyone seemed to agree with the view later voiced by noted Realist Grant Gilmore of Yale Law School: "It is unlikely that the nineteenth century idea of freedom of contract will have any role to play in the twenty-first century."

Other courts soon followed with an air of overdue relief, as if Judge Wright had belled some long-feared cat. From here on out, in the many courts that adopted the *Williams* standard, an undefinedly large assortment of contracts would be up for open-ended voiding, revision, or expansion on the basis of their reasonableness, a quality that would itself be determined, or rather guessed at, by the use of a balancing test of an almost dreamlike floating indeterminacy.

It helped a lot that the new Uniform Commercial Code, meant to bring state commercial laws into harmony with each other, was spreading around the country at this time. (It was eventually adopted in substantial form by every state except Louisiana, with its Napoleonic Code tradition.) The chief drafter of the U.C.C. was none other than Professor Llewellyn, who thoughtfully inserted a clause inviting courts to strike down contract terms that seemed to them unconscionable. Other U.C.C. clauses provide for a long list of contract issues to be handled by way of vague "reasonableness" or "good faith" tests, and—the kicker—provide that attempts by the parties to give meaning to those phrases by ruling out particular interpretations should be declared invalid.

The more ambitious judges were soon feeling the exhilaration of hunters on the first day of the season: targets seemed to be behind every tree. Consumer loans were only the first to come under the gun. Soon courts were tearing up and rewriting home mortgages as well. They declared that even if a mortgage had been issued on the explicit condition that it could not be assumed by a later buyer of the home, it was indeed ordinarily assumable anyway. Lucky sellers found they could ask well above the going price for their houses if they had a mortgage at 3 or 4 percent to pass on. It took an act of Congress to reverse this particular frolic, and in the meantime the nation's savings and loan industry, stuck with low-interest mortgages that were now taking much longer to turn over than expected, had slid further toward its spectacular collective insolvency.

A few courts geared up for the daunting task of developing price controls. A New York court declared it unconscionable to sell a freezer from door to door at three times the price of a similar unit available elsewhere; a New Jersey court soon raised (or lowered) the ante by throwing out the sale of some educational books for around two-and-a-half times the going rate; commentators urged that the threshold be cut to twice fair market value or less, or even that courts go all the way and undo any sale of an item for more than a "reasonable price" related to a merchant's imagined or expert-sworn costs.

Insurance policies became another prime target of the

great judicial eraser. Bartholomew Burne was crossing a street
when he was struck by a car and horribly injured. He continued "in a vegetative state" for four and a half years before
finally succumbing. The Franklin Life Insurance Company
paid his widow JoAnn the $15,000 face value of his policy
but disputed the added $15,000 that she asked for under a
"double indemnity" clause covering accidental death. Franklin conceded that the accident had been the cause of Burne's
death. But it stood on the language of a provision stating that
the bonus would be paid only if a death occurred "within 90
days from the date of the accident."

Franklin won on summary judgment in a lower court.
But the Pennsylvania Supreme Court, over strong dissents
from two of its justices, reversed in a 1973 decision and ordered the company to pay Mrs. Burne the extra money. However clear the clause might have been, the court said, "public
policy" forbade enforcing it. When terribly hurt people lin-
gered on for years before dying, their loved ones suffered far
more grief and expense than when they perished at once. It
would be a "gruesome paradox," the court concluded, to
afford more reimbursement for the lesser tragedy than for the
greater. And so the figure of 90 days would have to be
stretched to 1,640.

The language of insurance policies is full of "objective
triggers" because insurers want to avoid spending their time
in court arguing. As the courts have sliced away at one such
clause after another in search of fairness, insurance litigation
has soared. And premiums have risen to cover three distinct
costs: of the newly created coverage, of the possibility of other
policy-language erosion in unexpected places, and of all the
anticipated litigation.

New Jersey courts led the way in rewriting agreements
that oil and fast-food companies had signed with their service
station dealers and franchisees; the usual ploy was to declare
that a franchise explicitly cancellable by either side at short
notice was in fact cancellable only by the franchisee, and for

the parent company was in the nature of a permanent obligation unless it could convince the courts otherwise on a case-by-case basis.

The next and much more momentous step was to apply the same lock-in principle to ordinary jobs, by forbidding employers to fire workers without what a court determines after the fact was "good cause"; only one or two states have at present gone to that extreme, but many have moved in the general direction. Henry Nozko, president of Acmat Corporation, laments that under the new regime it took three months to drop a "boozing" employee who "would have been fired on the spot" in an earlier day. A study by Wyatt Company, consultants to employers, found that half of surveyed workers believed that "poor performance is tolerated too long in my company."

Nor were ideas of consent and individual responsibility faring well in more intimate entanglements. Many courts have turned their rewriting skills to prenuptial agreements, which, although never really popular in this country, did surge in some states after vague equitable-distribution laws put marital property up for grabs. Separation agreements between spouses have also come under attack, especially on custody matters, where in several states whichever parent changes his mind can get *de novo* (from the ground up) review.

Theories of the wickedness of adhesion contracts play a role here too. Courts are more likely to strike down a pre- or postnuptial pact if the couple came to an agreement and brought in a single lawyer to write it up for them without any record of dickering. In short, those who want to use such a device are pressed to choose between full two-lawyer negotiations, with all their expense and relationship-killing potential, and a risk that the device will not hold up. The inevitable explanation is that no one who signs away valuable rights without calling in a lawyer could possibly have understood their value. A more cynical view might be that our legal system is very efficiently organized to encourage the use of its own services.

If advance agreements on the substance of deals are to
be thrown out, it can hardly be expected that agreements on
procedural matters, or on which state's law would govern, will
fare much better. Thus a federal court explained that it would
be unconscionable to hold a Mississippi farm couple to the
livestock lease they had signed—including a provision specifying that the lease was to be construed under Kentucky
law—because they were of low education, had paid no serious
attention to what they were signing, and "had no idea they
were dealing with a Kentucky company."

A 1981 case shows many strands of the new approach
converging at once. Grove Textiles, Incorporated, was a company that sold yarn on the same general terms of sale as its
competitors. Customers had fifteen days to complain if they
found anything visibly wrong with its wares, and sixty days
to complain about any less-than-obvious ("latent") defects.
Grove's sales contract provided that disputes were to be submitted to arbitration, and then, if dissatisfaction persisted, to
the courts of Pennsylvania, where Grove was located.

Next thing Grove knew it was being sued in New Hampshire. One of its customers there, the Pittsfield Weaving Company, was irked to discover what it said were latent defects
in Grove's yarn after processing it. The sixty-day deadline,
Pittsfield said, was unconscionable because its own production process took longer than sixty days. And the requirement
to arbitrate before suing was unconscionable too. And so for
good measure was the requirement to sue in Pennsylvania.

The New Hampshire Supreme Court, in an extreme
decision even by today's standards, agreed down the line with
its local plaintiff. It noted that Pittsfield had more than once
tried to get other yarn sellers—though not, it turned out,
Grove—to negotiate their arbitration clauses, without success.
Moreover, it pointed out, one witness had testified that Grove
"was a larger company than" Pittsfield and had refused to
ship on anything other than its standard terms. Citing little
beyond the above facts, the court concluded that such take-
it-or-leave-it behavior was "so coercive and one-sided as to

prevent [Pittsfield] from having voluntarily assented to its terms."

Observe that in following the standard terms of its trade, Grove not only did not gain points in the court's calculations, but actually lost them. In a curious way, it had now begun to count against a disputed custom that it was universally adhered to in a business or profession. A standard tenancy clause, for example, might well be upheld in court if not all landlords put it in their leases. But if it were so important to them that they unanimously insisted on it, the prospective tenant might be said to have little real choice but to go along. The more vital a custom was to the carrying on of commerce, the lower its score on the "absence of meaningful choice" part of the unconscionability test. The harder the market pressed for a certain result, the harder the courts would shove back.

Unconscionability and related legal methods of second-guessing contracts couldn't effectively be confined to cases where a "little guy" was facing some sort of big, powerful institution. The legal precedents introduced by populist judges were promptly deployed by wealthy businesses that wanted to escape their own commitments. Delta Air Lines cited "public policy" in trying (unsuccessfully, but quite expensively) to get out of a perfectly clear contract with aircraft maker McDonnell-Douglas over the cost of some repairs. The techniques invented to allow welfare tenants to ditch their apartment leases were soon latched onto, with some success, by national businesses that wanted to ditch their own commercial leases. Before long, the original monopoly explanations having been turned very nearly on their head, courts were being asked to rule that the huge company that provides Washington, D.C., with electricity had been the hapless victim of an unconscionable contract with one of its equipment suppliers.

By the 1980s the revolution was more or less complete. The magic bag of tricks for interpreting a contract into or out of thin air, long kept under the judge's desk for rare, surreptitious use in the distressingly hard case, was now prominently displayed for the requests of everyday customers with their varied litigation problems. The unconscionability doctrine provided an all-purpose wrench with which to pry off any contractual language that did not yield to subtler methods.

Inevitably, the courts' approach to contract "remedies" changed as well. Contract had formerly served as a haven from the war of all against all that was ordinary litigation. It was accordingly designed (in line with the normal before-the-fact wishes of rational parties) to solve problems in predictable ways with a minimum of acrimony and recrimination. Punitive, emotional-trauma, and pain-and-suffering damages were all out. Obligations tended to hinge not so much on fault, negligence, or even intentional wrongdoing as on one side's objective failure to perform as specified. In commercial settings, cash damages, followed by a parting of the ways, were nearly always preferred over "specific performance" that might keep parties in each other's hair and on each other's nerves.

Now the war of all against all is back in full swing: contract remedies have become as combative and uncertain as other legal remedies. Punitive and subjective damages have flourished. Experts and discovery have proliferated. Trial lawyers, now increasingly working on contingency, demand that their opponents be taught a lesson.

There is no need to overstate the case. Every day even the judges most distrustful of markets still enforce contracts that they themselves would never have signed, and even those most driven by sentiment continue to sigh and let the less sympathetic side win many cases. To do otherwise would mean to abolish the legal framework of a capitalist economy entirely, and hardly anyone wants that. In countless cases the actual verdict of a case that reaches trial turns out no different than it ever would have. The problem is not so much that any one deal is dead certain to be struck down. It is that fewer and fewer deals are dead certain to stand up.

By invoking the new doctrines, either side in countless disputes can threaten a messy and expensive look into all the circumstances surrounding the course of dealings between the parties. And that puts an enormous tactical weapon into the hands of those who are willing to litigate. The lawyers for Ivana Trump who denounced as unconscionable her $20-million-plus-mansion-in-Connecticut postnuptial agreement with husband Donald may not have had much expectation of proving it so, but the chance of getting a court to consider such a theory at all provides a bargaining chip of considerable value.

All this second-guessing of contracts and encouragement of extra lawyering is astonishingly expensive. It is also in the main self-defeating. The more the courts look as if they may excuse a group from its undertakings, the more reluctant others become to accept the promises of that group as a basis for their own commitments. When it got harder to fire middle-management employees without setting up a long paper trail, employers became more cautious about hiring them. When it got harder to contract around personal-injury lawsuits in such inherently dangerous fields as vaccination, rock climbing, sport aviation, and obstetrics, providers raised prices and pulled out of markets in droves. When prenuptial agreements began toppling in court, many persons with property to protect began finding it advisable to keep separate bank accounts or even, in extreme cases, to cohabit rather than marrying at all.

The death of contract (as Gilmore famously called it) was full of implications for the sense of individual responsibility. If courts no longer thought it as important as they once did that people live up to their solemn promises, at least when the promise in question was a promise not to litigate in some way, people would themselves come to attach less importance to choice and agreement as sources of rights. And the major source of rights other than choice and agreement is the litigation industry.

The death of contract was of broad significance for the litigation explosion in another way as well. The self-correcting tendency, the resilience, of the old legal system had been undercut; a penny had been put in the fuse box. Henceforth lawyers could ask courts not only to decree a vague duty or a procedural imposition, but to squash all responsive attempts to provide specificity to the new duty or waive the burdensome procedure. The last and most important exit from litigation was now closed.

· T H E ·
CONSEQUENCES

11

⚖

THE RACE TO THE GUTTER

*We lawyers know well, and may find high authority for it if required,
that life would be intolerable if every man insisted on his legal rights
to the full.*

—*FREDERICK POLLOCK*,
Jurisprudence

The scene was a Dallas office
tower where a deposition was being taken in a big-ticket
commercial case. Lawyers from two Manhattan firms, Milgrim
Thomajan & Lee and Weil Gotshal & Manges, were arguing
over a document when tempers flared. "Somebody pointed
a finger," as the account in *Newsweek* put it, "another grabbed
at a piece of paper, and suddenly three grown men in tailored
suits were squirming around the floor, fists aflying among the
bodies."

Brutality in litigation is nothing new, but by 1990 senior
legal ethicists and judges were saying that it had never been
as bad in memory. Yale's Geoffrey Hazard, Jr., writes of the
influx of " 'Lord of the Flies' lawyers." "Many depositions,"
he says, nowadays "contain as much argument between the
lawyers as questioning of the witnesses. Motion papers reek
of adverbial abuse and recrimination. Oral argument is as
much concerned with putting down the other lawyer as getting

the merits across to the judge." "Some firms are even conducting in-house courses on what they call 'sharp tactics,' " complains Texas Supreme Court Justice Eugene Cook. "These tactics involve intimidation, with one lawyer telling another, 'If I ever get the chance, I'll sue you.' They involve a lack of civility. They mean filing motions on everything possible and running up the tab."

None of this would have surprised legal thinkers of the past. From the very start it has been noticed that even good people tend to behave badly when they get into lawsuits. The traditional rules were under no illusions about the perfectability of human nature in this regard. Instead they tried at every turn to keep the cost and ferocity of legal combat from getting out of hand and to steer fighters into relatively cheap, low-intensity modes of conflict.

The peacemaking efforts began with limits on the size of the fought-over territory. Pleadings to form issues promptly cordoned off the battlefield, defining the larger countryside that did not have to be fortified, where a semblance of civilian life could continue. Many potential clashes were presettled through clear demarcation of legal borders and adherence to contractual treaties. Limits on guesswork, especially on guessed-at damages, were also crucial. People tend to fight harder when inflamed by dreams of riches or fears of ruin. So the reparations paid would be high enough (it was hoped) to conciliate the victor's tangible grievances, but not so vast or uncertain as to stoke projects of empire or last-ditch resistance.

Another important restraint was one of timing. The old system compressed the fighting into two intense but closely supervised showdowns, pleadings and trial, with a quiet spell between in which each side could prepare its case and negotiate toward settlement; the parties were restrained from discomfiting each other by the use of compulsory process during this cease-fire period. At trial the rules of evidence, like a disarmament pact, kept out many missiles of dubious accuracy, high cost, or wide swath of collateral destruction. (Justice Holmes called the law's refusal to accept low-grade evidence a "concession to the shortness of life"; it was also a concession to the shallowness of wallets.) The reducing of evidence rules to a system also made it easier to prepare for trial by giving lawyers some idea what information they would be allowed to get on the record, and how.

Finally, the method by which lawyers were paid was meant to keep them attentive to the fighting but not obsessed by it. Much of the ethical tension in lawyering is between the obligation to provide effective advocacy for the client and the obligation to behave as an "officer of the court," a quaint phrase that sums up many ways lawyers are supposed to hold in check their urge to win at all costs. The traditional taximeter fee reflected this precarious balance. It came from (and could be cut off by) the client, so it reminded lawyers of their first obligation; but it did not depend on the outcome, and so did not tempt them into betraying their second.

The partisans of the invisible-fist theory tended toward impatience with rules that seemed to hobble the profession deputized to search for truth and enforce public norms. They were quite willing to see more shavings fly and more hours billed toward the goal of a more perfect imposition of society's presumed will through its courts. The more lawyering went on, surely, the more justice would be done; and what price was too high to pay for justice? Writings on legal ethics began to stress the lawyer's obligation to push clients' rights to the edge of the envelope through full, ardent, fiery, red-in-tooth-and-claw advocacy, as if the besetting sin of the modern American litigator were an excessive scrupulousness. Less and less was written about the obligation not to harass opponents.

For good measure, it was also claimed at first that the new litigation-made-easy procedures would actually lower the expense and acrimony of legal battle. Reducing pleadings to a trip-wire alarm would save one expensive step in a lawsuit. Opening private papers and files on demand would get the facts on the table, making it cheaper to prepare for trial.

Letting in hearsay, opinion, and not-very-relevant evidence would cut down on the need for laborious circumlocution in leading courts toward desired factual conclusions. Admitting more grounds to balance in controversies and more guesswork as to what actually happened would let courts bypass technicalities and head straight for their intended result. Wider use of class actions would save money compared with all those single suits, and long-arm jurisdiction would make for economical one-stop shopping by the person with multiple beefs who might otherwise have to pursue suits in several courts. Contingency fees were thrifty because lawyers who work on that basis put in such Herculean efforts.

Like all legal reformers, those of the invisible-fist school declared their heartfelt opposition to gamesmanship and mere "sporting" theories of justice. And like all legal reformers, they redirected without in the least quelling the strategic behavior of the players. All they could ever provide was a game with different rules.

The early promises were soon forgotten. It was soon apparent that the new system would have made for expensive litigation even if run by saints. Every change meshed with the next. Slippery legal standards called for more discovery. Open-ended damage theories called for more use of experts. Did lawyers begin trying to cash in lost-profits claims for gleam-in-the-eye start-up businesses? Then, as IBM's Nicholas Katzenbach has written, defendants must "scrutinize every possible business problem of the plaintiff" that might have accounted for its not becoming the next McDonald's or Federal Express, a task that will require heavy-duty discovery. Did lawyers begin throwing in emotional-distress claims in wrongful-firing disputes? Then since their client's mental state had been placed "in controversy," the next step was to call the dueling shrinks.

Even when no one consciously abuses the process, legal fights are prone to tit-for-tat escalation. If you are fighting over a dollar bill, the economic logic by itself will not prevent you from spending sixty (or ninety-nine) cents on litigation if that is what it takes to secure victory. Few tactical choices are quite that stark, but arms races can creep forward by degrees. Any good lawyer can find ways to spend a nickel to shift the odds a bit in your favor. The problem is that your opponent can so often spend a counter-nickel to shift them right back. Sometimes the bidding and bluffing take on a life of their own, poker-style, to go far beyond the original stakes. Thus (if the account in *People* is to be credited) did a fight between a divorcing Washington couple over who would get the Redskins season tickets wind up costing fifty thousand dollars apiece.

The weapons with the greatest potential for mischief are those that are more expensive to respond to than to deploy, which describes much of the arsenal of discovery. In its early days discovery had taken place by turns, which tended to curb it to some extent; round-one disclosures might make it clear that an issue was irrelevant, thus heading off many round-two requests. Now the process has been made a free-for-all pushed forward by simultaneous motions and notices filed by each side. The first-order offensive sorties—notices to depose, document requests—can be met with various defensive enfilades—motions to block a deposition, or seal documents against public exposure. The offense can strike back with third-order strafing in the form of demands to compel a resisted disclosure, unseal documents, and so on.

In larger cases some flyway plan is needed for the criss-crossing lawyer-squadrons in their buzzing dogfights, so courts came up with the *discovery scheduling order* which by inevitable back-formation had to be hammered out at a *discovery scheduling conference.* The scheduling conference itself has to be scheduled in advance, and needless to say each stage provides something else for the lawyers to fight over and bill for, in the various stages of what is called motions practice.

Inevitably, perhaps, pretrial litigation has become a much bigger source of legal business than trials themselves. Between the warrior-lawyers who try cases and the diplomat-lawyers who advise clients in times of peace has arisen a sort of Pentagon bureaucracy of litigators spending whole careers on motions and discovery. Some rise to eminence without ever having argued a case before a jury.

The random visitor to today's civil courtroom may hope to see one of the archetypal cathartic excitements of trial: an advocate is tearing apart a witness on the stand in cross-examination, or casting a spell over a rapt jury in final argument. Far more likely he will walk in on a disorderly scene with no jurors, witnesses, or even litigants in sight, only a row of lawyers popping up and subsiding like so many Dickensian piano keys. In a well-known article in the *New York University Law Review*, Philip Schrag described his first encounter with the clogged New York courts. Arriving to press a modest consumer complaint, he found that 250 motions were scheduled to be heard that day, and that this was an average calendar. "My second shock was the sight of the courtroom; as the clerk called the calendar, he could hardly be heard over the hubbub, as dozens of attorneys engaged in last-minute negotiations." The judges were too busy to hear oral argument on the motions or even read them. Instead they handed them over to assistants and took them back only to sign.

The idea of all this is to move cases along to resolution, but it is in fact fantastically dilatory and time-consuming even when played straight. Under no-horizon discovery, lawyers need extra time to digest the material they dig up and assert new issues based on that material, which leads to new discovery requests by the other side, new responses to those requests, and on and on. Motions nest within motions like Russian dolls. Prominent among them are motions for continuance: judges wrestling with unwieldy dockets can be happy to grant delays, reasoning that if trial is put off maybe the sides will settle. An antitrust suit against the American Academy of Orthopedic Surgeons was stuck in the discovery/motions phase for eight years, not unusual in the realm of antitrust.

It's an odd way of doing justice. Fearful that the high jump of pleadings would overly tax the strength of litigants' cases, we have replaced it with a grueling pretrial steeplechase that instead tests their endurance. In the war of attrition that is American litigation today, there is constant sniping between the trenches but seldom a knockout. The old joke is that the law can take a fifty-page document and call it a brief. Now it can take a stage on the way to complete paralysis and call it a motion.

Nor, when trial finally arrives, is it cheaper. Since marginal issues and evidence are admitted, it takes longer to get through cases. But the legal system actually found the most expensive way of all to handle evidence: it made evidence rules broad but also subject to wide judicial discretion. "The federal rules," as Cornell evidence specialist Faust Rossi has put it, "bristle with language granting discretion to the trial judge." So although most evidence will in fact be admitted, lawyers must fight many motion battles over its admission anyway and prepare for every variation just in case a piece is rejected.

All this would have made lawsuits costlier and messier even if all litigators were saints. But some are not.

Discovery and motions practice provide a near-inexhaustible repertoire of ways for litigants to tease, worry, irk, goad, pester, trouble, rag, torment, pique, molest, bother, vex, nettle, and annoy each other. Discovery is generally acknowledged to be worst. When allowed to rifle their opponents' confidential memos, grill their terrified employees, put their board chairmen through depositions that last longer than most trials, and take a look-see around their research labs, all with no judicial officer in attendance, litigators just go ahead and do it. And for some reason the targets simply will not relax and cooperate. So long as they can resist, they do. As a federal court noted, "hostility and bitterness" came to be "more the rule than the exception in unsupervised discovery."

Researchers for the American Bar Foundation surveyed Chicago litigators and found out quite a bit about the common tactical uses of discovery. Several respondents said they made a point of deposing witnesses that they knew their opponents did not want "dragged in." Others boasted of arranging to inflict discovery demands at what they knew were inconvenient times. Also popular were "harshly aggressive styles of questioning designed to make the opposing party decide he never wanted to repeat such an experience." The idea is to "see if you can get them mad," as one lawyer described it, to put them "through the wringer, through the mud," so that "they are frightened to be a witness and . . . are a much worse witness."

As for the targets, one of the Chicago lawyers expressed the attitude that became typical: "Never be candid and never helpful and make [your] opponent fight for everything." Sluggishness in answering requests can be a powerful tactic of delay, just as the requests themselves can be; nearly all the surveyed litigators said they had used discovery for this purpose and most said they had done it often. Most also admitted using the process to "distract" the other side. One proudly recounted how he couched requests so as to trick opponents into hustling to meet an argument "when you aren't even going to use [it]. This is pure joy."

By wide majorities, federal and state judges polled in a 1988 Harris survey said that lawyers' use of discovery "as an adversarial tool to intimidate or raise the stakes for their opponents" was a source of major costs in litigation. Fully 77 percent of the Chicago litigators acknowledged that they had done this, in an average of 28 percent of their cases. "I use discovery to hurt my opponent and help my client," explained one of them in tones almost of innocence; "it's something that's second nature to me."

The endless pretrial motions are likewise useful to keep a cause in the newspapers; to impress the adversary with willingness to fight or punish him for not conceding an unrelated point; to run up his costs and keep him off balance scrambling to respond. They also help in playing for time. For defendants who face incomprehensible legal jeopardy, as for Death Row convicts, the last defense is to stall and stall and stall. "I was born, I think, to be a protractor," a senior partner of Cravath, Swaine and Moore told a Stanford Law School audience. "I could take the simplest antitrust case and protract it for the defense almost to infinity . . . [One case] lasted 14 years . . . Despite 50,000 pages of testimony, there really wasn't any dispute about the facts . . . We won that case, and, as you know, my firm's meter was running all the time—every month for 14 years."

"Politeness Sometimes a Liability, They Say" runs the headline over a *National Law Journal* profile of Bickel & Brewer, an upstart law firm that is changing the way commercial litigation is done in Dallas. In one case that won fame, the firm obtained a temporary injunction against a software maker accused of taking trade secrets from a Bickel client. "The hearing lasted eleven weeks," reported Lisa Belkin in *The New York Times*. "The average temporary injunction hearing lasts three to ten days." Soon thereafter the defendant company went bankrupt; its president said its legal expenses had reached $1.8 million, almost equaling its $2 million annual profits. Messrs. Bickel and Brewer deny that driving the firm broke was part of their intent.

Detractors call Bickel & Brewer "hardball," "bare-knuckled," and the "Rambo firm." Asked about the firm's reputed "take-no-prisoners" approach, partner William A. Brewer III quips: "That's not true. We've got a cell in the back where we keep them." In another sign of a flip willingness to boast of what might ashame others, the firm has "adopted" the snake collection at the Dallas Zoo, chipping in $1,600 toward the care of the diamondback, boa, and others along with their habitats, *The Wall Street Journal* reported. "They are the least popular animal we have," a zoo spokeswoman said, referring to the snakes as distinct from their patrons, "so we really appreciate the law firm doing that."

232 • THE LITIGATION EXPLOSION

Bringing this approach to what had previously been considered a genteel city has paid big dividends. Bickel & Brewer at last report was racking up per-partner profits in the $400,000 range and offering the highest starting salaries in the nation, at $90,000. It had signed a roster of big-name clients that included Motorola, jeans maker Farah, and the Texas Commerce Bank. And inevitably other Dallas firms were adjusting in the direction of its standard of practice. For as tropical-fish fanciers know (to vary the animal imagery), adding an ultra-aggressive new specimen to a tank changes the behavior of all the existing inmates. The accepted rule in litigation is that a lawyer cannot afford to play nicer than the most un-nice lawyer in the case. Which is one reason the influx of contingency-fee lawyers into commercial and family litigation has begun to transform the style of practice in those fields.

It is sometimes imagined that the way to rectify these ills is to encourage lawyers to think of themselves as representing the general public in addition to, or instead of, their particular client, as the invisible-fist theory suggests. A depressing light is cast on this notion by the internal documents that Rael Jean Isaac uncovered from the Legal Services Corporation, whose federally funded but privately directed lawyers form the largest corps of ostensible "public interest" litigators. One in-house manual, calling litigation an "important bargaining technique," reminds Legal Services lawyers that "the opposition's costs may be significantly higher if it has to defend itself against a lot of small suits which are factually distinct . . . and this can enlarge [your] organization's bargaining power." "A lot of small suits humming away, where each time they have to file a response, each time they have to answer interrogatories, increases the pressure," explains another training program. What about the cost of filing these? "Lawsuits are expensive only if they are taken seriously. . . . Win or lose, you start to escalate the cost of resistance to [your] group's demands." It also advises: "The way to cause pressure on [the opponent's] in-house counsel is to bring actions in out-of-the-way places (make them travel) or generate a lot of action (make them work hard to keep up)." Yet another Legal Services training piece recommends demanding the hour-by-hour programming logs of TV stations as "a charming harassment technique . . . even though you won't ultimately get their license, you will have a chance to threaten to hassle them to death."

Of course, some professed idealists feel entitled to take special tactical liberties by reason of the overall moral grandeur of their cause. But how far do workaday litigators in conventional practice feel permitted to go in these battles? Federal judge and former Harvard law professor Robert Keeton has written that the answer "implicit in prevailing practice" is probably that it is okay to use "any legally supportable ground" in your fights, so long as you believe in the *overall* rightness of your client's position. This is far from comforting, since most lawyers do not find it hard to muster such a belief. And the competitive pressure of the litigation industry tends to weed out softness. Increasingly lawyers are found who take the view that they owe opponents no ethical obligation at all beyond "strict legal duty."

What does "any legally supportable ground" mean in a litigation struggle? Some of the common tactics might be grouped under the headings of trade-ins and add-ons.

The trade-in emerges when a lawyer can sue for a nonmonetary benefit and then trade it in on the settlement market for cold cash. Recall that the main effect of giving fathers wider rights to challenge mothers' custody of children has not been so much to take away custody from mothers who want it as to undercut their bargaining position on money issues. The classic trade-in pattern arises when a threatened court action is of more burning significance to its target than to the person who has a right to ask for it. At the extreme, the lawyer can manage to turn a small deposit of original merit into a treasury of settlement value.

A rich source of trade-in potential are laws that let people sue for injunctions or license denials that block other people's economic activities. If any neighbor among thousands can go to court to stop the siting of a utility transmission line, the demolition of a historic building, or the expansion of an airport runway, some lawsuits will come from persons who sincerely want to save their threatened amenity. But others will be filed with at least half an eye to how much the opponent would pay for the right to finish a half-done construction project, with the interest clock ticking. (The neighbors say they want money to drop their suit against the airport. Fair enough; jet noise can depress property values. You say their lawyer wants *how* much?) This is one reason injunctions are normally discretionary with judges instead of automatic.

Trade-ins are frequently based on lofty-sounding laws with many references to the public interest, but for most litigators they are just another weapon to pack in their violin cases. Big-city governments can gain leverage over the development of shopping malls in outlying suburbs by filing challenges to the projects' environmental impact statements, though ecology may be the last thing on the mayor's mind. From there it is only a light skip to withdraw the suit in exchange for a cash payment by the developer to a job-training or business-development fund run by the city or perhaps, depending on the local ethical climate, by a community group with links to the mayor's relatives.

The add-on allows the lawyer to take a claim that itself might or might not have been worth filing and stretch and extend it, bulk it up, and puff it out by adding charges, defendants, theories, and damage assertions that would never have been tenable on their own. A well-founded breach-of-contract claim can thus go into the word processor and emerge as a headline-grabbing mail fraud and racketeering case. Creative orthopedics experts can turn a genuine knee injury into a can't-be-ruled-out suggestion of spinal-cord injury, the thigh bone being connected to the hip bone and all that.

One devastatingly common add-on, made infinitely easier by the combination of long-arm jurisdiction and un-informative pleadings, is the attachment of miscellaneous third-party bystanders as defendants. By now it is perfectly routine for a malpractice suit to list every doctor whose name is found in the patient's file, sometimes along with nurses and maybe the hospital's volunteer board members (no doubt there's an insurance policy there). The parents' suit over the sports injury can likewise name not only the deep-pocket school district and the maker of the sports equipment but also the shallower-pocket coach or adult team adviser. The lawyer will explain that these peripheral claims can always be bargained away when you start talking settlement, and what makes a better bargaining chip than personal discomfort?

Any well-trained lawyer can come up with rationaliza-tions for the use of trade-ins and add-ons. The wholly legit-imate, sure-to-win-at-trial claim, pressed honorably, will seldom command a settlement value as high as the lawyer thinks it deserves, and after the legal fees are deducted the client will get less still. Throwing in a few junk charges might bring in enough to make the client whole, maybe with enough left over to pay the fee. Meanwhile the other side, which may differ on the merit of the underlying claim, is certainly going to be nettled by the add-ons, and reaches for the junk-iest defenses.

The contingency-fee bar has helped perfect the practice of putting grievances on an assembly line from which they emerge with every option included. The process begins with the initial client interview. *American Law of Product Liability 3rd*, a standard multi-volume reference for injury lawyers, starts with the basics. It warns that "your client's first reaction may be to blame himself for the injury rather than relating product misadventure to the manufacturer. The initial reac-tion of your client might well be that of the [judge or jury]. It is important, obviously, to overcome this."

After the client is made aware of the probable culpability of suitable defendants, he must next be made to realize the severity of his injuries. The first step is to put him through a suggestive "head to toe" checklist of physical complaints, starting at the scalp and proceeding through each and every body part on the way down, followed by more systemic woes (insomnia? weight gain? lack of energy?). Then comes emotional trauma (any feelings of humiliation? anxiety?) and other perhaps previously unsuspected sources of compensation rights.

Then it's on to long-term disability. The client's doctor may say he seems to have come through fine, but a leading article on how to interview injury clients, in the *American Jurisprudence Trials* series, tells lawyers not to be discouraged on that account. "The initial medical reports often disclose little as to possible functional or organic disabilities," it explains. "Indeed, it is not unusual for a nonspecialist to report that he can find no cause for a patient's symptoms. Such a report should not be conclusive insofar as the attorney is concerned," because, after all, "even a minor physical injury may bring on a functional disability, or aggravate a pre-existing one, although no trace of the physical injury remains."

What if the client seems to be exaggerating or malingering? The article continues: "The fact that there appears to be a strong desire for gain in the client's claim, or that the physical aspects of the injury do not seem to bear out the degree of disability or pain, should not lead [the lawyer] to a conclusion that the claim is unworthy." In fact, the client may be acting out a neurosis brought on by the accident itself and thus deserving of compensation just the same—a wonderful all-purpose theory, that one.

These methods work. One study compared traffic claims in North Carolina, where lawyers are called in on only a third of injury cases, with New Jersey, where they get into more than three-fifths. In North Carolina, 41 percent of complainants reported back problems and 51 percent neck problems as a result of their accidents. In New Jersey the respective figures were 70 and 73 percent. All told, of crash victims with similar injuries, those who hired a lawyer ran up about three times the medical expenses of people who didn't.

The lawyer will usually want to send the injury client to a new "good" doctor, and also advise him to keep a diary of any and all symptoms and complaints from here on in. In his book *The Lawsuit Lottery,* University of Virginia law professor Jeffrey O'Connell quotes a widely used trial-lawyer handout that is careful to shoo clients away from claims that can too easily be falsified:

INSTRUCTIONS TO CLIENTS
"MY DAY"

> . . . 5. DON'T USE THE WORDS "I CAN'T"—Please do not use the words "I can't," because "can't" means physical impossibility. . . . We would prefer you would use such words as "I am not able to do it as well" or some other words meaning the same thing. . . . Everyone will admire you more if you try.

For many an injury claim, the fortune inside the cookie is pain and suffering. (Leading New York trial lawyer Robert Sullivan has explained that "you really gotta whip that jury into a frenzy to goose up the damages for pain and suffering.") Yet many clients don't spontaneously describe their woes in the vivid and graphic terms that grab jurors, warns the *American Jurisprudence Trials* guide to client interviews. For instance, clients will vaguely refer to their head pain as "bad." "The necessity of using meaningful and descriptive terminology must be emphasized to the client." Saying his pain is like "having the top of his head blown off" or "having his head squeezed in a vise" will get a much more appropriate award, the article advises.

"However," the author goes on, "the attorney must not place himself in the position where he *is suspected* [emphasis added] of having coached his client in the use of an apt word or phrase. The jury might suspect this if an illiterate or unintelligent witness uses language not in keeping with his vocabulary limitations."

If this is what injury lawyers are telling each other with a wink and a nudge in the widely circulated *American Jurisprudence Trials* reference volumes, what on earth are they saying off the record?

The client who seems unwilling to pick up on the suggested wordings on pain can be given a good long wallow in this gruesome subject by way of another of the checklists in the product liability lawyers' manual. The following are fairly typical of its dozens of harrowing questions: "30. Does constant worrying about your health tend to tire you out? 31. Does your health make you generally miserable? 32. Does it seem that suffering is your way of life? 33. Are you miserable and unhappy? 34. What do you think is the cause of your pain? 35. Do you think that the pain is due to something more serious or different from what the doctors have told you?" And so forth, for pages.

With proper encouragement even the least hypochondriacal among us can fall into a luxurious obsession with the inherent unfairness of suffering. Professor O'Connell remarks in *The Lawsuit Lottery* that "many in the medical profession are understandably shocked by a system that, contrary to all medical wisdom, encourages accident victims to preserve, hug, and indeed nurture and memorialize every twinge and hurt from an accident."

Studies agree that the intense focus on the legal form of "recovery" actually tends to delay an accident victim's medical recovery. Harvard psychiatrist John Nemiah, writing in (of all places) the magazine *Trial*, notes that in the "limbo of indecision and idleness" before trial or settlement it often happens that "the patient remains an invalid until legal elements emanating from his injury are resolved." Nemiah explains that "the adversary nature of a tort [claim] . . . heightens the patient's sense of grievance, entitlement to redress, and revenge—which tends to foster his aggressive drive and to shift his attention away from the goals of rehabilitation and eventual regained independence."

Betsy Clarke, reporting in the magazine *Chronicles* on a continuing-education seminar for Missouri disability-claim lawyers, found that "an innocent observer of this seminar would have concluded that deceit and subterfuge are more important than disability in getting a person compensation." One panelist noted that judges often grow skeptical of a claimant who testifies that he is in constant pain but then sits comfortably during the trial. A second panelist explained how he overcomes this problem: "he and his client practice interrupting the trial every thirty minutes to ask for permission to stand up or sit down." He rationalizes the little game by explaining that if not for this sort of encouragement many litigants in unendurable pain would not be assertive enough to fidget.

The magazine *Disability Rag,* published by activists for the handicapped, has excoriated trial lawyers for their practice of playing victimization for all it is worth. Its May/June 1986 cover story quotes a typical trial summation by a lawyer who tells a jury that his client "will never work a day in his life again. His life, for all practical purposes, is over." Jill Robinson, a lawyer for injury plaintiffs who is herself disabled, chides her fellow practitioners for evoking "a powerful, swirling array of dark and distasteful emotions in the jury," so as to inhibit their "ability for rational analysis. . . . The sooner the verdict is returned [with a high award], the sooner they are released from their confrontation with the unbearable." Lawyer Deborah Kaplan says some of her colleagues "tell their clients to avoid anything—such as learning to drive a car again or getting their own apartment—that might lead the jury to suspect that they're 'less disabled' than they are." A *Disability Rag* writer reluctantly spiked an article about a disabled woman after the woman's lawyer wrote to demand prior review of the article lest it make her look "too competent." For the client it can all provide a paralyzing diagnosis of hopelessness and helplessness, made in his own name, to live down to.

Other lawyers should not feel complacent, since questionable techniques of client preparation are hardly confined to injury law. Houston lawyer David Berg writes that "most of us trim the sail of the testifying client a bit too much . . . who among us has not warned the client, 'Before you tell me your side of the story, let me tell you what the law is in this area,' or 'If you say that, you'll lose.' Or who, wincing at his client's explanation, has not reminded the client, 'Well, that's not how your boss remembers it,' or 'Aren't you really telling me . . .' "

Only a minority of lawyers spend their time litigating. But litigation casts a long backward shadow over all the advisory and negotiating services that lawyers provide. And as litigation rises in cost and intensity, so must these earlier stages of legal work.

A fair bit of defensive and preventive lawyering begins with the observation that organizations keep getting sued on the basis of items in their own files. "I get so many phone calls from managers wanting to fire somebody for poor performance," said Gloria Shanor, a labor law executive with Georgia-Pacific, the big forest products company. Managers may have been dissatisfied with a worker for years, she says, but often have kept putting kind remarks in his file in hopes of being constructive. These days, such remarks make it very hard to fire the worker without legal jeopardy.

The solution is not hard to find: control what goes into the file. At some point managers will learn exactly how much praise they may safely dispense, and in what terminology, to any employee the company doesn't plan to employ for life. Other documents come under similar pressure to be emptied of meaningful content. The Nordstrom clothing store chain kept getting sued for failing to live up to all the rules in its twenty-page handbook of employee discipline procedures. It reportedly replaced the booklet with a one-page sheet and one rule for managers: "Use your good judgment in all situations." "Our wrongful termination problems have gone way down since we got rid of that darn handbook," explained cochairman Jim Nordstrom.

Reading documents written in the expectation of confidentiality is a thrill that every lawyer can enjoy, once. After that, the documents start changing. In one widely publicized case an Oregon doctor won a $2.3 million treble-damage antitrust verdict against eleven of his fellow doctors, who were uninsured against this calamity, on the grounds that their peer review criticisms of him constituted unlawful restraint of trade. In practically no time the recommendational climate in the medical world turned mute and wintry. Hospital lawyer Frank Cielsa said he "used to get phone calls from people who said: 'I got your letter but I'm not going to respond in writing because the doctor is no good.' Now I'm not even getting the phone call." "It is becoming so that it takes a very courageous or perhaps stupid individual to say what he really thinks about another," said Dr. Bryant Galusha, executive vice president of the Federation of State Medical Boards. "People are just refusing to put things in writing that will put them in legal jeopardy later."

One 1989 survey by a recruiting outfit found that although 81 percent of companies try to check out references before hiring, 41 percent have established formal policies against giving out anything beyond the bare confirmation that someone is a former employee. When the process of reference fails and problem employees get into positions where they can do grave harm, litigators naturally proceed to sue on the theory that the problems should have been caught. Injury lawyers had a field day denouncing the evils of medical malpractice in 1986 when a court-martial sentenced Navy Commander Donal Billig to four years in prison for involuntary manslaughter and negligent homicide after the deaths of three heart-surgery patients at the Bethesda Naval Hospital. (The conviction was later overturned.) Billig had earlier lost his operating privileges at a New Jersey hospital and been fired from a medical group in Pittsburgh, but his fellow doctors kept writing him upbeat letters of reference.

Paper trails documenting dissent within organizations create countless leads for opposing lawyers, so at least the trails if not the dissent must be expunged. If every unheeded suggestion from an internal ethics or safety officer is going to be a time bomb in the files, whether it is sensible or misguided, then internal ethics and safety officers are not going to be left free to make all the suggestions they might like, at least not in forms that get written down. "It's a dirty secret of the takeover wars," writes Gordon Crovitz in *The Wall Street Journal*, "that lawyers often now prepare the board minutes *before* the board meets. Directors can then read scripts lawyered to meet the current Delaware case law." Candor is for out in the corridor, and pieties are for print.

Eventually, in organizations fully accustomed to the glare of hostile scrutiny, nothing spontaneous or natural is permitted to happen at all; when the flash bulbs go off every few seconds, the legal paparazzi no longer get any candid shots. The bureaucratic style of communication—meant as much to conceal information as to convey it—is sometimes attributed merely to defective grasp of prose style. But in fact nothing could be a more rational response to an organizational environment where privacy is impossible, heavy penalties attach to saying the wrong thing, and the rules on what is wrong to say are muddled if not incomprehensible.

In oft-sued organizations a strange linguistic stratification can take hold. A perfectly opaque language will be used to compose permanent written documents. A second, Mandarin language of euphemism and indirection is used for conversations where less than fully reliable persons are present. And actual frankness is reserved for the hearing of those judged capable of forgetting it if necessary. It is a state of affairs entirely familiar to immigrants from the unfortunate sorts of societies where the authorities inflict harsh punishments for the use of the wrong word or phrase.

THE RACE TO THE GUTTER

Bureaucracies also need a Memory Hole. Of course destroying or concealing data once a lawsuit begins is taboo. Kodak dropped a $113 million antitrust verdict after one of its lawyers falsely stated that certain documents no longer existed when in fact he had a copy at his office. But there is no way to attach an inference of guilt to routine periodic destruction of data before disputes arise. Customer complaints are "highly inflammatory" and much sought by lawyers and should be thrown out as soon as possible, urges George Flynn of Minneapolis's Faegre & Benson.

On advice of counsel American institutions have thus begun shredding campaigns, in the manner of besieged embassies, to destroy file contents promptly and regularly—to the despair of scholars who know that institutional archives can be valuable resources for future historians, social scientists, and epidemiologists. The *Cleveland Plain Dealer* is one of a number of publications that have begun ordering reporters to destroy notes shortly after a story runs, according to an article by Betty Holcomb in the *Columbia Journalism Review*. Again and again, once the system adjusts to the loss of privacy, the net effect is to reduce the amount of information on hand. "Discovery," as a country lawyer once put it, "is only as good as what a lawyer leaves around to be discovered."

The invisible-fist school is of course dismayed at the drying up of the hidden evidence springs with which it had hoped to run the millwheels of eternal litigation. Some of its members have responded with proposals for widespread mandatory document retention, prison terms for persons who fail to step forward to denounce their working colleagues, and similar steps to perfect the administration of justice. Yet such harsh measures will never bring back the sense of unconstraint that once tended to produce genuinely informative documents back in the days when litigation was truly unusual and unexpected. Once the citizenry is made forcibly aware that everything it says will be held against it, some people are bound to clam up, others to say the opposite of what they mean, and very few to be prepared for calm and rational discussion. An inquisition can make liars, or secret-keepers, of even a population known for plain speaking and square dealing.

Gratuitous belligerence and cost infliction, witness coaching and information control, may to some degree be inevitable in any system of justice. But they have been made much worse than they need to be by rules that encourage the pursuit of litigation as total war. It would be a mistake to imagine that the answer is simply to exhort lawyers to be more considerate and conscientious. Within the American legal profession, probably a solid majority already would like to see the fighting deescalate. Even many lawyers who are doing well financially out of the strife would be happy to make a bit less money if a more rational and civilized style of practice could result.

Those who like the system the way it is, however, are rapidly coming into their own as leaders of the profession. Andrew Patner and Wayne Green of *The Wall Street Journal* reported in 1989 on a fascinating debate between members of the family-law bar at its annual meeting in Chicago. The top guns in the field pressed for new big-ticket theories by which money could be extracted from ex-spouses, such as the "tort of fear" seeking punishment for the emotional distress of the client. "I find your promotion of torts to be really, really pernicious," replied Diana Richmond of the San Francisco firm of Richmond & Chamberlin. Richmond, to loud applause, said her colleagues should be "disengaging our clients from horrendous situations and intense litigation," rather than seeking maximum dollar return.

"That's fine if you want to take the social worker's point of view," shot back Houston's J. Lindsay Short, head of the Texas chapter of the American Academy of Matrimonial Lawyers and editor of its journal. "I have to take the trial lawyer's point of view." He warned that " 'disengagement' could lead you to malpractice." "You all can go pick up your 'being-a-nice-guy' medals the same day you turn in your law licenses," said Sanford S. Dranoff of New York, named president-elect of the 1,200-member academy. "What we are doing is making sure that our clients know what their rights are," said Stephen A. Kolodny of Los Angeles, citing the Marc Christian/Rock Hudson case. "We have an obligation to provide effective representation."

In a gesture toward pacifism, Texas, Los Angeles, Chicago, and other jurisdictions known for unpleasantness have adopted what are called courtesy codes of behavior for litigators. One of the first legal bodies to feel the need for such a code was the A.B.A.'s torts and insurance group, home coliseum of the guessing-for-dollars bowl and an area where as *Newsweek* (reflecting the general view) puts it, "nasty tactics are an art form." But so long as more and more litigation is driven by the interplay of subjective and speculative legal standards with contingency-fee advocacy, it is unlikely much will change. The only real hope in lowering the steam levels is to turn down the fire under the pot.

The law school commentators in their abstract way describe the modern trend in legal procedure, evidence, and jurisprudence as being to encourage the "free and full exploration of a dispute." More bluntly, it is to let the lawyers beat up on each other and each other's clients to the utmost degree, in hopes that the hotter the fray the more truth and justice will emerge. It would make a good subject for a macabre cartoon: a child is pounding a playmate's head against the schoolyard asphalt, while in the distance one progressive educator is telling another, "Oh, look—they're fully and freely exploring their dispute."

The old restraints and inhibitions may not have been such a bad idea. Some degree of strife is inevitable in this fallen world, but not every border skirmish need degenerate into all-out war. At their creakiest, the old procedures may have resembled a caricature of a duel, bringing the well-chaperoned parties together at dawn with a pair of antique foils. Perhaps that stylized mode of combat needed updating.

What we got instead was a gangland war where the weaponry and tactics are varied and imaginative, spies are everywhere, all sorts of bystanders get mowed down, and the fighting continues around the clock for years. In hope of getting justice, the American law deregulated combat.

12

⚖

JUNK LITIGATION:
What's Merit Got to Do With It?

Whether you win or lose the suit, you'll still lose.

> —*Washington, D.C., trial lawyer John
> Coale, threatening to sue the K-Mart
> Corporation on behalf of a handi-
> capped child, quoted in John
> Jenkins,* The Litigators

The unique discovery immun-
ities accorded to lawyers and their work product enable the
litigation business to keep its internal workings out of the
public eye and off the public record to a remarkable extent.
So it was noteworthy when in the early 1980s an unusual
falling out between trial lawyers brought to light the backstage
goings-on behind one good-sized class action called the *Fine
Paper* case.

The case arose from reports of possible price-fixing in
the paper industry in the 1970s. A veteran Chicago class-action
lawyer named Granvil Specks decided it would be a great
thing to represent paper buyers who might have paid more
than they should have as a result of any violations that might
be proved. He proceeded to file two treble-damage antitrust
suits in federal court, one in Illinois on behalf of an obscure

client from New York, the other in Connecticut on behalf of an equally obscure client from Louisiana. The suits purported to represent not only the named clients but everyone else in the country who had bought office stationery and other better grades of paper. Specks then circulated copies of the complaints to various lawyers with whom he had previously worked in class actions, many of whom soon joined the action on behalf of clients of their own. One lawyer later testified that Specks "begged" him "over a period of several months" to come on board with a complaint.

Before long more than a dozen suits had been filed in eight federal courts around the country. They were consolidated into a single suit against fifteen paper companies and assigned to a federal court in Philadelphia, where a grand jury was investigating the price-fixing rumors. The suit was also certified as a class action on behalf of all those who had purchased fine paper from any of the defendants over a twelve-year period.

As it happened the grand jury never returned an indictment; a probe by the Federal Trade Commission was equally unproductive. But by this point the civil lawsuits were picking up a head of steam, with more and more law firms joining in. (The number eventually reached forty-one, representing a diverse assemblage of clients that included the Archdiocese of Philadelphia and the American Lutheran Church board of publications.) About half the fifty state governments filed suits of their own in their capacity as buyers of fine paper. Some of these states joined the main class action, but fourteen others chose to go it alone in their own separate lawsuit, also in the Philadelphia federal court.

An organizational meeting of the plaintiffs' lawyers in the main suit was called in Chicago. Michael Spiegel, a California deputy attorney general who was there, later testified how incongruous it all seemed. Among those leading the discussion were "three or four of the most prominent antitrust attorneys in this country representing a mom and pop greeting card store, a fishmonger from Fort Bragg, California who buys wrapping paper to wrap fish," and so forth. Some of the tiny clients were shared by several law firms. The lawyers running the show were claiming to represent the Fortune 500 companies that buy office paper and all the other members of the vast class.

To manage the suit, a lead counsel team and a larger steering committee were picked in what those present seemed to consider a highly democratic manner: one lawyer, one vote. So, as Spiegel recounted, "the mom and pop greeting card store with four attorneys got four votes," while, say, the state of Colorado got one vote. "I could have brought a 400-man staff out there and packed that meeting if I wanted to." This might explain the organizers' scramble to get friendly lawyers into the suit at the outset.

The tension between lawyers was already building at this stage. Philadelphia lawyer Aaron Fine says he complained to Specks at being kept off the steering committee in favor of a lawyer who had been less active in the case and was told that the other man had been put on in recognition of his "position in the industry." The paper industry? No, Fine was told, the antitrust-suit-filing industry.

Specks and other members of the newly elected leadership had by then begun the allocation of work assignments to participating lawyers, a cozy process that Judge Joseph McGlynn, Jr., later referred to unkindly in his opinion as the "distribution of patronage." Some lawyers who had taken an active role at the start began to be "frozen out of the case," again to quote Judge McGlynn.

Up to now the lawyers had been scrounging about for evidence to prove their conspiracy charges against the companies, and frankly there wasn't much. Now came what seemed a stroke of luck. Two personal-injury lawyers named Walter Riordan and Stewart Perry produced a witness named James Nelson, president of a bankrupt paper-distributing company in Minneapolis, who said he had personal knowledge of wrongdoing by paper-company executives. What a break—it seemed the charges might pan out after all! One by one, nervous defendants began to buy their way out of the lawsuit. The St. Regis Paper Company settled for $2 million, the International Paper Company for $5.2 million, and several others followed.

In lawsuits charging business conspiracies a curious dynamic often works to encourage the accused to surrender. Individual defendants will frequently be offered a chance to buy their way out relatively cheaply at an early stage. But as they do so, those who might prefer to hold out for trial are left on the hook—should they lose—for the entire pot of damages, minus whatever sums the departed firms have paid in settlement. In treble-damage cases especially, where the potential exposure is enormous, this creates great pressure not to be the last holdout. Conceivably the smallest of the fifteen companies might have been hit with the bulk of a massive verdict based almost entirely on the activities of larger firms that had bailed out earlier.

As the settlement money piled up more new lawyers kept jumping in and being assigned work; eight of them joined after $30 million was already in the bank. Judge McGlynn later concluded that the "only logical reason" for these filings was to allow these lawyers "to participate in the case and thereby to obtain attorneys' fees." Finally, on the first day of trial, the remaining defendants offered enough money to bring the total kitty up to a bit over $50 million. The plaintiffs' committee accepted the offer and the suit was settled.

Except for the fees. The plaintiffs' lawyers filed petitions for a total of $20.2 million in fees based on what they said were 97,000 billable hours spent on the case. The Specks firm alone asked for $4.4 million. Counting a million in expenses, the combined requests came to more than 40 percent of the stated recovery, to be skimmed off before any paper-industry customers saw a penny. Incidentally, several of the toy clients the lawyers were claiming to represent had not even bothered to file claims against the resulting settlement fund.

Usually fee requests like these sail through uncontested; the lawyers lock arms to declare them reasonable and the presiding judge, with no adversary process to spotlight weak points, can give them at best light scrutiny. But this time something went terribly wrong. Prominent plaintiff's lawyer Harold Kohn of Philadelphia had done early spadework on the suit but was not pleased with the way it was then run. As the time for petitioning approached Kohn warned that he would not stand for fee requests that totaled more than 20 percent of the recovery. His colleagues refused to come down that far—they had already reached what Specks viewed as a consensus on where to pitch the collective fee amount—but launched overtures in hopes of averting what one lawyer called a "blood bath" over the fee applications.

Too late. Kohn proceeded to lay out to a fascinated Judge McGlynn a scathing analysis of his colleagues' fee requests, which he said had been systematically padded in collusion by the leading lawyers. Five law firms, he charged, had brought in friends and voted as a bloc to seize control of the suit and parcel out its work assignments. If one competent firm had done the work, Kohn said, it would have taken 5,000 to 15,000 hours, not 97,000. His critique was lent force when a group of outside companies that buy huge quantities of fine paper intervened with their own detailed challenge to the size of the fees for work supposedly done on their (among others') behalf.

More than $1 million, it turned out, had been billed for 4,500 hours allegedly spent drawing up a pretrial memorandum, although the state governments going it alone in their separate suit had already filed a similar document that dealt with most of the same issues. Another 4,200 hours were charged to the development of a damages theory, although the judge said the lawyers had not managed to come up with a viable one by the time of trial. Nine law firms had billed 1,500 hours for depositions of James Nelson alone. Bills for first-class restaurants, hotels, and travel dotted the petitions, along with claims for work contracted out to teenage sons and other family members.

The ruling group soon "returned the volley," as the judge put it, with a flurry of objections to Kohn's own fee petitions, on grounds that however tended to backfire. They decried as "scandalous" his high hourly fee request, although one of their own number, a San Francisco lawyer named Guido Saveri, was asking even more. "The lawyers also attacked Kohn on other fronts," Judge McGlynn wrote in his opinion. "In class action antitrust cases, such as *Ocean Shipping Antitrust Litigation* and in the *Corn Products Derivative Antitrust Litigation* in which Kohn and other *Fine Paper* lawyers are presently involved, retaliatory measures against Kohn such as removing him from the executive committee have been taken by Specks, Saveri [and other lawyers] allegedly because of Kohn's objections to their fee petitions in *Fine Paper*." The same pressures, the judge suggested, had been brought to bear to prevent defections by other *Fine Paper* lawyers, who "refused to trim their fee requests because they feared they would be excluded from further antitrust cases by Specks, Saveri and Sloan."

There was something deliciously ironic in all this. Colluding to divvy up a market, pressuring competitors to keep their prices high, harassing defectors and retaliating against them in distant markets—these were the very practices that the antitrust laws were supposed to be saving us from in the first place. And here, looking like the reddest-handed offenders caught in years, were the very same lawyers who had made a fortune in fees by their lugubrious talents in denouncing workaday businesses for supposed anticompetitive sins.

A break between the two Minneapolis lawyers, Riordan and Perry, once good friends, shed yet more unwelcome light on the behind-the-scenes goings-on. Perry thought he deserved credit for discovering and priming the star witness, Nelson, but said his colleagues (whom he compared to "sharks in a feeding frenzy") had in effect stolen the fellow for their own use. He also said he had observed Specks promising to get Riordan into bigger suits in the future; Riordan himself, he said, had referred to the *Fine Paper* suit as a "gravy train." Riordan for his part described a colorful scene at a restaurant where Perry had allegedly slammed his fist on the table, called the suit a "money tree," and said "I'm going to shake it, I don't care what you guys say." It was further alleged that Nelson had requested money in exchange for his testimony, and that he and his family (one of whom was hired as a consultant by the lawyers) had been promised large sums.

After more than a month of eye-opening revelations along these lines, Judge McGlynn slashed the fee request by more than three quarters, to $4.3 million (the expenses he allowed came to another million). An appeals court backed his basic findings but ordered the sums recalculated on various grounds, which allowed the lawyers to get somewhat more. The squabbling went on for years, however; in 1988, more than a decade after the case began, the appeals court was resolving yet another dispute between Riordan and the other lawyers over the recarving of the fee pie, by now virtually mashed to crumbs.

The unusual insight into litigation practice in this case, entertaining though it was, was also expensive: the fee battles took up more courtroom time than most trials. The first-round fee hearings alone consumed 73 hours, as compared with 198 hours for the whole trial on the merits concerning the alleged fine-paper conspiracy.

Trial on the merits? Who said anything about a trial on the merits? But it was true: only weeks after the larger case was settled the fourteen state governments that had chosen to go it alone presented the evidence to a jury in a trial on the merits. Their case was so weak that the paper companies did not even bother to introduce evidence in their own defense, and a jury gave them a hands-down victory. Since settlements are forever, there was no way for the companies

254 • THE LITIGATION EXPLOSION

to get back any of the $50 million they had forked over under threat of identical charges in the other suit.

Concern about less-than-meritorious lawsuits is nothing new. Back in 1927 H. L. Mencken noted how often established playwrights and scriptwriters were being hit with plagiarism suits from mostly unknown writers in "embarrassing actions, costly when won, and ruinous when lost." Some of the complainants were honest but naive folks who saw that a hit play or film followed the same plot as one they had written, not recognizing that every good plot gets used again and again. But others were opportunists with "nothing save a yearning to get a whack at what seemed to be very opulent royalties" by way of "threats and intimidations," egged on by "lawyers who know that the average man, rather than stand cross-examination about his private and professional acts, will commonly pay substantial damages." (This was back when cross-examination on the stand was still the worst of a lawsuit's invasion of privacy; modern discovery came later.) One dramatist, Mencken said, was wholly exonerated but nearly bankrupted by the legal fees; another by his recollection was sued six times and managed to lose once though plainly innocent. Already, movie studios were refusing on advice of counsel to read scripts sent in over the transom by strangers, not only returning such scripts with the envelope unopened but also keeping records of having done this.

The older law was by no means immune to the problem of meritless suits, but it did go to some lengths to discourage them. Pleadings focused immediate attention on the merits of a case. Objective triggers and no-guesswork rules of evidence and damages gave both sides a better idea of which cases belonged in court and which did not. Procedural rules tried to keep in check the cost impositions litigants could inflict on each other.

Perhaps most important of all was the combination of client control of suits with lawyer independence. Most lawyers know far better than most clients how to abuse the system.

If clients have to instigate suits of their own accord, many will never notice the opportunities for abuse. Even clients eager to file an abusive suit may not readily find a lawyer willing to play along if all they can offer to overcome misgivings is a ho-hum hourly fee. Under a regime of client instigation and lawyer independence, the idea of filing suit has to pass two separate sniff tests.

Abuses accordingly seem to cluster in areas where the normal check that lawyer and client provide on each other breaks down. Lawyers who represent a dead person's estate, a bankrupt business, or an incompetent resident of an institution can be on their honor as to how to proceed. Murray Teigh Bloom, in his 1968 book *The Trouble With Lawyers*, quotes an official who explained why some of the less savory New York lawyers liked to get themselves appointed "special guardians" to tend to the interests of orphaned children:

> A special guardian wants a particularly fat fee out of an estate. He goes to the executor or attorney for the estate and holds him up. How? He just says, look, I want so much. If I don't get it I'm going to tie up this estate in objections for the next five years. And he could. Any lawyer could find *some* reason why there should be a delay in the interests of the children he's supposed to be "protecting."

Even in the older law vague standards of conduct, lopsided cost impositions, and lawyer initiation of suits could combine to form an environment for filing meritless litigation. Consider shareholder lawsuits against corporations.

The "fiduciary" standards that govern a management's obligations to its stockholders have long been slippery and amorphous, a problem that developments in modern corporate law have tended to worsen. A shareholder can sue, for example, over a management's failure to disclose some "material" fact about its business prospects, a term that is rich in potential for disagreement. (Shareholder lawyers, like the singer Madonna, have done well out of living in a material world.)

The cost structure of shareholder litigation tilts heavily as well. Discovery is perfectly lopsided, since nothing useful can be asked of the plaintiff. (Yes, I own ten shares of stock. Any other questions?) In "derivative" suits launched by a stockholder against a company's executives personally, the targets may have to run three or four sets of lawyers' meters: one for the company, one for the accused executives (who are defended at company expense), one for the "outside" directors who are supposed to screen the suit, and sometimes others as well.

Under these conditions a shareholder-lawsuit industry came to be organized along lines similar to those of the antitrust-lawsuit industry. As we saw in Chapter 3, it is amply supplied with obliging clients. Some dear old friends of leading lawyers hold one or a few shares apiece of countless listed stocks and mutual funds and turn up as client of record in suit after suit against different companies.

Shareholder lawyers, like class-action antitrust lawyers, tend not to be keen on doing a lot of research. More often they wait for a government agency to announce some enforcement action, or for a scandal or corporate embarrassment to hit the newspapers, and then piggyback on the bad news. "Every time a company coughs wrong, I file a complaint," boasts Seymour Licht, who according to *Forbes* quit a professorial job to become a full-time investor/litigant and "churns out lawsuits as fast as his IBM PC can print them."

Columbia Law School professor Jack Coffee, who has written a series of influential articles on the problems with this kind of litigation, says the extensive, costly preparation that is seen on the defendant's side may contrast with "a form of feigned litigation that sometimes occurs on the plaintiff's." Although the shareholder lawyer may launch massive discovery demands, it does not follow that he "will always review carefully the documents he requests," Coffee says. "To be sure, he must appear to be serious about the case or he will sacrifice some negotiating leverage, but the distance between appearance and reality can be considerable."

Why wouldn't a lawyer bother to read the documents? Simply put, because he never intends to let the case get to trial. Most defendant companies buy off most shareholder suits most of the time. A survey by Thomas Jones of the University of Washington found that plaintiffs got settlements in 70 percent of all such suits, while winning trial judgments in a mere one percent. The result is what has been called shareholder greenmail, or, cornily enough, "feemail." Some of the lawyers are also nicknamed "pilgrims" because they are noted for their early settlements.

What about the need to submit the settlement agreement and fees to a judge for approval? The truth is that the first precondition of negotiation is bound to be that the defendant go quietly, swearing along with the shareholder lawyer that the settlement serves the best interests of all concerned. Faced with a united phalanx announcing a truce, it takes a brave judge to insist that the two sides go back to slugging it out.

In practice many judges, like many corporate defendants in these suits, reluctantly approve settlements that they privately suspect are sheer and utter shakedowns. As we saw in Chapter 3, the one figure judges can readily watch in the absence of an adversary challenge is the ratio of the fee to the total recovery for the class. So settlement negotiations often drift, consciously or not, toward a range that allows the desired fee request to seem not that far out of line—perhaps 25, 30 or 35 percent, depending on how generous a court the lawyers have found in their shopping.

Some courts also allow the defendants to make later, private side payments to the lawyers. And in a twist that can really make the system work for the clever lawyer, some courts have ceased to demand that the settlement be a literal monetary multiple of the fee, instead counting toward its size what Professor Coffee calls "corporate therapeutics." These are promises to revamp the target company's procedures or hierarchy, sometimes in not-very-onerous ways that might have been considered anyway, but that both sides can argue with a straight face are really worth a fortune to shareholders.

A suit against General Tire brought as its only apparent tangible benefit the company's promise to appoint two independent directors to its RKO subsidiary; stockholders got no money, but the plaintiffs' lawyers waltzed off with half a million dollars, approved by the Sixth Circuit Court of Appeals over a strong dissent. Lawyers got more than $200,000 in fees from Coastal States Gas for inducing it to revise various procedures and disclosure policies; again no cash went to shareholders. A suit against Texaco brought $700,000 in fees for another form of "nonpecuniary" relief. It was found that at least a third of settlements in the Jones survey were of this flexible kind.

Of course, sometimes the corporate defendants in these suits are genuinely sincere about being glad to settle, because they think they really might lose at trial. But that is hardly a reason to feel more comfortable about these suits; indeed, it is a reason to feel more nervous. If the suit is dismissed "with prejudice"—meaning it cannot be filed again—the defendants may be getting off very cheaply for an act of real malfeasance.

The rise of the vision of litigation as a way of doing good coincided with a decline in the suspicion with which it was viewed as a way of doing bad. Many in the law schools and some on the bench came to dismiss concerns about meritless litigation as mere professional "folklore." Two leading commentators on corporate law, for example, have called the securities "strike suit" filed for nuisance value "an over the hill dragon, puffed up to keep the courts from dealing with substantive issues." The prospect of trial, it is constantly asserted or at least assumed, is enough to winnow the chaff. When West Virginia's Supreme Court decided to let spouses sue each other on injury claims—a development that many insurance defense lawyers see as a virtual Valentine's Day invitation to fraud and collusion—it confidently pronounced that "it is a rare occasion when the false or collusive claim escapes [the defense's] searching examination. We do an injustice not only to the intelligence of jurors, but to the efficacy of the adversary system, when we express undue concern over the quantum of collusive or meritless lawsuits." Only "upon the anvil of litigation," it said, working itself up to a fine rhetorical pitch, is "the merit of the case . . . finally determined. Forged in the heat of trial, few but the meritorious survive."

This confidence was to be sorely tested. Every step toward unleashing America's litigators worsened the dangers. The spread of contingency fees immeasurably sharpened the incentive for lawyers to participate in abuse. Solicitation allowed lawyers who had figured out how to fiddle one part of the system to reach the right sorts of clients to do so again and again. Wider use of class actions and similar devices meant more lawyers were operating without clients who talked back.

The ease of getting past pleadings and to trial multiplied the chances to impose costs on an opponent by way of a flimsy case. (When Judge Charles Clark in dissent voted to give Cole Porter a summary judgment in the plagiarism suit against him, he wrote that forcing a trial on the charge "seems to me an invitation to the strike suit *par excellence*.") Long-arm jurisdiction and especially the unlimited use of discovery and experts tremendously raised the ante of cost imposition. Resisting suits, never a cheap matter, got much more expensive. Laurence Bodine of the trial lawyers' newsletter *Lawyers' Alert* says it costs between $500,000 and $2 million to defend a "big" injury case involving burns, paralysis, or major birth defects. Not-so-big cases still cost plenty. Rand Corporation studies found that the average cost of defending a California wrongful-firing suit had topped $80,000 in the early 1980s and was rising at around 20 percent a year. In 1985 veteran Kansas City defense lawyer William Sanders reportedly estimated that for a purely innocent defendant it was worth $75,000, or around $90,000 in 1990 dollars, to get out of a medical malpractice or product liability case.

′ No one at ground level actually believes that defendants stalwartly resist all meritless claims or that the filers of those claims then give up and withdraw all of them. Study after study confirms that after initial bluster about refusing to pay nuisance value defendants proceed to do just that rather than sink a small fortune into making their point. Some trial lawyers have cheekily turned around and argued that defendants have no one but themselves to blame for failing to resist being taken to the cleaners on probably-false claims. The rhetorical ploy is, of course, wholly disingenuous. No one would be more upset than plaintiffs' lawyers if defendants started stonewalling all of what they thought were bad claims and the system ground (as it quickly would) to a litigation-choked halt. Anyway, some random if small percentage of the stonewalled suits would inevitably emerge from courtroom guesswork in plaintiffs' verdicts and lawyers would then demand the most scarifying sorts of punitive and bad-faith damages to chastise the stonewallers for their unreasonable resistance.

When a defendant or group of defendants does adopt a policy of stonewalling claims it considers bad, it tends to be recognized as exceptional. One medium-sized business that adopted this policy, the Standard Brands Paint Company, was considered unusual enough to rate a *Wall Street Journal* news profile. The company, which runs a chain of paint stores, says it refuses to make settlement offers on the sixty or seventy suits it considers meritless that are pending against it at a given time. An executive with another retail chain called the company's policy "gutsy" but isn't recommending that his own firm adopt it: "In the short term, it's a more expensive route to take."

This of course is just the point. Even if the food company suspects that the customer put the dead mouse in the ketchup bottle himself, it's worth sending him a few hundred dollars lest he call the newspapers. Collectively, the policy may encourage false claims; but the individual company is all too likely to calculate that at least this guy will go elsewhere with his next complaint.

It is a maxim of all practicing lawyers, anyway, that there are no sure things at trial. To the irreducible uncertainty of jury behavior, a given of the system, has been added vast and unnecessary uncertainty over wild-card experts and wheel-of-fortune damage theories. Believing strongly that a suit is unfounded does not mean believing that a ruinous split-the-difference verdict between the two sides' positions can always be averted.

Many defendants that settle what they consider nuisance claims are reluctant to talk about the experience, whether from embarrassment or simply because they do not want to encourage more of the same. The litigation arising from the Dupont Plaza hotel arson case in Puerto Rico, however, brought rare expressions of indignation. Lawyers for the fire victims did not of course sue the disgruntled unionists who had actually *set* the fire, their pockets not being very deep. Instead they went after the hotel itself, the target as opposed to the perpetrator of the attack, along with many related individuals and business entities, for not having built the structure so as to resist deliberate torching. They also—here is where long-arm jurisdiction came in handy—sued scores and scores of companies that manufactured or distributed anything flammable among the hotel furnishings: wallpaper, paint, floor wax, carpeting, bar stools, even the dice used in the casino, along with the makers of component parts.

The miscellaneous defendants bought their way out of the suit at rates from $250,000 to $500,000 on up. They began settling with special alacrity after the presiding judge ruled that defendants large and small had to contribute equal shares to "joint defense activities"—which meant the dice makers and the rest were suddenly looking at hundreds of thousands of dollars of legal expense, quite apart from hiring their own lawyers and paying some share of any resulting verdict if the flammability theories convinced a jury. "We settled principally because of the absolutely astronomical defense costs that were imposed because of the joint defense activities," said a lawyer for Nevamar Corporation, which reportedly settled for $400,000. Nevamar supplied laminates used in the hotel's dressers.

In unguarded moments even some plaintiffs' lawyers will make it clear what is going on. One reason contaminated land sites are such money mines for litigators is that courts have shown themselves willing to subject just about anyone remotely connected to such a site to protracted litigation. The state of California ponied up $300,000 to be let out of a typical toxic-site case, even though in the view of many there was no real case against it. In a 1987 speech, Jeffrey Matz, a lawyer with the plaintiff's firm in that case, told fellow litigators some of the secrets of his firm's success. It is "imperative," he advised, "to consider a wide range of possible defendants." His firm had named realtors and lenders as well as the city and state governments. The advantages of taking "a broad stroke approach to the selection of defendants," he said, include an "enhanced potential for settlement":

> [I]t is this writer's experience that even those defendants whose liability is somewhat remote will contribute sums to a settlement which are significant. . . . Many of the peripheral defendants can be settled with at an early stage and for relatively substantial sums (at least enough money for the purpose of financing the case) when they realize the massive effort and expense that will be required to defend themselves in the course of the litigation. A sum on the order of $300,000.00 to $500,000.00 may very well represent nothing more than defense costs when evaluated over the full effort and the full five-year period.

The spread of entrepreneurial litigation in the intellectual-property field has brought with it a wave of complaints of "patent blackmail." The Refac Technology Development Corporation buys up and litigates to the hilt what are mostly seen as marginal or low-value patents, according to a revealing report by *New York Times* technology correspondent Edmund Andrews. Refac claims to hold "basic" patents underlying such everyday technologies as liquid crystal displays, automatic bank teller machines, videocassette recorders, bar-code scanning and credit-card verification systems, and spreadsheet software. As of early 1990 it had filed infringement suits against two thousand companies and threatened to sue a thousand more. In some cases judges have thrown out its cases as frivolous with strong comments, but not before the company has in the meantime extracted royalty settlements from other defendants. Enough targets have come across with royalties that Refac's revenues have surged from $3.2 million in 1985 to $10.5 million in the first nine months of 1989, with its reported after-tax profit margins standing at a voluptuous 25 percent.

Most patent holders who plan to go into business selling their designs do not take advantage of their right under current law to sue retailers who sell allegedly infringing products, probably because they do not wish to alienate potential distributors of their own products. Refac, because of its specialty in suing instead of manufacturing, has targeted retail defendants heavily, suing Sears, Macy's, J. C. Penney, and many smaller chains. As usual the migration of claims to a litigation machine removes the inhibitions that might arise from expectations of good will and mutual benefit.

Times reporter Andrews found that Refac's lead litigator had gone on record with his approach to patent law in an obscure industry journal read by many of those he sued (but not, of course, by many in the general public). Making due allowance for a lawyer's possible tactical interest in scaring his opponents, the comments were still exceptionally illuminating. "It only makes sense," wrote the litigator, Philip Sperber, "to view the cost of litigation as bargaining leverage to force a settlement on terms favorable to the party that can litigate the matter to death without worrying about the cash flow." On the importance of insisting on jury trials rather than arbitration:

> If patent validity or infringement is questionable, why take a chance with an arbitration expert who will know exactly how weak the patent is and how dubious infringement is? It makes sense to take one's chances with a judge inexperienced in the technical and legal aspects involved. If the infringer is much bigger than the patentee or an entire industry has copied the patent, a jury trial would be much more beneficial than arbitration because of the sympathy and deep-pocket doctrine that can be played to the hilt.

Refac's president, Eugene Lang, like some other entrepreneurs of litigation, has made a name for himself with splashy philanthropic ventures, a step that has helped to deflect public criticism in advance (and can't hurt in the jury box either). Still, his firm is unusually controversial in the business community: reporter Andrews found many opponents willing to name names. "I believe this has been a scheme from day one, a concerted plan to extort money through the abuse of the legal system," declared Surjit P. Soni, who got a Refac suit thrown out on behalf of electronics importers. "They are trying to live off industry by using fear and intimidation," said Radio Shack president Bernard Appel. "It's a disgrace of the legal system."

In areas of the law where absolutely anyone can sue, of course, litigators need not go to the trouble of buying up complaints. Challenges to radio and TV licenses are an example. Under a 1966 federal court ruling, anyone at all can file a "citizen complaint" against the renewal or transfer of a station owner's broadcast license. Costs are as lopsided as can be wished: a complaint copied out from a form book or from earlier legal filings can trigger a full-dress hearing, and although station owners hardly ever lose their licenses in such hearings they are put to enormous expense, none of which is shouldered by the objector no matter how ill-founded the complaint turns out to be. The inevitable happened: people arrived on the scene to file complaints and withdraw them for money. One outfit set up to do license objections on a regular basis was last reported to be raking in settlements of as much as $250,000 from station owners around the country in exchange for dropping or not filing its challenges. The Federal Communications Commission has lately been trying to curb the abuses, but with what success is not yet clear: the commission has no direct power over the "citizen" objectors, and as with shareholder suits part of the art is getting the target to go quietly.

Even as more and more areas of legal endeavor have come to resemble the shareholder lawsuit, the shareholder lawsuit itself has been pushed to new heights of creativity, as the Ford Motor Company had occasion to learn in 1978. In that year Ford was going through a bout of bad publicity on various matters. Then came a new jolt: the celebrity lawyer Roy Cohn filed a lawsuit alleging that Henry Ford II and other executives had looted the giant company. The suit, on behalf of aggrieved shareholders who also happened to be children of Cohn's law partner, alleged that Mr. Ford had accepted a $750,000 bribe from a food concessionaire. Waving documents in his hand, Cohn told a reporter that he had "an open and shut case."

   The scandalous charges against the head of one of the world's largest companies made instant headlines. Then a surprise: the suit was thrown out; it had been filed in the wrong court. At which point Cohn quietly approached Ford to ask if it wanted to talk settlement, threatening to sue again in the right court and promising a fusillade of new publicity when he did.

   Ford went along and gave Cohn $100,000 in what were called legal fees provided he would go away and sue it no more. Cohn proceeded to declare that "it now appears" that Mr. Ford had not after all engaged in any wrongdoing. Hughes, Hubbard and Reed senior partner Jerome Shapiro, who cut the deal for Ford, said the company vigorously denied that there was any substance to the charges. "We were buying off Roy Cohn. It's Cohn we're interested in, and what he said he could do to us in the press. . . . He can get a headline in *The Wall Street Journal* or the *New York Times* by picking up a phone. . . . These papers printed uncritical, big headline accounts of Cohn's charges."

Steven Brill of *The American Lawyer* summed up the outcome: "The lawyer's supposed clients—the shareholders— get nothing. Nor do they give up anything: the shareholders can sue again on the same charges. It's just that the headline-making lawyer can't represent them." There was one new fillip: "Contrary to what would be required in any other shareholders' suit, a judge does not have to approve this settlement. With the first suit thrown out and the second one only threatened, there is no suit pending, and, therefore, no judge with jurisdiction." Brill added mildly: "In many circles this would be called extortion."

The most unusual feature of this lurid tale is that Cohn— widely seen even by his fellow hardball litigators as a one-man ethical disaster area—didn't get away with it. At the behest of a third party, a federal judge in New York eventually ordered his and another law firm to return $230,000 they had obtained between them. But the wider questions refused to go away. It was nice to think that as litigators grew rich some sort of wider ideal of justice was also being incidentally advanced in the process. And indeed the defenders of the invisible-fist theory were committed to this just-because-the-slaughterhouse-is-sickening-doesn't-mean-the-product-isn't-wholesome line. Whatever the failings of individual litigators, they felt, litigation itself was productive and beneficial. Maybe the new impresarios of litigation did not make ideal candidates for the Supreme Court, but because of them paper companies would sure think twice about trying to fix prices.

Of course, sometimes—as in the two Philadelphia suits—the court outcomes diverged so oddly from each other that it was hard to believe an injustice had not been done in either the one or the other case. If the evidence was flatly insufficient to condemn the paper companies of wrongdoing, as the one court found, what did it mean that they had paid $50 million to get out from under the larger suit? These rather embarrassing questions led to what might be called the fallback don't-worry-be-happy position. Yes, any single trial verdict you might examine might be a fluke or a plain injustice. But what really counted was that most cases were settled out of court. This vast system of negotiated plea bargaining not only saved huge amounts of money, compared with holding all those trials, but was also in some ultimate sense more rational because it smoothed out the averages. One jury might award five million dollars against the vaccination program for the alleged side effect and the next ten juries might award zero, but experienced lawyers would tend to converge on a settlement value of a few hundred thousand per case. And that value (it seemed, when you didn't think about it very hard) was not a bad stand-in for the severity of the underlying misconduct, if misconduct was the right word. Maybe the system as a whole was more sensible than the sum of its case-by-case parts.

An unnerving thing for this Candide's-last-stand theory is that settlement values seem to depend so much on factors that have nothing to do with guilt or innocence. The charged act of medical malpractice can't really be three times as severe just because it occurs in the Bronx rather than across the river in Queens or New Jersey. (A study funded by the American Bar Foundation of early 1980s cases found that Bronx medical malpractice cases had a success rate nearly three times those filed in Denver, at 56 percent versus 21 percent, and that median awards were more than eight times as high, at $602,000 versus $70,000.) A case's inherent merit can't depend heavily, as its settlement value does, on which lawyer files the suit, which judge it is assigned to, or whether the doctor carries a lot of insurance, or is from out of town. Intrinsic underlying validity is certainly one possible ingredient in a case's settlement value, just as milk is one possible ingredient in a fast-food "shake." But the uneasy feeling persisted that other ingredients might dominate by weight.

If meritless cases have positive settlement value, it will be up to lawyers to prevent injustice by keeping them from being filed. It used to be hoped that a lawyer would look at a prospective claim as a judge might look, and not just ask if it had raw settlement value. And yet every step toward the modern law tended to deflect and postpone this hard look. The acceptance of guesswork up and down the line meant that only the most glaring indicia of meritlessness had to be considered fatal to a claim. The spirit of the procedural changes was one of sidestepping consideration of the merits for as long as possible. Notice pleading was meant to get people into court based on a hunch that they had been wronged, an inability to rule out misconduct by the chosen defendants, a Micawber-like hope that something would turn up in discovery. Nothing could have been better calculated to bring up litigation from the debatable zone between definite merit and definite meritlessness, from the murky underworld of half-seriousness and demi-plausibility.

And if lawyers do not give hard thought to whether positions are justified or not, clients usually will not either. Into the law office walks the worker fired for flunking a drug test, the parent whose child was bounced from the amusement park for pulling a knife, the car buyer who regrets having bought such an expensive new model and wishes to return it. They are perhaps unsure whether their position has legal pith. The lawyer can do ten minutes of research and treat them to a boring dissertation on how judicial doctrine as it currently stands in their state affords them no relief. Or he can lean back and observe, innocently, that many persons in just the same situation as theirs have won concessions or cash compensation; shall he ask for it? He need not raise as a question, and it may not occur to the client to ask, whether such concessions were forthcoming in acknowledgment of legal merit or from the imposition value of litigation.

Once a case gets to court, the rules conspired again to encourage lawyers to leave for the jury the question of whether it had merit. Instead of a duty not to accuse someone without a firm basis, litigators were given at most a duty to withdraw their accusations if the evolving evidence established beyond dispute that no basis would ever be found. (And even if the first ten expert witnesses turned down the case, who was to say the right one wouldn't come along?) Slender though it was, this duty to withdraw a suit found to be baseless was far from easy to enforce. Even if the discovery dredge yields no plausible pistol from the riverbed, a lawyer can be tempted to put off withdrawing the suit day after day in hopes a settlement offer will come in. And even if the facts can't be fit into any accepted legal theory to justify keeping a suit going, they can always be fit into some unaccepted or newly invented theory. So long as a lawyer can muster a degree of sincerity about it, pushing one of these novel theories against a chagrined opponent can be held up for applause as a public-spirited reform campaign (are you against change and growth in the law, or what?) instead of a venture in harassment or greed.

And so the idea grew up that one of the rights of a litigator was the right to try, to push a position at each stage of a lawsuit while stifling any inward doubts or pangs of conscience about it. Indeed, new-style legal ethicists were on hand to explain that pushing at all doors was an ethical obligation and not just a right. Clients were entitled to every profitable step a lawyer could take on their behalf. The increasing pressure of litigation as a competitive business presses in the same scruple-smothering direction.

The invisible-fist theory provides a key ethical bridge toward such a style of practice by resting the moral basis of lawyering on presumed group interests and general deterrence rather than on achieving particularized justice between a pair of litigants. Even a suit that probably will lose can be said to deter misconduct and focus useful social scrutiny on doctors, corporate managements, or whomever. And if a claim or add-on happens not to have a factual basis, so what? This opponent or another very similar one has gotten away scot-free on other occasions and has a large overdue account to pay to the class of which this plaintiff is a member.

The lawyer who fights an endless series of battles against one basic opponent, losing a number of rounds unfairly along the way, convinced that bloodsucking creditors/goof-off dead-beats/grasping bosses/gold-digging workers are getting away with murder, can find it all the easier to reach for and savor an undeserved victory on the grounds that the whole adverse class had it coming. A Harvard study of medical malpractice in New York found that in the overwhelming majority of cases where suits were filed the doctor had *not* been negligent. But trial lawyers nonetheless trumpeted the study as a great vin-dication for them because it also found that in the over-whelming majority of cases where doctors had been negligent they got off without being sued at all. "When I was a young lawyer," as the old line runs, "I used to lose a lot of cases I should have won. Now that I'm an old lawyer, I win a lot of cases I should have lost. So, you see, there is justice in the system *as a whole*."

13

⚖

NAKED TO MINE ENEMIES

This man should be left naked, homeless and without wheels.

> —*Securities and Exchange Commission Chairman Richard Breeden to his staff, on a respected Minneapolis lawyer charged with trading stock on inside information*

In 1975 a troubled young woman tried to commit suicide by jumping off the roof of her Chicago apartment building. She survived but was hideously injured. Under the tutelage of a flamboyant trial lawyer, she proceeded to sue her former psychiatrist, Dr. Sara Charles, claiming that had she been put under more aggressive therapy she might never have tried to kill herself.

"My first feelings after being charged with medical malpractice were of being utterly alone," Dr. Charles wrote. "Suddenly I felt isolated from my colleagues and patients." Later she learned that "almost every physician accused of being negligent has a similar reaction."

For the four years that the case dragged on, "it swallowed up my own life completely, demanded constant attention and study, multiplied tension and strain, generated a pattern of broken sleep and anxiety" by its challenge to "my integrity as a person and as a physician." These, too, she found after surveying colleagues, "are the common reactions of most doctors accused of negligence."

Especially troubling was the unveiling of the opposition's planned expert testimony. One hired expert had testified in hundreds of cases before; he interviewed the wheelchair-bound young woman for an hour, reviewed her records, and then opined that it had been a mistake not to have ordered her drugged and hospitalized at early signs of trouble. Aghast at the thought that her judgment might somehow have been wrong after all, Dr. Charles went back and plunged into the relevant professional literature in great detail, but after long reading concluded that it fully backed up what she had done and in no way supported the expert's view. That was comforting in one way, but in a different way terribly debilitating. The feeling began to set in that the truth itself had ceased to matter; the case had taken on a life of its own and would be decided on grounds other than the best opinion of her professional peers. She vowed to her husband: "If I am found guilty of malpractice over this, I will never practice medicine again."

Few steps on the road to civilization were as important as the gradual growth of the idea that accused persons have certain distinctive rights. A society cannot be secure from arbitrary power unless its members are secure from being charged with or convicted of wrongdoing in circumstances of error, unfairness, oppression, or prejudice. Thus the familiar protections of the Bill of Rights summed up in the phrase *the rights of the accused*.

The rights of the accused in criminal law begin with the accusation itself. Under the Fifth Amendment, the charging of a person with serious criminal offenses must be approved not only by a public prosecutor but also by a judge or grand jury. Under the Sixth Amendment criminal defendants must be told, promptly and in detail, of the nature of the charges against them: "In all criminal prosecutions, the accused shall enjoy the right . . . to be informed of the nature and cause of the accusation."

The privacy of criminal defendants is likewise protected. In particular, their papers may not be seized without an advance finding of probable cause and a particularity of request. "The right of the people to be secure in their persons, houses, papers, and effects, against unreasonable searches and seizures, shall not be violated," reads the Fourth Amendment, which goes on to specify that "no warrants shall issue, but upon probable cause, supported by oath or affirmation, and particularly describing the place to be searched, and the persons or things to be seized." As for the extraction of oral and written confessions, the Fifth Amendment guarantees criminal defendants the right to remain entirely silent at and before trial without adverse inference being taken: "nor shall [any person] be compelled in any criminal case to be a witness against himself."

Criminal defendants are protected by absolute (and highly simple) rules on which courts can try them, lest they be victimized by forum-shopping. "In all criminal prosecutions," the Sixth Amendment specifies, the accused shall enjoy the right to a trial by a jury of "the State and district wherein the crime shall have been committed; which district shall have been previously ascertained by law." If a defendant is outside that state when apprehended his distant accusers must set in motion the elaborate process of extradition, outlined in Article IV, Section 2 of the Constitution.

A crucial part of due process is clear advance guidance as to what is unlawful conduct and what is not. One of the oldest and most widely recognized principles of civil liberty is that criminal defendants can be punished only for offenses that have been clearly marked out beforehand as prohibited. As the Supreme Court noted in 1926, it violates the "first essential of due process of law" to forbid or require the doing of some act "in terms so vague that men of common intelligence must necessarily guess at its meaning and differ as to

274 • THE LITIGATION EXPLOSION

its application." "No one may be required at peril of life, liberty, or property to speculate as to the meaning of penal statutes," the Court explained in 1939. "All are entitled to be informed as to what the state commands or forbids."

Under the old established maxims, American courts were first supposed to read a vaguely worded criminal law as narrowly as they could, so as to penalize as little or permit as much activity by citizens as possible; if such narrowing did not dispose of the ambiguity, the only thing left was to throw the law out as unconstitutionally "void for vagueness." "It would certainly be dangerous," as an 1876 Court observed, "if the legislature could set a net large enough to catch all possible offenders, and leave it to the courts to step inside and say who could be rightfully detained, and who should be set at large."

A famous 1931 case shows how seriously these rules were taken. Congress had made it a federal crime knowingly to take across state lines a stolen automobile, motorcycle, truck, or "any other self-propelled vehicle not designed for running on rails." The defendant, McBoyle, had taken a stolen airplane. That form of conveyance was not mentioned in the law but (prosecutors argued) would not unreasonably be covered by the "any other self-propelled vehicle" language.

The Supreme Court threw out McBoyle's conviction. A law whose literal wording "calls up a picture of a thing moving on land," wrote the great Oliver Wendell Holmes, "should not be extended to aircraft simply because it may seem to us that a similar policy applies, or upon the speculation that, if the legislature had thought of it, very likely broader words would have been used." "Although it is not likely," Holmes noted, "that a criminal will carefully consider the text of the law before he murders or steals, it is reasonable that a fair warning should be given to the world in language that the common world will understand, of what the law intends to do if a certain line is passed. To make the warning fair, so far as possible the line should be clear."

Decisions like *McBoyle* show the most admirably objective, one might say the most majestic, face of the law—even though (or perhaps because) no one much likes their immediate result. (In this case, the defendant presumably had to be brought to justice under some less effective state law.) If the courts will not stretch their authority even to reach a plainly culpable character like McBoyle, they are not likely to stretch it to reach a citizen whose actions are more defensible.

When standards of punishable conduct are vague and shifting, some defendants will be punished retroactively for conduct that was not clearly unlawful at the time it was taken. Article I, Section 9 of the Constitution restrains a similar abuse by forbidding the passage of *ex post facto* laws or bills of attainder, which are essentially laws inflicting retroactive liability on specified persons.

The protections of civil liberty extend to the realm of evidence. A virtual fortress of formal evidentiary restrictions protect criminal defendants from being convicted in circumstances of guesswork or prejudice, by way of flimsy, second-hand evidence or evidence more potent in angering juries than in shedding light on the truth. The conservative *Frye* rule keeping marginal expert testimony out of court got its start in criminal law, for obvious reasons. Criminal defendants, of course, go free unless their guilt is proved beyond a reasonable doubt—the most dramatic possible rejection of speculation.

Guesswork is equally rejected in sentencing—in the determination of how high a price someone should pay for overstepping the line of propriety. The Eighth Amendment provides that "excessive fines" shall not be imposed, "nor cruel and unusual punishments inflicted." Arbitrary, pick-a-number punishments are antithetical to the principles of due process; they recall the cartoon where a judge, glancing up at a clock that reads 11:50, tells the defendant: "I sentence you to . . . oh, ten to twelve years." Wildly varying punishments for identical conduct are equally inconsistent with principles of fair play: it would be quite tyrannical to sentence the occasional first-time shoplifter to life in prison so as to keep all the others from treating their smallish penalties as a "cost of doing business."

Another part of due process is the right not to face prosecution under the law of an inappropriate state—not to get sent up for driving at seventy miles an hour or drinking at age nineteen while on visits to states or countries where such behavior is legal. Equally violative of the rule of law would be to export a more stringent penalty for an act that was criminal in both places, by, for example, executing someone for a crime that he had committed in a state without a death penalty. And so the Supreme Court enforces simple, rigid rules on choice of criminal law. It would certainly never listen to a prosecutor's argument that conflicts between state criminal laws should be resolved in favor of more guilt-finding and longer sentences by reference to an underlying "policy" of nailing as many defendants as possible.

Perhaps the most important safeguard of all is one of the least obvious, so ingrained in the system that it hardly seems a matter of deliberate choice. That is the placement of the function of prosecution in a single, unitary office, paid on flat salary, accountable to public control and sworn to high duty.

Prosecution is a fearsome power. Those who wield it are constantly approached by persons in government and private life who would like it deployed against their enemies. Many times the filing of charges does turn out to be justified. But life would quickly become intolerable if prosecutors started launching all colorable prosecutions that some vindictive or self-interested party wanted them to, relying on judges and juries downstream to avoid injustice. The principle of prosecutorial discretion is understood to operate in the direction of mercy and forbearance, as an essential abatement from the intolerable harshness of full prosecution on demand of every defendant who might conceivably be gone after.

A blameworthy refusal to exercise this discretion, an insistence on going after a defendant who is probably innocent or whose offense is merely technical, is generally accounted prosecutorial abuse. Fortunately, several safeguards work to curb this abuse. First and most obvious, the function is kept under public control, prosecutors being either elected directly or appointed by elected officials. The tenure of a prosecutor who embarks on a career of abuse can thus be brought to a speedy halt. Second, the function is unitary or close to it. If dozens of D.A.'s in a town roamed freely with no coordination among them, prosecutorial discretion would soon be close to a dead letter; nineteen prosecutors might be too scrupulous or merciful to go after a particular defendant, but the vindictive complainant would need to convince only a twentieth. Finally, and most fundamental of all, prosecutors are kept fiscally independent of the results of their efforts. Sometimes ambition for higher office spurs them to a binge of scalp-taking, but at least they are not paid per scalp.

The office of the flat-salaried, publicly accountable, unitary prosecutor is thus a familiar part of the American scene. Courts have repeatedly struck down arrangements that threatened to evade these safeguards by entrusting prosecutorial powers to self-seeking private parties.

In 1985 the California Supreme Court came down hard on the ultimate subversion of prosecutorial independence: contingent pay. The town of Corona, east of Los Angeles, was trying to close two pornographic bookstores. It enacted into law a civil nuisance ordinance aimed at the bookstores drafted by James Clancy, a private lawyer associated with a group called Citizens for Decency through Law. It then retained Clancy to bring civil abatement proceedings under the ordinance, his fee to vary from thirty dollars an hour if he was unsuccessful at closing the stores to sixty dollars if he succeeded. The California high court struck down his appointment. It singled out the contingency arrangement for reproach as "antithetical to the standard of neutrality" required of a lawyer purporting to represent the interests of the public at large, even in a civil case as this was.

Two years later a not dissimilar case reached the U.S.

Supreme Court. The handbag-making enterprises of the Klaymine family had allegedly violated a court order prohibiting them from infringing the copyrights of the Louis Vuitton luxury goods company. A federal court had then appointed a lawyer from the Vuitton company to prosecute the Klaymines for contempt of court. The Supreme Court struck down the appointment as improper. "Even if a defendant is ultimately acquitted, forced immersion in criminal investigation and adjudication is a wrenching disruption of everyday life," noted the opinion of Justice Brennan. "For this reason, we must have assurance that those who would wield this power will be guided solely by their sense of public responsibility for the interests of justice." Allowing a lawyer both to demand punishment and to represent a private party that benefited from the imposition of punishment would be improper, ruled a plurality of justices, because "such an attorney is required by the very standards of the profession to serve two masters." Justices Powell, Rehnquist, and O'Connor agreed that appointment of interested parties as prosecutors posed a "significant" danger to justice but wanted to order the gathering of more information about the case at hand. Justice Scalia found the appointment unconstitutional on separate grounds that did not reach the issue of who could be appointed. Only Justice White saw no constitutional problem with the appointment, and even he said he would "prefer" that it not have been made.

In short, in criminal law, where we care about individual rights, we make sure people are not lightly accused, tried, or convicted, most especially at the behest of self-interested private parties. But of course civil litigation and criminal prosecution are different things. Lawyers are nowadays trained in the idea that the two are completely unrelated; some seem to find it dizzy-making even to mention them in the same sentence. The two bodies of law, we are meant to think, are run from wholly separate lobes of the legal mind whose once-connecting synapses have been severed beyond all relinking.

Criminal defendants are accused of misdeeds against society, but civil defendants are just accused of owing money or some other obligation to some complainant. And so while criminal defendants deserve ironclad due process rights, civil defendants deserve no rights at all.

No one would deny that there are important differences between the two halves of the law. Criminal law can drag people through nightmarish and expensive legal process, stigmatize them as terrible wrongdoers, take away everything they have, and send them to jail. Civil law can drag people through nightmarish and expensive legal process, stigmatize them as terrible wrongdoers, and take away everything they have, but (so long as they avoid contempt of court) it will not send them to jail. It will leave them on the street, and they will have to find their own place to stay.

Perhaps in view of this supposed mildness of sanction, defendants in civil law used to get due process protections that although recognizably similar to those of the criminal law were more modest in scope. Civil pleadings were a less solemn cousin of arraignments; civil law afforded many privacy protections, but fewer than criminal law; and so on down the line. To take another example, the principle of *res judicata* gave some protection against being hit with repeated lawsuits over the same grievance, but not as much protection as the principle of double jeopardy gave against being hit with repeated criminal indictments over the same misconduct.

The makers of the modern American law, as we have seen, relentlessly stripped away the due process rights and safeguards that had once protected the targets of civil litigation. One might have expected therefore that they would have pared back the role of blame-finding and punishment in civil lawsuits, so as to make its sanctions milder and less threatening, lest the place to which people were being railroaded be a bad place.

There were some grounds for thinking this might happen. Many legal scholars of the early twentieth century took the view that the real point of civil litigation was not to punish anyone for past wrongdoing but to adjust disputed rights rationally for the future. One of the implications of this theory should have been the gradual disappearance of what are known as punitive damages, damages meant to set an example of the loser as opposed to compensating the winner.

Punitive damages were seen as a peculiar holdover from the law's moralistic past. They cropped up most often in suits over assaults, false imprisonments, and other outrages where hurting someone had been the whole idea of the misconduct. Seldom were they awarded in cases of negligence, even where it had been gross; most drunk drivers, for example, apparently did not face them in civil suits. Their amounts were small by the standards of an earlier day, and infinitesimal by our own. They had never been common in Britain or Canada, and are virtually unknown in the Continental civil law tradition.

Where allowed at all, punitive damages were sharply limited. They could be levied in some of the "tort" injury cases that mostly arose from unchosen interactions, on the road or elsewhere, but not in contractual settings where a mishap had occurred in the course of voluntary undertakings, or in family law. (The same restrictions applied to damages for emotional distress and related ills.) The distinction made some sense. Terror of legal liability makes people shy away from contact with each other, which may be just what we want between strangers on the road but is quite counterproductive in business, employment, or family settings.

Punitive damages were plainly on the decline. Several American states had abolished them entirely or in large measure, preferring to leave the mission of punishment to the criminal law, with its long-grown safeguards, and the omission did not raise any special stir in legal circles. Not improbably this vestigial tailbone of the civil law would soon vanish for good.

There was just one problem. The last thing the emergent sue-for-profit industry wanted to do was get rid of the element of accusation and blame in the lawsuits it pressed. A sedate jury, a jury teetering on the verge of boredom, is a jury that hands in tepid awards that produce measly contingencies. The way to make money is to get jurors truly furious, to turn the dryest and most technical commercial dispute into an arm-waving indignation contest.

As the burgeoning litigation business began feeling its accusatory oats, it was observed that punitive damages were not wasting away as predicted but were in fact showing signs of great vigor. Various changes in courtroom rules were helping out. Edward Imwinkelreid of the University of California at Davis observes that "dramatic changes" in evidence law have lately made it far easier to introduce evidence into civil litigation of a defendant's other crimes and torts—a prime example of the sort of evidence that the law has always handled gingerly because of its explosive potential for prejudice, and against which there are strong rules on the criminal side. Some courts in civil cases have even let in evidence of uncharged misconduct that has been alleged but by no means proved.

One of the great advantages of a punitive-damage demand is that it allows a lawyer to introduce evidence of his opponent's income and wealth, a type of evidence that is otherwise largely excluded because of its obvious prejudicial danger and its low usual level of relevance to the question of whether someone has misbehaved. Without access to such data, it is argued, a jury could not figure out how big a punitive fine it should impose to carry the proper sting. Lawyers discovered early on that throwing in a punitive claim against a deep-pocket opponent, even when there was no real hope of making it stick, could magically improve their client's chances on the seemingly unrelated issues of whether compensatory damages were owing and how much if so.

Courts also began letting punitive damages into contract litigation. For a while the favorite method of doing so was to declare that a seemingly contractual situation was in reality, if peered at through the proper lens, a case of tort. In the Dold family's lawsuit, mentioned in a previous chapter, the Hawaiian courts found that by overbooking its rooms in a "wanton and reckless" manner the hotel had departed the realm of contract law and exposed itself to tort liability. As time went on courts shunted more and more buyer/seller, worker/employer, and landlord/tenant relations into the tort category. The California courts invented a whole series of new torts with names like "bad-faith denial of the existence of a contract." Then courts began awarding punitive damages directly in contract cases, ending the little games. Other courts were finding ways to move the myriad physical and psychological interactions of husband and wife or parent and child into the realm of civil punishment.

Punitive damages can be a more than attractive reason to sue on cases where actual compensatory damages would be quite low or perhaps nil. A 1985 case against Union Oil of California over an implied covenant in an oil and gas lease resulted in $22,807 of compensatory damages and $3 million in punitives, reduced to $2 million after two rounds of appeals. Merrill Lynch was ordered to pay punitive damages on charges that it had overtraded a widow's account to churn up commissions even though the account had risen by a more than satisfactory 50 percent over the two-and-a-half-year period in question.

It will surprise no one that punitive damages have become a way for plaintiffs who are themselves quite affluent to add to their cash holdings. The enormous GTE Corporation won a $100 million jury verdict from the much smaller Home Shopping Network, later settled for a mere $4.5 million, for the personal-sounding tort of defamation, after Home Shopping claimed that GTE had sold it an inadequate phone system. Actor Timothy Hutton was awarded $7.5 million in punitive damages on top of $2.2 million in compensation after M-G-M backed out of an agreement to make a movie with him. (The studio settled the case for an undisclosed sum.) Pennzoil got its $11 billion award from Texaco, including $3 billion in punitive damages, on a theory of tortious interference with a contract.

For trial lawyers, punitives have an incomparable practical advantage. More even than emotional-distress damages, they lack any objective referent or yardstick: they are essentially the inscrutable emissions of mysterious black boxes of punishment. Juries can be invited to pick a number between zero and infinity, and at least a few very large numbers are likely to result from time to time. (In effect punitives can be said to measure the emotional distress of the jury itself, a body that does not even go on the record with a vivid description of its mental state.) Rand Corporation researchers found that average punitive damages in Cook County, Illinois, in the early 1980s ran at $1.9 million.

In addition, since juries are told about past awards by way of trying to afford them some yardstick, new record verdicts tend to have a bootstrap effect on future awards. By 1989 around ten percent of California jury verdicts led to punitive awards, and the average award stood at a whopping $3 million plus, up 178 percent in only two years. Lawyer Theodore Olson of Gibson, Dunn & Crutcher found that the California record on punitive damages upheld on appeal rose from $10,000 in the period between 1922 and 1959 to $250,000 in the 1960s, $740,000 in the 1970s and $3 million in 1986. In 1988 two awards of $14 million and $15 million were upheld, both in economic claims over contracts. Over six times as much was awarded in Cook County punitive verdicts between 1980 and 1984 as was awarded in the previous twenty years combined.

Business defendants have repeatedly been tagged with punitive damages for actions that had been specifically contemplated and approved by government regulators. That is what has happened in a string of vaccine and contraceptive side-effect cases, some but not all of which have been overturned on appeal. Juries have likewise hit drug companies with punitive damages in cases where federal agencies and the scientific consensus in general flatly denied that a compound caused a claimed side effect at all.

Punitive damages are now routinely awarded in cases that experienced lawyers had expected not to lead to liability of any kind—amounting in all but name to *ex post facto* punishment. "Too many criminals are on the street," said a juror in a landmark "lender liability" suit against Bank of America where the finding of liability itself astonished banking lawyers. "They get off too easy . . . so I saw to it that the bank didn't get off." Plaintiff's lawyers in the ComputerLand promissory note case recounted in Chapter 3 had portrayed the defendant "as a rich, cutthroat businessman," according to a member of the jury that awarded $115 million in punitive damages. So in "the damages, we wanted to make it hurt him."

The partisans of the invisible-fist theory, as usual, had rationalizations for what was going on. They thought punitives might help solve an intractable phenomenon. The consensus through many ages has always been that only a tiny fraction of all potential lawsuits and claims actually get pressed. Even in our own age of litigation, where a hundred policies combine to encourage legal resort, most civil wrongs are still not corrected in any visible or formal way. If civil law is truly supposed to achieve "general deterrence" of unwanted conduct—that is to say, if it is to consist of criminal law carried on by other means—this lack of litigation is baffling and even sinister. Something must be hamstringing the prosecution; wrongdoers must be paying less than what theorists have assured each other is the full cost of their mischief.

There were a couple of unexamined leaps of logic here in this assumption of pervasive underenforcement of legal norms. For one thing, it is hard to disentangle the give from the take in many of the complex relationships that lead to actual lawsuits, to tell, for example, what benefits A may have been obtaining in exchange for tolerating B's periodic breaches in dealings stretching over years before the relationship curdled. For another thing, the really flagrant sorts of rule-breaking tend to backfire on rule-breakers in ways aside from their being sued. But the invisible-fist partisans saw underdeterrence as a dreadful problem and punitive damages as part of the answer. The prospect of such damages encouraged more complainants to go to court and frightened defendants into better behavior. And they made up for all the times this defendant or another just like him had gotten away without being sued at all.

The enthusiasm for punitive measures, however, soon ran into a serious obstacle: judges. With some regularity judges tend to reduce or strike down punitive awards, often expressing their distaste for what they see as the lawless infliction of draconian punishments on the basis of guesswork. (In fact many of these awards amount to guesswork on stilts: the jury is invited to guess first whether this defendant actually harmed this plaintiff, and then guess how many other undetected misdeeds of the same sort have gone on.) News stories about high punitive awards were still very effective in panicking defendants into settling cases for large amounts. But the oft-set-aside awards themselves were not nearly a reliable enough source of income for the litigation industry.

Some more efficient juicing attachment was needed, with more automatic features. The idea was hit on of using multipliers. As so often, the earliest precedent here had come with the antitrust laws, which popularized the idea of triple as opposed to actual damages, along with one-way attorneys'- fee awards. Over the years several other laws picked up the triple-damage idea, usually with the explicit rationale of encouraging more litigation, an aim that always seemed to meet with success. Academics were soon coming up with mathematical proofs that if two of every three softball-playing kids went unapprehended after breaking windows, the way to ensure optimal safety was to make each kid who got caught pay as if he had broken three windows. Presumably if nine of ten went scot-free the multiple should be set that much higher. As with punitive damages, the logical conclusion again seemed to be that the less interest offended parties showed in enforcing a rule, the more hair-raising the penalties for overstepping that rule ought to be. But few people wanted to inquire overmuch as to where the logic led.

———

Meanwhile a powerfully converging trend was developing on the other side of the law's divided empire. The idea was gradually being accepted in civil law that undefined legal standards, due-process-less procedures and guesswork-ridden fact-finding methods were compatible not only with punishment, but with punishment of the utmost severity. Inevitably these ideas would seep into the criminal law itself.

The long-established Rule of Law protections for criminal defendants, in the form of the void-for-vagueness and narrow-construction-of-penal-statutes doctrines, began to erode. Perhaps the earliest major hole had been punched in them to authorize the sweeping criminalization of—what else?—antitrust violations. Way back in 1913 Justice Holmes himself okayed the conviction of a man for violating the Sherman Act, which had in deliberately opaque language declared unlawful "every contract, combination . . . or conspiracy in restraint of trade or commerce."

In a 1950 case the focus was on another unpopular kind of businessperson, the vendor of pornography. A near-replay of the *McBoyle* situation came up: a law had banned the shipment of obscene books, pamphlets, films, and so forth, words that call up the image of visual media; the defendant in the case at hand had shipped obscene phonograph records, not mentioned in the statute. This time the Court limbered up for the trifling stretch and upheld the man's conviction.

The Court's 1973 decisions on pornography, fully influenced by the new thinking, were widely seen as a new high- or low-water mark for vagueness in criminal law. A bookstore owner can be convicted, under the Court's formula, for selling a work that "taken as a whole, lacks serious literary, artistic, political or scientific value," so long as "the average person, applying contemporary community standards," would find that it appeals to prurient interest. The majority blithely allowed as how the reckoning of guilt would inevitably vary from one jury, defendant, and occasion to the next. A horrified Justice William Brennan declared in dissent that the Court was leaving obscenity law in the form of a hodgepodge that "even we cannot define with precision. . . . To send men to jail for violating standards they cannot understand, construe and apply is a monstrous thing to do in a nation dedicated to fair trials and due process."

But sending men to jail on exactly that basis was soon to emerge as a central prosecutorial strategy in the ever-widening crusade against "white-collar crime." Much was being made, for example, of the federal laws that ban mail and wire fraud, laws that have been called the "prosecutor's friend" because it is so easy to charge people with them. Their boundaries, always hazy at best, began to expand in scope case by case: by the 1980s they were impossible to know with any certainty. In the 1989 federal indictment of Chicago commodities traders, for example, the asserted mail fraud offense was to "defraud the investing public of its right to the honest functioning of the marketplace," which could mean just about anything. "They are criminalizing the Boy Scout oath," says Columbia professor Jack Coffee. "People should be brave, clean and reverent, but I don't think we can criminalize the failure to meet such a standard."

Likewise, federal law enforcers began to charge persons with varieties of "insider trading" that are mentioned nowhere in the underlying securities laws and that had previously been widely considered lawful. In the most scandalous case, they charged investment analyst Raymond Dirks with inside trading for uncovering and alerting his clients to the Equity Funding financial scandal, an action for which wide sectors of the financial community believed he deserved a presidential medal of honor rather than an indictment. (Dirks was vindicated, but only after a lengthy ordeal.) When defense lawyers pleaded with Congress to clarify the law by spelling out which sorts of trades and types of investment advice were forbidden and which allowed, the Securities and Exchange Commission staff actually opposed the idea.

Then came the crowning culmination of the punitive trends in civil and criminal law: RICO.

For many years the vague federal mail and wire fraud

laws had one saving grace: they could be invoked only by public prosecutors. Their use was therefore subject to the very important restraint of prosecutorial discretion, not to mention the myriad protections of criminal procedure. They could not be used in private lawsuits at all. Then in 1970 Congress passed the Racketeer Influenced and Corrupt Organizations Act. The criminal law half of RICO attaches severe new penalties to the commission of a loosely defined "pattern" of so-called predicate acts, themselves unlawful. Some predicate acts, such as arson and kidnapping, are of an unmistakably criminal nature, but mail, wire, and securities fraud are all included as well; the latter is almost as amorphous as the first two.

RICO's other half, "civil RICO," allows private litigants to file civil claims for damages arising from violations of RICO's terms. Successful claimants can obtain triple damages and attorneys' fees. The defendant need not have been the subject of any earlier conviction, indictment, or even prosecutorial attention: a case that would be laughed out of an actual D.A.'s office is perfectly ripe for civil RICO. Suddenly contingency-fee lawyers could file suits under the ultra-vague mail and wire fraud laws, and for fabulous triple-damage-plus-fees sums. Most states adopted similar "little RICO" laws.

As the name of its umbrella statute implies, RICO was sold to a credulous public on the idea that the emerging litigation industry was among the few groups powerful enough to take on and defeat organized crime. But in fact backstage congressional staffers cunningly drafted the law to open up an infinitely broader range of targets for that industry. According to an A.B.A. study, more than 90 percent of the targets of civil-RICO lawsuits have no connection whatsoever with organized crime. Nearly half of civil RICO suits rely solely on mail or wire fraud charges, and another third rely at least primarily on securities fraud charges. By now lawyers have deployed civil RICO in divorces, will contests, and landlord-tenant disputes; against abortion protesters and others demonstrating on the street for their political beliefs; and, of course, in countless straight money suits over commercial disagreements. Among the companies solemnly charged with "civil racketeering" in American courts are ABC, GM, Ford, Citibank, Morgan Stanley, Allstate, State Farm, the big accounting firms; the list could be extended for pages.

Many times RICO can be invoked by *both* sides in a routine business dispute or in other contexts absurdly removed from the sleep-with-the-fishes ambience of a word like *racketeering*. Pro-censorship groups used threats of civil RICO to harass Florida convenience stores into dropping sales of *Playboy*, whereupon the publisher of that magazine fired a RICO suit right back at them in Miami federal court.

With the twin weaponry of RICO and punitive damages, America's trial lawyers have set themselves up as "private attorneys general" of a uniquely privileged kind. They can charge opponents with shocking-sounding wrongdoing under the vague, shifting, and retroactive legal standards that typify life after the triumph of Legal Realism. They can build cases on a scaffolding of the merest guesswork and supposition, junk science, and prejudicial tidbits. They can compel defendants to testify against themselves and pull new charges out of a hat at the last minute. They can bring a long line of plaintiffs to court to challenge the same underlying acts of a defendant, and if ten juries find no guilt they can call on an eleventh. At the end of it all they can pocket for themselves and their clients fines of a magnitude with not much limit outside the indignant imagination. No voters or governors look over their shoulder to fire them for using threats of this process to extract money from a defendant who is too palpably innocent.

Is it any wonder so many ambitious persons want to become lawyers?

When asked why due process has been done away with in civil litigation, plaintiffs' lawyers wheel in their tracks and fall back on the idea that litigation is in no way accusatory, that it aims only to restore people to their rights and not to punish anyone. If a lawsuit were seen as a reckoning of guilt, accused persons might have distinctive rights; but it isn't, so they don't.

Law school writers have helped out with theories that explain why, in their view, error in one direction in a civil lawsuit is no more serious a matter than error in the other. The model is supposed to be the lawsuit asking that title be fixed to a confused land boundary, where neither landowner is necessarily pointing a finger at the other, but both need to know who owns what. On such a model (it is claimed) society has no special interest in keeping the one in possession if the other can muster even a feather's-breadth better showing of title; possession should be zero points of the law. Nor is there stigma involved in a switch, even where it might seem to be. The civil court hears the story of the brawl only so that it can decide whether Hatfield should continue to retain in his possession a certain property that rightfully belongs to McCoy, namely the sum of money that would compensate him for having been hit over the head with a beer bottle. No one is actually being accused of anything.

None of this makes the slightest sense to people who actually get sued. They know full well that they are being accused of something. Like Dr. Charles in the vow to her husband, they will slip into what lawyers will tell them are errors of terminology, such as by swearing they are not "guilty" in a civil suit when the more correct phrase is that they are not "liable." (Dr. Charles held on until trial and won a hands-down acquittal—or, as a lawyer would instantly say in correction, a verdict of no liability.)

Litigation is much talked about as if it were a sort of surrogate social insurance program, just to move money around to those who need it, without warning or apology. Nothing could be more fallacious. The underlying structure of a lawsuit as a showdown between two versions of the truth means that the court that wishes to take someone's money must also utter an assertion about their conduct. Sometimes (by no means always) the targets can write off the sky-high

insurance premiums and the residual monetary risks as a cost
of doing business. Money is, after all, just money. What can
never be made routine, short of a truly deadening cynicism,
is a sustained sniper fire of allegations that one has acted
wrongly, even monstrously, that one is personally responsible
for the misfortunes of others. Accusation hurts. A National
Institute of Medicine study found that the sheer experience
of being sued, "always disruptive and often agonizing," was
of at least as much concern to obstetricians as the financial
outlay, which was itself fairly staggering: many paid more
than a hundred thousand dollars a year in insurance. Even
suits that were won, the Institute found, could be "devastating."

The wonderful, calories-without-guilt feature of suing a
big organization is supposed to be that no one will take it
personally. Maybe so if the organization is brain dead, if no
one feels responsible for its performance. But if it is alive and
well run, someone or other—a scientist or sales rep, product
designer or claims handler, the CEO or the newest young
trainee—will feel ultimate responsibility for the particular
lapse that is charged. The trafficking is always in reputations
as well as more tangible commodities: at law it is hard to steal
a purse without also filching a good name.

When it's time for a drink in the bar after a trial, plaintiffs'
lawyers are perfectly capable of downplaying this matter of
odium and stigma. As Dr. Charles wonderingly observes in
her book, many of them "readily tell doctors that they should
not take negligence charges personally." They explain that
their suits "are not indictments of physicians' integrity" but
"simply means of securing recompense in specific situations
for their legal clients." Thus can leading trial lawyer Philip
Corboy assure doctors that filing malpractice suits against
them is just his colleagues' way of getting a second opinion.

No more profound hypocrisy can be found in our legal
system. When a client has suffered heart-wrenching injuries,
but no real misbehavior can be shown, of course trial lawyers

will invoke Compensation to justify suing. But when the opponent's conduct can be made to look bad, even when it is doubtful that their client suffered any real harm as a result of it, it's back to Deterrence to justify suing all the same. When the angry, jabbing pick of Fault does not look as if it will get them into the strongbox, naturally they are happy to employ the flexible, insinuating metal strip of No-Fault. And when the best strategy (as usual) is to try some of each, that is what they will do.

The same have-your-defendants-and-eat-them-too dialectic pervades the wider arguments used to rationalize the litigation industry. When asked why four times as many innocent as negligent doctors get sued, trial lawyers invoke the idea of litigation as surrogate social insurance. When it is asked why suing doctors should ever be considered a rational way for society to get money to injured patients—it takes years and the fighting eats up most of the money changing hands—the lawyers switch back and proclaim themselves society's only line of defense against bad doctoring.

The odd, ever-shifting mix of Fault and No-Fault elements in the arguments of plaintiffs' lawyers may from a distance appear a mere jumble of contradictions. But like the eccentric eating habits in the household of Jack Sprat, it makes perfect sense when viewed as a way of extracting every last bit of sustenance from the fare on hand. Anything nutritious left on the platter by the Fault theory will be efficiently vacuumed off by No-Fault.

It is bad enough when individuals say what is necessary to rationalize their will to power. But our law itself has been made to weave back and forth from fault to no-fault rationales as necessary to defeat defendants. It resorts to ideas of cost-spreading and social compensation to justify hyper-relaxed standards on letting lawyers into court to sue. But once they are in court on that basis it lets them whip juries into a frenzy with the idea that a defendant is guilty of heinous crimes against society. It promulgates vague rules that allow virtually any family, commercial, or employment relationship to be turned into a lawsuit on the it's-only-a-title-dispute theory. Then it gives lawyers both the means and the fiscal incentive to run those suits as straight-out assaults on reputation, to attack and besmirch opponents whose conduct has seldom come anywhere close to what society has chosen to designate as criminal. It furnishes ultra-loose procedures and evidence standards on the theory that society doesn't care which direction errors take, and follows them up with ultra-strict pains and penalties on the theory that society's most precious values are at stake in private litigation.

And so it has drifted into one of the most appalling evils that can disgrace a legal system: railroading defendants to punishment under conditions in which no one can be sure they are guilty.

· THE ·
WAY OUT

☫

THE POWERS OF IMPOSITION

The only prize much cared for by the powerful is power.

—OLIVER WENDELL HOLMES, JR.

Leona Serafin had come into Detroit's Outer Drive Hospital for what was supposed to be a routine kidney stone removal. Instead, uncontrollable hemorrhaging set in on the operating table and she died a few days later. An autopsy found the cause of death to be thrombotic thrombocytopenic purpura, a rare and nearly always fatal blood disorder whose origin is unknown.

Two years passed, and a pair of lawyers representing the Serafin family filed malpractice suits against the hospital and three doctors. After another three years the case went to trial in Wayne County circuit court. The lawyers could not offer testimony that the doctors or hospital had fallen short of any accepted standards in recommending or conducting the surgery. Upon hearing their case the judge promptly ordered a verdict for the defense. There was an appeal, but without success, and the Michigan Supreme Court denied review.

On the normal plan, the defendants in a case like this are supposed to go back to practicing medicine and try to forget what has happened to them. One of them, Dr. Seymour Friedman, could not forget. He filed a lawsuit against the two lawyers, who he said had good reason to know their action was groundless. Because of it, he said, he had been put to direct expense; he would have to pay higher insurance rates for as long as he practiced medicine; he had lost two young associates who could not afford to pay the higher premiums being charged to his office; his professional reputation had been defamed; and he had been put through intense personal embarrassment and anguish.

The Supreme Court of Michigan declared that the doors of the state's courts would be locked against him. It said Dr. Friedman could not get anywhere even if he could prove the lawyer knew the claim was false: the authoritative Second Restatement of Torts explains that a lawyer cannot be sued for malicious prosecution even if he "has no probable cause and is convinced that his client's claim is unfounded," so long as "he acts primarily for the purpose of aiding his client in obtaining a proper adjudication of his claim." That these lawyers were alleged to be angling for a settlement, not an adjudication, part of which would go to them on contingency, did not seem to matter. The majority's thirty-three-page opinion could not agree on reasoning—in fact it was split four ways—but it all came down to one sweeping assertion: a lawyer has no "duty of care" to avoid hurting the person he litigates against.

Around the country, other doctors who tried to fight back against groundless malpractice suits were learning the same lesson. Some sought relief under defamation law, reasoning from the burgeoning line of cases where complainants were winning fortunes from former employers and others who had given them bad references. They were thrown out of court. Others pointed to the frenetic pace at which courts were creating new "duties of care" between total strangers—such as a landowner's new duty toward strangers who might slip and fall while trespassing on or burgling his property—and said it was high time lawyers acknowledged a duty not to inflict easily foreseen harm on named, known opponents. That didn't work either.

A Illinois doctor invoked a clause in the state's constitution instructing its courts to provide a remedy for every wrong. He was told that the wrong done by litigation would just have to remain an exception. Allowing redress to the targets of wrongful lawsuits, he was told, might deter someone somewhere from launching a rightful lawsuit. The state's high-minded policy was to encourage the universal seeking of redress, and so the seeking of redress would just have to be forbidden to him.

America is the litigious society it is because American lawyers wield such unparalleled powers of imposition. No other country gives a private lawyer such a free hand to select a victim, tie him up in court on undefined charges, force him to hire lawyers of his own at dire expense, trash his privacy through we-have-ways-of-making-you-talk discovery, wear him down on the perpetual-motions treadmill, libel him grossly in documents that become permanent public records, and keep him scrambling to respond to Gyro Gearloose experts and Game of the States conflicts theories. Other countries let lawyers or litigants do some of these things, but never with such utter impunity.

The prosperity of large sectors of America's litigation industry is built on these impositions. The guessing-for-dollars tourney would soon adjourn if the lawyer who filed ten long-shot suits in search of one lucky break had to pay the full costs of the other nine. Most of the nuisance claims would go back to nuisance-land. Without the impositional value of add-ons and trade-ins many an otherwise legitimate lawsuit would not turn into a race to the gutter. Lawyerly demands and negotiation tactics in out-of-court situations would lose much of their bullying tone if stripped of the underlying threat of imposition.

Legal reforms can be roughly grouped into three broad classes: those that would expand the impositional powers of litigators, those that seek to sidestep or evade the issue, and those that would challenge and roll back that power.

The steady expansion of lawyers' powers of imposition is the stuff of daily headlines. It is the substance of a hundred new laws creating sweeping but undefined new obligations and liabilities, often accompanied by triple and punitive damages. It would be interesting to know how much of this wave of vague and punitive legislation arises merely from inattention to the principles of the rule of law and the rights of the accused, and how much derives from the behind-the-scenes lobbying of self-interested lawyers, contingency-fee or otherwise.

What is known is that the litigation industry has not simply sat back to enjoy the billions that have rolled in from its extraordinarily lucrative trade. It has shrewdly invested its newfound wealth and power in the currency of political and ideological influence. Plaintiffs' lawyers prefer to keep a low collective profile, lest they attract organized criticism; but their profound and wide-ranging power can no longer be denied. In state legislatures across the country, as well as in the U.S. Congress, they sit astride key committees that determine whether and how the legal system will be reformed. They number among the top givers to local campaigns, often chairing candidates' and parties' fund-raising committees. They hold special sway among the state judiciary, many of whose members must run for reelection and often have few places to turn for campaign funds other than the local trial bar.

The power of the litigation industry is likewise felt strongly in the realm of ideas and ideologies. Plaintiffs' lawyers swarm into movements for social reform of all sorts, often outmaneuvering and easing aside nonlawyers whose preferred reform strategies do not emphasize the widening of litigation opportunities. And although these lawyers claim to be the tribunes of all the put-upon underdogs of the world, they have every motive to sabotage proposals, however advantageous to those underdogs in other respects, that threaten to shut down their own cash machine. Their sway is felt especially in the "consumer movement," which lacks a strongly based popular constituency to act as a counterweight to lawyers' counsels.

By and large, the reform proposals most feared by the imposition industry are those that would cut into the powers that have brought it to its present peak of power and affluence. Yet many of the common suggestions for curbing the litigation explosion seek to avoid confronting the question of whether those powers should be permitted to expand further.

One of the most commonly proposed nostrums for curbing litigation is also one of the very weakest. It is for the government to dispense more benefits to cover the ills that people sue over, without changing anything in the legal system itself. The conventional wisdom, for example, blames America's epidemic of injury litigation on its lack of national health insurance and the inadequacy of other government programs that cover disability and loss of work. How can you expect people not to sue, it is asked, without making sure they have some other way to pay their bills? By analogy, it is argued that the answer to the waste and destructiveness of divorce battles is to provide more social services for broken families; that the way to cut down on the torrent of wrongful-firing litigation is to mandate more unemployment benefits to take the sting out of being let go; and so forth.

There is much less to these arguments than meets the eye. In the first place, huge quantities of government aid and private insurance are already on the table to compensate people for misadventure. They sue anyway. They walk straight from the workers' compensation, unemployment insurance, Medicaid, or disaster relief office to the lawyer's office. Neither is private insurance by itself effective in staving off lawsuits. George Priest of Yale Law School points out that very few American accident victims nowadays pay the bulk of their medical costs from their own pocket, and that the large majority have some coverage against disability. They keep right on suing.

In a convenient exception to the generally liberal *zeitgeist* on evidence in civil lawsuits, as it happens, most American courts have, at least until recently, flatly refused to let in evidence about whether sued-on losses have already been paid from some "collateral source" such as an official or charitable pocket. One survey estimated that of the money changing hands in California injury litigation in 1987, between $500 million and $1 billion went to duplicate prior payments. Most of the earlier payors did not attempt to reclaim the money, leaving winning litigants free to enjoy the proceeds of what can only be called double-dipping.

The second, lawsuit-obtained scoop in double-dip injury compensation must be considered dessert, because it provides little in the way of balanced sustenance. The lawsuit award often comes many years after the sued-on injury; by the time it arrives its effect is often to bring unexpected affluence to a person who has long since recovered from the financial adversity of the original injury. Many of today's awards compensate plaintiffs who suffered no out-of-pocket expense at all, turning them from formerly troubled middle-class people to formerly troubled rich people. This is the precise reverse of a sensible insurance policy, which would provide money when people need it. It is worth noting that when people buy insurance for themselves, they do not buy coverage against hazards of pain and lost potential, partly because difficulties in measurement and proof would make the coverage a bad buy, but mostly because the rational course is to insure not against catastrophes in general but against catastrophes that create a need for cash.

Most "social insurance," like most private insurance, seeks to replace basic out-of-pocket expenses rather than compensate people for intangible and speculative harms. And that points up the real reason more social spending will do little to curb litigation. American courts are crowded with money demands over pain and suffering, loss of time spent with family members, loss of projected incomes as top tennis stars and violinists by teenagers who break their arms at summer camp, and so forth. Not even the most dogmatic Swedish welfarist would think of setting up a government program to compensate people for these ills, at least not at the levels of cash entitlement plucked from a spinning barrel by American courts.

So long as people can sue for a million, no modest check from a social-insurance fund is likely to keep them from dialing 1-800-L-A-W-S-U-I-T. If anything, getting unearned money from the government seems to whet the sense of entitlement that often leads to litigation. Doctors reportedly view Medicaid patients as more likely than other patients, not less, to sue if something goes wrong; there is no "gratitude effect."

A more promising scheme to lure business away from litigators goes by the name of alternative dispute resolution (ADR). ADR is a shorthand term for a range of dispute-settling methods, from informal mediation through arbitration all the way to "private courts" staffed by former judges that mimic their official counterparts in everything but the crying of oyez-oyez-oyez at the beginning of a trial.

ADR has most of the advantages that are advertised for it. It usually offers quicker, cheaper, and more reliable resolution than court trial, with less inflaming of tempers, which is helpful in divorces, ongoing employment cases, and other cases where mending a frayed relationship can do good.

Mediation and arbitration should be especially powerful when both sides can agree by contract to submit to them before disputes arise. But as the Grove Textile Company learned in Chapter 10, lawyers have ways of striking back. They can always complain of some asymmetry in that amor-

304 • THE LITIGATION EXPLOSION

phous quantity known as bargaining power. And although the attacks do not always succeed in derailing ADR, they do affect the nature of the experience itself.

The Supreme Court's decisions on arbitration in the securities business typify the problem. In the 1987 case of *Shearson/Amex* v. *McMahon,* the Court by a vote of five to four upheld the standard-form agreements by which stockbrokers and their clients agree to arbitrate rather than litigate disputes. But the narrowness of the margin and the language of the decisions make it plain that the arbitrators' work can go forward on the understanding that its outcomes will not diverge all that drastically from those the courts see as acceptable.

Each extreme new development in the courts thus tends to be followed, a few respectful paces behind, by the substitute courts. If a claim has some settlement value as a lawsuit, an arbitrator had better accord it some value too, or the pressure back to court will start up again. Punitive damages are now regularly used as the basis for arbitration awards, and now racketeering charges are beginning to appear as well. A process that was supposed to reduce acrimony and blame-mongering has itself become steadily more suitlike: the arbitrators find themselves in some objective sense an extension of the courts, with no real choice when to jump, but at most some discretion as to how high.

ADR has another big problem: in the minds of lawyers it is usually competing not with trial but with settlement. Most cases do settle, whether justly or not, and if the clients are feeling calm and rational enough to consider ADR, won't settlement come all the sooner? Settlement has the obvious advantage to the lawyer of leaving him in more control of the process, and there is no mediator to pay.

It is hard, too, for ADR to compete with today's litigation-promotion machine, with its sophisticated marketing campaigns. Mediation services cannot afford to fly teams of runners to disaster scenes or run elaborate press operations with leaked documents. The modest fees to be had in keeping marriages, civic ties, and therapeutic relationships together will not pay for blanket ad campaigns or saturation political contributions.

More fundamentally, ADR is selling a product that many customers don't want to buy. Countless litigants, not to mention their lawyers, would actively resist being shunted off into something more quiet, private, and predictable than today's courts. They wish to pursue the heady allurements of getting rich or getting even, the glamor of publicity, the grim satisfactions of ideological combat. The sober advocates of alternative dispute resolution can preach only the less passionate virtues of thrift, reliability, and repose. Trying to attract converts amid today's bazaar of litigation opportunities, they stand about as much chance as the proprietors of a Christian Science Reading Room amid the fleshpots of old Naples or Port Said.

The social-spending approach tries to end the gang fighting by offering hot lunches; the ADR approach invites the combatants to work out their hostilities in a nice game of bridge. The next major category of reform proposal is, by contrast, quite bold; it tries to wrest valuable turf away from the litigators without actually taking away their switchblades.

For decades bright minds in law schools have been coming up with "no-fault" proposals that would remove major areas of injury and conflict from the courts. Nearly always, these plans promise big cost savings along with much faster and more predictable payments to a larger number of injury complainants.

And then the litigators strike back.

Consider what has happened to the classic no-fault plan, workers' compensation. Workers' comp laws were supposed to end litigation over on-the-job injuries. On-the-job injuries have nonetheless reemerged as a huge category of litigation both within and, more significant, without the formal workers' comp system.

Perhaps the best-known occupational health calamity of the last half century has been that of asbestos exposure. Much of the problem dates back to the crash program to turn out Navy ships during World War II. Large numbers of shipyard insulation workers came down decades later with serious illness linked in most cases to the combination of highly concentrated asbestos exposure with smoking. Under workers' compensation and federal government immunities, they could not sue the employers or government departments whose full-speed-ahead decision to tolerate dangerous working conditions (in the interest of getting vessels into service) had actually exposed them to harm. Instead lawyers came up with the idea of suing the companies that mined and distributed the asbestos, although few of those companies had any real control over whether the products they shipped would be used safely or unsafely. (Indeed, since the Navy requisitioned asbestos supplies, most could not have refused to deliver the mineral had they wanted.) The legal community cleaned up to the tune of billions of dollars, and claimants got a fair bit of money too, but the results bore little relationship to actual responsibility.

It is the rare on-the-job injury or illness that *cannot* be taken out of the workers' comp system by clever lawyering. In most sudden on-the-job accidents workers' comp laws prevent direct suit against the employer. So instead lawyers blame the outside companies that supply conveyor belts, power drills, forklift trucks, or construction scaffolding. Some expert can always be found to question the product's design, or at least swear that it should have come with a different, stronger warning label. And that is all it usually takes to get to a jury. In 1985, counting asbestos, three fifths of large product liability claims were paid on injuries that happened at workplaces—the very same injuries that reformers once thought they were taking out of the lawsuit system.

Sometimes the third-party defendants targeted in this litigation find ways of dragging in the second-party employer who had supposedly been protected against suit. New York, for example, allows the outside manufacturer sued on a workplace product-liability claim to turn around and sue the employer whose conduct it says contributed to the accident—perfectly re-creating the employer liability that workers' comp was thought to have done away with, except that two expensive lawsuits will now go forward instead of one. The Alabama high court came up with a different twist when it ruled that injured workers could sue allegedly negligent supervisors and managers *personally*, a stratagem well calculated to panic their parent company into a preemptive cash offer.

Other loopholes eliminate the middleman and simply allow direct suits against employers. Several courts have accepted the imaginative theory that the physical features of the workplace are in effect designed "products," thus allowing their designer, the employer, to be sued under the no-holds-barred law of product liability. Another favorite gambit is to argue that a broad category of employer lapses formerly viewed as negligent should be considered "intentional" and thus fair game for lawsuits under another of the exceptions to workers' comp. In 1982 the Ohio high court was prevailed upon to rule thus; amid mounting chaos the state's legislature had to reverse the decision, but by then the tactic had been carried with success to other states.

Lawyers in many states are also allowed to use the loophole shown by a 1986 Texas case. The family of Wilbur Jack Steen had sued his employer, the Monsanto company, blaming his early death on exposure to chemicals. Under the terms of workers' comp, they were not permitted to accept a Galveston jury's award of $8 million compensation. But Texas law barred only the collection of *compensatory* damages. Which meant they were perfectly free to keep the *punitive* portion of the award—set by the jury in this case at a staggering $100 million, a sum larger than the gross national products of several member states of the United Nations.

Creative litigation, then, is dragging American business defendants into the most expensive of all possible worlds. They are increasingly exposed to ruinous verdicts for sympathetic cases of on-the-job injury; but they also continue to pay cash on the barrel through conventional workers' comp for all the cases too weak to be taken to juries.

And the workers' comp system itself has proved highly vulnerable to litigation pressure. Much of the idea of the system was that its rights to compensation would be well enough defined that lawyers would not be needed. Even today, workers' comp works reasonably efficiently at covering sudden, acute injuries: when there is no doubt which ladder someone fell off or which furnace burned his hand, the check can go out at once. But the grayer zones of causation attract lawyers and their experts, especially the foggy outlying benefit-frontiers of stress, back strain, sleeplessness, and above all what is called permanent partial disability. Most of these conditions, while often quite real as sources of misery and disability, and frequently job-related, baffle attempts at objective measurement, arise from stimuli outside as well as inside the workplace, and can feed on themselves so that the more they are probed for the more they are found.

The advent of lawyer solicitation has massively increased the pressure on workers' comp systems. In California stress-at-work claims emerged as a major topic of lawyer advertising, the category multiplying sixfold during the eighties to reach a quarter of all workers' comp claims. Outlays nationally for stress claims rose to around $200 million a year. And yet only a tiny share of all workplace stress and emotional trauma was being paid for through such channels, or ever could be. Over-all, workers' comp outlays rose 76 percent nationally in the four years to 1988, from $13.8 billion to $24.3 billion, pushing the system to the brink of insolvency in many states.

No-fault laws must be written very strongly if they are not to succumb to the death of a thousand loopholes. Consider no-fault auto insurance, which is conceived again as a deal: drivers give up the right to collect from other drivers' insurance companies after many accidents—a process that is slow, chancy and lawyer-ridden—and in exchange get the right to collect pre-set benefits from their own insurance company, a process that is usually speedy and litigation-free. Drivers save a great deal of money in states with what are called strong no-fault laws, the kind that fence lawyers out of all but the gravest accidents. But trial lawyer lobbying has helped convince other states to enact what is called weak no-fault—which is actually worse than none at all. In weak no-fault states the threshold of accident seriousness is set so low—sometimes at a mere few hundred dollars of medical bills—that any lawyer can get his client into court just by sending him to a cooperative doctor for a battery of tests. The upshot is that drivers get to collect money from their own insurance company if they wish (if, for example, an accident was obviously their own fault) but can still sue whenever the equities fall or can be arranged in their favor. Insurance rates rise to cover the costs of running two compensation systems at once. Trial lawyers and their allies among supposed consumer advocates then gleefully proclaim that no-fault has failed.

The no-fault idea is readily adaptable to air disasters, where there is seldom much doubt about the names of the victims or the severity of their injuries and the same few defendants tend to get sued every time. The rest of the world long ago saw the folly of litigating every crash to the hilt at enormous expense. Under the 1929 Warsaw Convention, accordingly, airlines agree to accept absolute liability in most specified situations for crashes of international flights. The cap on compensation is set at a very low level: a mere $75,000 apiece for most American flights.

Wealthy Americans shudder at the seeming stinginess of this limit: how dare anyone value their lives at less than the cost of their houses? But people from other countries fly on international routes, too, and to many of them the arrangement appears eminently fair. Under a regime of unlimited litigation, the survivors of the seasoned American tourist on the flight from Karachi to Istanbul could collect millions in home courts for lost income, lost enjoyment of life, and other Yankee concepts of litigation entitlement. The survivors of the Pakistani guest worker in the next seat would get a tiny fraction of that sum. And yet the two may well have paid the same price for their tickets, and thus the same premium toward their litigation-driven insurance policy. The Warsaw Convention does not prevent anyone who wants to from spending a few bucks extra to buy a million dollars' worth of flight insurance. What it does do is spare all travelers from having to pay the costs of a "policy" whose benefits would go mostly to the well off.

Still, American lawyers constantly probe loopholes in the Convention. One such exception allows suits against airlines over willful misconduct, which lawyers are accordingly extra-quick to charge. (Public-indignation campaigns are whipped up much more often on crashes of international flights than on crashes of domestic flights, where big awards are routine whether willful misconduct is shown or not.) In the first trial of what was expected to be a series, filed by different surviving families, a Washington, D.C., jury awarded $50 million in punitive damages against Korean Air Lines for having had the temerity to let its airliner be shot down by a Soviet fighter plane in 1983. Part of the wonder of punitive damages is that lawyers can collect them again and again in successive trials over the same charged act of wrongdoing.

Another tactic in Warsaw Convention cases is to sue the aircraft manufacturer whose fuselage should have been less vulnerable to terrorist action, or the federal air traffic controllers who should have helped in some way. Liability lawyers indeed live on loopholes. Does an auto no-fault plan bar suit against the negligent driver in an accident? Then they will sue the automaker whose vehicle should have been more "crashworthy"—a term whose meaning is as eye-of-the-beholderish as any trial lawyer could wish—or the city highway department that should have laid out or landscaped the road to provide better visibility.

Undiscouraged by the ways lawyers have found over, under, around, and through so many previous no-fault plans, reformers gallantly keep coming up with new ones. But unless the fury of litigation itself can be made to subside, the prospects for success cannot be accounted good.

The latest wave of interest is in extending the no-fault idea to medical malpractice claimants. And yet the borderline problems are considerably worse in this area than in workplace, highway, or aviation accidents. An official malpractice board or compensation fund would come under inevitable pressure to pay claims based on guesswork about medical negligence that could not be absolutely ruled out as provably unfounded. That would lead down the slope to compensation for bad results in medicine generally, at untold expense. In the meantime, litigation pressure would increase on drug and medical-device makers and other likely bystanders.

Conceivably lawmakers could define "compensable events" with great care and order officials to pursue a hard line against doubtful claims. But to judge by recent experience, any political willpower that might be asserted at the outset would be hard to sustain. The federal black-lung program was launched as a way to help underground coal miners who suffer from pneumoconiosis and related disabling conditions specific to their demanding and unpleasant work. The program was soon unable to resist paying for a very wide range of health problems among not only retired miners but also chain-smoking bookkeepers and typists for coal companies who developed emphysema or bronchitis. Expenditures spun completely out of control, rising from $14 million to $731 million in the four years to 1980; by 1981 a cumulative $3.7 billion had been appropriated from the federal budget to cover shortfalls in the fund.

Lawyer assaults bedevil even those no-fault plans that are drawn up with extreme care by lawyers skilled at avoiding litigation. The havoc is far greater when the drafting of a law is less careful, or bad by design. The federal Superfund program to clean up hazardous waste sites was advertised as mostly a get-things-done expenditure program with a small liability component. But that small liability component was crafted into a most incendiary litigation fuse. The statute deliberately left it uncertain who would be held liable for what, or how much anyone would have to pay; it applied severe retroactive sanctions to conduct to which no liability of any sort had attached years earlier when it was taken; it consigned difficult scientific questions to unending contests of guessing experts.

And so the Superfund program almost immediately descended into a fantastic snake pit of legal strife notable both for its injustice and for its uselessness in actually cleaning anything up. Thousands of peripheral businesses and landowners are dragged in as defendants who didn't realize they had done anything wrong at all. They are sued for the disposal of not only their own long-forgotten wastes but also those of complete strangers that were carried to the same sites. In the face of an *in terrorem* threat of unlimited liability they dig in their heels and litigate the daylights out of the case, denying everything and admitting nothing. It is next to impossible to get the cooperation of all the various parties needed to do an actual cleanup—landowners, businesses, financing sources, engineers—because of all sides' well-founded fear that anyone who sticks his head above the trenches will get hit with flying liability shrapnel.

Nothing could be more understandable than the urge to escape from today's legal culture. But today's legal culture is well fortified against escape attempts. It besieges any little pockets of nonadversarialism that may establish themselves. It subtly undermines attempts at legislative compromise and transforms would-be limits on litigation into occasions for yet more litigation.

If the law provided a framework of reason and predictability, many no-fault systems could be made to work well, and alternative dispute resolution could be made to work more than well. By the same token, if the law did provide such a framework, people would be less eager to flee its domain, much as the yearning to get out of certain countries fell off perceptibly once those countries reached the level of civilization and tolerance needed to recognize emigration as a right.

There is, in short, no easy way to avoid the task of bringing sense back to our legal system. Litigation must be reformed from within, by rolling back the powers of imposition that make it so fearful.

A good place to begin is with the idea of due process. The U.S. Supreme Court is showing signs of reawakening from its long slumber as guardian of due process in civil litigation. An early sign came in three cases at the end of the 1970s, when the Court finally resumed serious constitutional scrutiny of the state courts' long-arm jurisdiction. The Court ruled that California could not levy child support payments against an out-of-state man whose contact with the state had been to send his daughter to live there with her mother; that Oklahoma could not grab an upstate New York car dealer and his regional distributor after a customer had driven one of their vehicles into the state and crashed it; and, finally, that a local Indiana driver could not be abducted to Minnesota on the ground that his insurance company did business there. The long-awaited ruling on the Minnesota law invalidated the similar New York law as well.

These isolated line-drawings may not yet add up to a consistent new philosophy of where state jurisdiction stops. But they do signal that it stops somewhere, and that is welcome news. The decision on the car dealer even bowed toward the value of giving people some chance to predict where they will get sued.

Also promising has been the Court's growing interest in applying due-process-of-law principles to the punitive side of civil litigation. At this writing the Court has agreed to consider whether some applications of punitive damages violate the Constitution's due process clause. In the meantime lower courts, often led by jurists who are known as liberal on other applications of liability, have been recognizing the need to curb the arbitrary and capricious award of punitive damages;

so have most of the state legislatures. Even the American Bar Association has called for giving civil defendants more protection in this respect.

The Court has also shown a dramatic new willingness to curb one of the key impositional powers in the litigator's arsenal: the power to force a trial on flimsy charges. For years the Court had seemed to lean toward the can't-hurt-to-go-to-trial view epitomized in Ira Arnstein's lawsuit against Cole Porter. But in 1986 it finally gave a ringing endorsement, as fully in the (changing) spirit of the federal rules, to the disposal of factually unsupported contentions and cases on summary judgment. In a trio of decisions the Court said that a judge can use summary judgment to isolate and dispose of contentions that are "factually unsupported"; that it is not too early to assess the credibility of each side's underlying evidence at this stage; and that a mere "scintilla" of evidence need not always get a case past this screening process.

The Court has also reined in a few of the wilder excesses of the class-action lawyers. It ruled that they could not evade the minimum dollar value needed to get a dispute into federal court by rolling lots of tiny disputes into one, and that to stay in federal court they sometimes had to go to the trouble of notifying the members of the class that a suit was being filed in their name. Organizers can still take nationwide class actions to state courts with more favorable rules, but the proponents of the device have definitely lost the strong initiative they had in the past.

Reform of expert-witness impositions is still mostly a matter for the future, but some state legislatures—urged on by outraged doctors—have made a start. Connecticut bars the use of malpractice experts who do not themselves practice medicine. Alabama now requires that the witness have practiced recently in the same specialty as the defendant whose decisions he is second-guessing. Maryland rules out malpractice testimony from any expert who spends more than 20 percent of his time in court.

Among the most crucial steps will be the reform of discovery. But this is an area where the litigation lobby jealously guards its privileges. Nothing has come, for example, of Chief Justice William Rehnquist's sensible proposal to do away with discovery entirely in federal cases with stakes below fifty thousand dollars. (The same information, of course, would be obtainable at trial.) Opponents have repeatedly managed to kill other ideas for narrowing discovery; a 1983 round of amendments urged courts to act against abuses, but by most reports they are still pretty much as bad as ever.

Rolling back lawyers' impositional powers is a crucial goal, but some residue will always remain. Litigators, like certain smokestack industries, can argue that without the right to inflict some irreducible level of unchosen discomfort on everyone else they could not carry on their in some cases useful work. The question is whether these remaining losses should "lie where they fall," on innocent opponents, or should instead be charged back to the lawyers and litigants who create them. No doubt it is impossible to ban imposition before the fact without banning litigation itself. But should litigators not be held answerable after the fact when their impositions turn out to have caused harm? That was what the Michigan court flatly denied in Dr. Friedman's case, and what American courts in general have long denied.

There is something fantastically ironic in all this. Litigators had built their fortunes on making every other profession and industry pay for its mistakes, real, alleged, and imaginary. Pursuing the invisible-fist notion of "cost internalization" to the end of its logical tether and miles beyond, they had asserted the right to hunt out and present to a jury any link between misadventure and money, between sorrow and solvency, between calamity and cash balances. They had brushed aside any notion that the value of a defendant's work in general was any mitigation of one of these "externalities," that the law should be one whit less severe on a doctor who needlessly lost a patient just because he had saved a hundred other lives. Nor did they accept as an excuse that an endeavor was carried on in a public-spirited or self-sacrificing way; they had indeed ruthlessly torn down the old "charitable immunities" that had once protected community volunteers and religious sisterhoods from being sued for accidents in the running of their nonprofit hospitals and schools.

But America's trial lawyers refused to apply any of these lessons to themselves. They had carefully arranged for their own industry a supercharitable immunity, a complete free pass to cover not only negligence but also wanton misconduct in the litigation that was making so many of them millionaires. The public benefits of their activity were too profound to ask them to disgorge a sou from their coffers to recompense those they had ruined through false accusation. Theirs, it seemed, was the only profession that never had to pay for its mistakes.

That is the assumption that has now begun to change.

15

⚖

STRICT LIABILITY
FOR LAWYERING

May you have a lawsuit in which you know you are in the right.

—*Gypsy curse*

It's not as if lawyers can't be sued. Indeed, they get sued all the time. But the major type of suit that is allowed against them actually tends to make matters worse. That is the malpractice suit from one of their own clients.

Today's law graduate can reportedly expect to be sued for malpractice at least three times in the course of his career. The *National Law Journal*, describing the trend as an "epidemic" and "deluge," has reported that in the two years up to June 1988 nearly 40 percent of law firms got sued. The average settlement per case has increased threefold over the past several years, according to Patricia Myers of Shand, Morahan & Company: "What used to be a $5,000 mosquito bite is now a $100,000 shark bite."

Record verdicts follow each other at a rapid clip. Texas

trial lawyer John O'Quinn, of the full-page Yellow Pages ad and telephone hotline, got a jury to hit the Houston law firm of Sewell & Riggs with a $17.5 million verdict, including $7.2 million in punitive damages, for allegedly giving bad advice that caused Ali Ebrahami and Yousef Panaphour to get sued in connection with a speculative real estate syndication deal. Local observers believed that the Houston verdict in part reflected jury hostility to lawyers as a group—a base sentiment that through the alchemy of courtroom advocacy could be transmuted into a golden contingency for, inevitably, another lawyer.

Not surprisingly, insurance rates for law firms went up six- or sevenfold over a decade, with deductibles doubling or tripling and policy limits cut back. A few trial lawyers have publicly hinted that the wicked insurance companies are to blame for this spiral, but inconveniently for that theory much of the coverage is in fact provided on a cooperative basis by lawyer groups themselves.

The rise in lawyers' malpractice suits does not appear to track any great surge in the number of incompetent legal practitioners; beginners' errors don't seem to be the problem, for example, since veterans in the business actually run into more claims. In language that other professionals would instantly recognize, lawyers' practice manuals are mournfully advising that no degree of care and precaution can wholly protect an attorney from these suits.

A good many suits are aimed at the less adversarial sort of lawyers, the ones who draw up trusts and foundation papers, give advice on taxes and estate planning, draft business deals, and so forth. But all in all the lawyers of peace get off relatively easy. With what might seem to be Homeric fitness, more than half the avenging fury is visited on the race of litigators themselves, especially the plaintiffs' accident lawyers, who are the targets of around a quarter of all legal-malpractice complaints.

This should come as no real surprise. Like amateur rugby, demolition derbies, and other hostility-releasing pastimes, litigation has been known to cause injury to its enthusiastic participants. The more restless contestants, recruited and warmed up with hints of gigantic purses in the offing, are put through the grueling scrimmages only to land, very often, in the most ruinous sort of "bad outcome" (as other professions have delicately come to refer to their clients' setbacks): in this case, a defense verdict. The question naturally arises: couldn't the lawsuit have been won if handled differently? Trial advocacy, with its skilled judgments under time pressure, will often yield to a second opinion in hindsight. And of course the client can ignore any papers he signed knowingly accepting a risk of loss; remember, contract disclaimers are unfair to consumers.

Resolving a suit charging litigation malpractice commonly calls for a technique known as the trial within a trial. The client's new lawyer argues that the original claim, which may have failed before an earlier jury, would surely have won if not for the original lawyer's sad lapse in judgment. Lawyer number one, now the defendant, may be reduced to arguing that the case he accepted and perhaps touted as unbeatable at the time was in reality quite spurious and would have been shot down no matter what. That requires him to reconstruct the case of the original (now absent) opponent, with little hope, of course, of getting much willing cooperation from the actual people he has so recently been suing.

Exotic damage theories have proliferated in lawyers' malpractice as elsewhere in the law. In the old days, when courts distrusted "speculation" in damage assertions, the client had to show that his claim would have been a virtually sure winner had it been handled properly. That kept out all but the strongest litigation malpractice claims. Now many courts are happy to turn probabilistic hurts and might-have-been injuries into cash; some of them have even embraced what is known as the "loss-of-a-chance" doctrine, which makes doctors pay if they did anything to worsen the chances of a patient who would probably not have pulled through anyway.

When it comes to litigation, unlike medical prognoses or

prospects of operatic stardom, it does not seem all that strange to reduce the vicissitudes of the future to a single dollar figure. Lawyers do it all the time when they calculate settlement values. So it has begun to be argued that to avert the need for the cumbersome trial within a trial, the lawyer who bobbles a claim should simply be made to pay over to the client the settlement value of that claim as gauged by (dueling hired) experts. The notion has a certain logic, but observe its odd result: it gives clients an enforceable right to cash in on a claim that was provably baseless but whose nuisance value gave it an undeniably positive settlement value.

Other generous damage theories also come back to haunt today's litigator-defendant. For example, the unhappy client may collect for his emotional distress in seeing his claim go down to courtroom defeat, on top of the inward trauma, if any, he suffered at the underlying injury. In much the same way, punitive damages can be stacked dizzily atop punitive damages. Or, more simply, the lawyer can be made to pay the punitive damages for which his original opponent could have been mulcted, though his own conduct would in no way have justified a punitive award. Racketeering claims, with their invigorating triple-damage entitlements, are of course being piled on, too.

Higher-order lawsuits over lawsuits do not yet appear common. Few clients line up lawyer number three to sue lawyer number two for blowing the malpractice case against lawyer number one. But Jonathan Swift had it all mapped out:

> *So, naturalists observe, a flea*
> *Hath smaller fleas that on him prey;*
> *And these have smaller still to bite 'em,*
> *And so proceed* ad infinitum.

This one particular outbreak of litigiousness is causing anxiety in some unlikely quarters. An article in *Trial*, the magazine for people who sue people, complains that the cost to a litigator of defending one of these suits can be even higher when the charges are unfounded than when they have substance. The author frets that the confused state of the law allows complainants "to throw in a RICO claim whenever a lawyer makes mistakes and to extort a settlement from a lawyer terrified of the racketeering taint." A former head of the Association of Trial Lawyers of America has said, rather defensively, that "obviously we are not responsible" for "mistaken judgment or shoot-from-the-hip calls during trial. . . . Just because our judgment was mistaken, just because the result was bad, that alone does not create liability."

It is certainly amusing to watch the high priests of recrimination gag as they drink from the chalice they have prepared for the rest of us. But *schadenfreude*—delight in others' well-deserved misfortune—is never a very reliable guide to policy. This mode of chastisement is not likely to teach its targets the desired lessons and is all too likely to worsen the plight of the rest of us.

Why? Because the whole point of a typical malpractice charge is that a lawyer did not fight hard enough. Many complaints arise from the failure to throw in a damage claim or legal theory that might have turned a modest jury award into a whopper. According to news reports, some lawyers reluctantly add RICO claims to their lawsuits because they fear that not doing so could open them to a malpractice charge. So-called discovery malpractice can consist of failure to depose an opponent or ransack its files with sufficient zeal. Some lapses that sound like instances of mere incompetence, such as missing deadlines, may in fact arise from shadings of professional opinion. A lawyer forbears to file papers in a suit, and a statute of limitations runs out; he may have been grossly forgetful, or may simply have felt in good conscience that the case at the time was not yet strong enough to warrant a claim. If later developments make it appear that the case had a good chance, he can be in big trouble.

In short, malpractice liability pushes lawyers to be even more combative and ruthless, more hostile to opponents' interests, than they would be of their own inclination. It is thus misleading to say that fear of malpractice charges encourages "defensive litigation," along the lines of defensive medicine: the better word would be offensive. Demanding extra crates of discovery documents helps forestall charges of being ill-prepared for trial. Filing lots of motions helps give clients a comforting sense that their suits are going somewhere. Not all the incentives, to be sure, cut toward hyperactive law-yering. Some malpractice-chary lawyers are turning away the most excitedly litigious clients, and others are more careful about spelling out why they advise not suing, which could be a good thing. But mostly the trend is perfectly consistent with today's lawyering excesses. In fact, some of the shrewder supporters of litigation have come out in favor of stringent legal-malpractice liability, however discomfiting it may be to their colleagues in strife.

Punishing lawyers for not beating up on their opponents thoroughly enough is not a very promising way to bring the litigation explosion under control. More constructive would be to lend a hand to those on the receiving end of the beatings. Not until 1983 did the first glimmerings of such help appear on the scene.

The 1939 federal rules of civil procedure had a few provisions meant to discourage false or ill-grounded pleadings, but they were essentially toothless. You could try to get an opponent's spurious pleading struck out, for example; but your proof on this point was not normally to be introduced until trial, and of course holding the case open for years until then might be the whole point. For a stronger remedy you basically had to prove your opponent was litigating in bad faith, which is hardly ever feasible. Litigators virtually never get caught on bad-faith charges unless they have been almost insanely indiscreet.

Why not? In the first place, part of a lawyer's training is in knowing how to couch actions so as to avoid crossing the line to provable bad faith. More to the point, bad faith among members of all other professions is commonly proved with the aid of discovery tidbits taken in or out of context. But the magic Cone of Silence of lawyer discovery privilege repels all such eavesdropping. Legal-malpractice suits, incidentally, are an exception to the normal rule of discovery privilege, because there the client waives the secrecy in his own interest.

The first serious attempt at reform came in 1983. It is called Rule 11, and it finally begins to hold lawyers and litigants accountable for the candor and plausibility of the accusations they hurl at their fellow members of society. There had been a rule numbered 11 in the Federal Rules of Civil Procedure all along, requiring lawyers to sign their pleadings, but no one had paid it much mind. The 1983 changes provided that by signing a pleading a lawyer vouches that its contents are well grounded in fact and law. If instead they prove unfounded, he or his client can be hit with real sanctions. Crucially, the rule was extended to cover signatures on motions as well as pleadings, providing a way for courts to curb abuse all the way through a lawsuit and not just at the start.

The requirement that a pleading be well grounded in fact does not mean a lawyer has to assemble proof of each allegation, let alone proof that will pass eventual courtroom muster, before filing suit. It does mean he must not ignore readily available proof that his suit is unfounded. Sanctions have been imposed in cases where a little basic checking would have found that a deadline for suing had expired, or that a claim had already been disposed of in court before, or that the opponent had not yet gotten around to committing the mischief he was suspected of planning.

Some courts have used Rule 11 to muzzle "shotgun" pleadings. The lawyers who filed one class action named as defendants everyone listed under the heading of mortgage lenders in the Philadelphia Yellow Pages; they were made to pay under Rule 11 to some of the miscellaneous defendants swept in. The same lesson was taught to three insurance companies that, after the collapse of the Continental Illinois bank, filed allegations of fraud against too wide a circle of persons connected to the bank. Federal Judge Milton Shadur said this "unexamined assertion of serious charges against innocent parties" had apparently been premised on the view that it cost "nothing more to have sued 36 defendants rather than 31"; he called it a "collective-farm approach to litigation, scarcely appropriate to the capitalistic free-market society in which [the insurers] function."

The requirement that a filing be well grounded in the law, as distinct from the facts, is a bit more complicated. Lawyers constantly urge courts to revise or extend existing law, and the rule does not penalize them on that account alone. What it does require, according to most courts that have ruled on the issue, is that they flag their argument as a departure from existing doctrine and alert the court to squarely opposed precedent. If consistently enforced, this might discourage the favorite ploy of leading courts into a virgin wilderness of new doctrine while assuring them that they are following the path of precedent.

Legal positions can be hit with sanctions if they are so outlandish that no reasonable observer could expect them to go over. Former Attorney General Ramsey Clark was penalized after he filed suit against President Ronald Reagan, Prime Minister Margaret Thatcher, and the government of Great Britain demanding reimbursement for residents of Libya who suffered losses from the 1986 U.S. bombing raid on that country. The rule has also been deployed against the tax protesters who urge for the umpteenth time that paper money is not legal tender or that the income tax is unconstitutional. Sanctions were likewise levied against a San Francisco lawyer/softball player who had been ordered out of the section of Golden Gate Park reserved for hardball and proceeded to sue the city and county, Mayor Dianne Feinstein, sundry police officers and officials, and the California Baseball Association on the theory (among others) that softball was symbolic speech covered by the First Amendment.

Rule 11 has brought relief to a long list of lawsuit victims who formerly had next to no effective recourse. Loyola University of Chicago was sued thirteen times by a woman whose medical-school application it had turned down; on the last round it succeeded in getting sanctions against her. An Arizona company had to go to Missouri to defend itself from a suit over a truck accident in Texas despite the complainant's "utter failure," as a court put it, to show that the defendant had even the "slightest connection" with Missouri for purposes of the suit; federal Judge John Nangle lambasted the opposing lawyer for not making a reasonable effort to look into the jurisdictional questions.

Rules against false pleading would have little bite if lawyers could get into court by saying nothing at all. So in line with the spirit of Rule 11, courts in a string of recent cases have been demanding more specificity in pleadings, especially where accusations are plainly invidious. Lawmakers in some states are helping out with measures aimed at identifying and screening out the weakest cases and issues at an early stage. Several states now require the complainant in a malpractice case to line up the opinion of an expert witness before, not after, filing suit against a doctor. Courts' new aggressiveness in granting summary judgment is part of the same trend. The 1983 round of rules changes also helped a bit in eliciting contentions by making pretrial conferences automatic within the first 120 days of a suit.

Equally welcome as a remedy for litigation abuse has been the application of Rule 11 to motion filings. Judges have started to grant sanctions against litigants who file time-wasting requests for summary judgments to which they are plainly not entitled, or spurious post-trial motions after an adverse verdict to stave off the day of ultimate defeat.

A crucial question is whether Rule 11 allows judges to do anything about filings with some basis in fact that are grossly exaggerated or bulked out with add-on charges. If not, much abuse will continue: lawyers will go on with their Rumpelstiltskin-like requests to have a straw pile of merit spun into a gold heap of remedy. But help may be on the way here too. Ida Hudson was suing the company she worked for when it struck back with a counterclaim to which it attached a terrorizing dollar value of $4.2 million. The judge applied sanctions to the company's law firm, not because the counterclaim had no basis at all, but because the damages asked for were so plainly and arbitrarily out of line with its allegations. The next step is to apply this principle to original claims as well as counterclaims.

Some prominent litigators and like-minded academics have reacted with dismay to these modest initial efforts to bring the litigation industry under control. Their arguments will seem curiously familiar to those who have followed the story this far.

The most outrageous thing Rule 11 does (they say) is to saddle lawyers with liability for missteps that, although sometimes gross, were committed in good faith. Maybe the profession can learn to live with some controls on willful wrongdoing. But what will happen to its morale if liability begins to be applied for mere negligence, or—the ultimate horror—without fault?

Then, too, it is complained that whatever assurances may be made to the contrary, Rule 11 inevitably puts its lawyer-targets under a cloud of stigma and bad feeling, seeming to label them as somehow unfit to practice after a single all-too-human error. The rule is furthermore said to stir up strife between parties who should stay on amicable terms because they may need to deal with each other in the future, namely opposing lawyers who are apt to meet again in negotiations.

The rule is also said to abet unfairness and discourage cooperation by leaving it uncertain who is liable for its penalties. Depending on a judge's sense of where responsibility lies, he can aim sanctions at lawyer alone or client alone or both together; at a lawyer who signed but did not prepare an offending paper or at one who prepared but did not sign it. For a while law firms themselves could be hit with sanctions, forcing the offender's partners to chip in, but the Supreme

Court ruled in late 1989 that only individual lawyers were responsible. In short, the rule menaces the co-participants and higher-ups in a wrongful filing with a version of what is elsewhere called joint and several liability or enterprise liability—although here at least there are no reports, as there are from the wider arena of litigation, of 5 percent wrongdoers having to pick up the tab left by 95 percent wrongdoers.

Even more fundamentally, the critics complain that Rule 11's standard for liability is vague and unpredictable. Judges have so much leeway in deciding what is sanctionable that they come out with rulings all over the map or even (some darkly hint) play favorites among classes of litigant. In many borderline cases it is not easy for a lawyer to predict beforehand what kind of shoddy filing will trigger sanctions and what will slip by. Fordham law professor Georgene Vairo warns that the result could be to "chill" creative litigation by making lawyers feel less comfortable in stretching legal principles to their limits or even setting their work to paper.

Finally, like all forms of legal activity, Rule 11 costs time and money to carry out and is sometimes used as a tactical weapon. The rule might seem like a bargain as procedural devices go because it is often aimed at very costly misconduct and yet seldom calls for barrages of discovery or pricey expert witnesses. Still, the time and money spent on this one form of "satellite" litigation deeply distresses some trial lawyers who otherwise are wont to deride complaints of the wastefulness of legal process. On this single issue, if on no other, they argue that the power of courts to rectify human failings has its natural limits, that the compensation of victims must be balanced by a due concern for freedom of action, that there must be an end put to conflict.

Now that all these arguments have at last been endorsed by litigators worried about their own liability, perhaps they will be taken with due seriousness when made by everyone else. If the imposition of Rule 11 is vague and unpredictable, revising it should be a high priority. But logic points toward revising it forward, toward fuller accountability for lawyers, and not backward to the days of lawyering with impunity.

One step toward making Rule 11's application more uniform and predictable would be for judges who have been ignoring the rule to catch up with their brethren. Courts are not only allowed but instructed to apply sanctions when they see a violation, and to do so on their own initiative, without waiting for an opponent to object. Some jurists have used the rule quite vigorously to raise the standards of practice in their courts. But others turn down nearly all requests. Many states have not adopted versions of Rule 11 at all, or enforce it only with great laxity, making it hard to get relief for misconduct in litigation however egregious.

It is important to draw a clean and predictable line on which victims of meritless litigation deserve compensation and which, if any, do not. One extensive survey reports that European courts have found it relatively hard to police distinctions between "frivolous" or bad-faith lawsuits and others. Rule 11 is sometimes spoken of, quite wrongly, as if it banned only "frivolous" litigation; but that word appears nowhere in the rule, and its coverage is plainly broader than that.

There is another place to draw the line on which litigants deserve compensation from their opponents, a line that is considerably cleaner and more intuitive. All that is needed is to recast the concept of meritlessness to reflect the best guess the legal system ever winds up making about the merits, namely the outcome of trial and appeal itself. Before describing the kind of rule that would emerge, however, it is well to step back and discuss one further facet of the Rule 11 controversy.

That is what might be called the issue of damages. How much should a wrongful litigator pay to the opponent he has harmed? Should he be let off with a warning or light penalty? (The lawyer who filed the softball suit was made to pay only a token fifty dollars.) Or should he be made an example of through punitive or treble fines, to avenge the court's dignity and achieve general deterrence of wrongful lawyering, much of which goes undetected? Or should he simply pay straight compensation for the knowable, nonspeculative expense to which he has put his opponent? Most trial courts to date have converged on this last answer. By far the commonest Rule 11 sanction in reported cases has been an award of the reasonable costs of response, mostly consisting of attorneys' fees.

The notion of awarding attorneys' fees to prevailing opponents is enough to trigger anxiety attacks in many American litigators, even those who are otherwise most hard-boiled (especially in them, in fact). It reminds them uncomfortably of the distinctive, peculiar American exception on lawsuit costs. Other civilized countries, with few if any exceptions, agree that the winner of a lawsuit deserves to be reimbursed by the loser for much if not all of the costs of the suit. Everywhere else it would be considered astounding and insupportable to afford no relief to the person or organization dragged into a civil lawsuit for years, made to unveil its internal secrets, and then vindicated on all issues.

Only America fails to recognize this right of redress. Both prevailing plaintiffs and prevailing defendants suffer from this injustice. Because attorneys' fees are normally unrecoverable in this country, plenty of valid, airtight claims trade at much less than 100 cents on the dollar on the settlement market, and others cannot economically be pressed at all: reportedly in Manhattan it is hard to get some contingency-fee firms to look at claims below $200,000. One leading commentator sardonically observes that under the "American rule" it is always irrational to pay a debt or carry out an obligation in full once the other side has finished its performance. The imbalance creates a field day for the chiseler or defaulter in any line of work where money is pocketed before service is provided or vice versa: the sloppy building contractor, the fly-by-night insurer, the crooked mail order house, anyone who lacks for one reason or another the strong aversion to being sued that most productive members of society share.

The contrary, "English" rule on costs, as it is called—

though it might just as well be called the rest-of-the-world rule—seems so intuitively appealing that there must be another side to the story. If the American rule is so patently unjust, why did it ever take hold at all? And why has it lasted for more than a century?

Two arguments sometimes made for the American rule fail to impress on inspection. First, fee-shifting might appear to raise the stakes in a lawsuit by widening its range of possible financial outcomes, thus intensifying the combat and making litigation even more of a terror to private planning. Second, it might encourage the running up of lawyers' bills, given a case of preordained size, since clients may not watch a meter closely if they know for sure that the opponent will be the one who pays it.

It is hard to get observers from other countries to take these arguments seriously, since American lawyering is known around the world as hard-fought, uncertain, and expensive. The arguments are flawed theoretically as well. European systems typically hinge their finding of whether a litigant has "prevailed" on how close he came to achieving his demands. This furnishes a strong reason for litigants not to demand ten times more than they think the court is likely to give them. The resulting moderation of demands and sobering-up of exaggerations means that litigation inflicts far less financial uncertainty in Europe than here even when fee shifts are factored in. Fee padding is more of a potential problem, but allowing the losing opponent to litigate against the fee request sets up very heavy pressure against that abuse, and as we shall see below European systems arrange their fee-shift formulas so that even clients who prevail tend to be on the hook for many of their lawyers' marginal expenditures, giving them good reason to watch the meter.

What now may seem the most perverse feature of the American rule—its denial of fees to winning plaintiffs—may account for its original evolution. A rule against fee recovery hampers the pressing of claims that are not at all speculative, that are sure to win at trial; it hampers, in short, the pressing of valid claims. And that was apparently its foreseen and intended effect in early America. The backers of the original American rule were in large measure farmers and frontiersmen who wanted to stave off the enforcement against them of debts and mortgages about whose face validity there was no real doubt.

Depending on how stringently the English rule was enforced in those days, the debtors might have had a point. Shifting *all* the costs of enforcing a valid claim can be almost unimaginably harsh. Debt collection is the classic example. A borrower has stalled or fallen behind, the lawyers swing into action, and before long they get a judgment against him for his two-hundred-dollar debt plus another eight hundred dollars in attorney fees. If every last dime in legal costs is recoverable from an opponent, lawyers can do a nice little business turning minor obligations into crushing burdens.

But European courts have found better ways to control such abuses than refusing fee recovery altogether. Their solution seems to be to low-ball the fee awards, so the winner can get back much but not all of what he paid his lawyers. In France some categories of costs cannot be recovered; in Britain the "taxing masters" (as the officials in charge of fee-shifting are known) are relative pinchpennies; and so forth. Leaving a portion of costs to fall on the winner sacrifices some of the fairness and incentive considerations that make fee-shifting so compelling in the first place, but the unpalatable alternative would seem to be the gross overkill of small claims. And in fact stinginess on winners' fee awards fits rather neatly into the view that litigation is an evil that should be discouraged. If courtroom strife is a costly and hurtful way of composing human differences, it makes sense to repress it to at least a small extent even for causes of undoubted merit.

Back in an era when most suits were predicated on a firm likelihood of success, the American rule probably cut down on the number of suits filed. What today seems strangest about it—that it actually encourages people to file doubtful and speculative suits—probably seemed like a relatively minor failing back then, if it was given much thought. An elaborate set of nonfinancial barriers still faced the feckless claimant, if not always the feckless claim-resister. In an age when pleading was strict, privacy until trial protected, home jurisdiction sacrosanct, legal solicitation forbidden, and so forth, the absence of one more major barrier to long-shot suits must not have seemed as significant.

But times have changed, of course, and the old barriers now lie flat on the ground. Rule 11, welcome as it is, does not in itself provide a comprehensive deterrent to wrongful litigation, or compensate all of its victims. And so the pressure to expand winners' fee recovery will inevitably grow.

In point of fact, it cannot be said that American law still hews to the principle of making each side pay its own costs. Fee-shifting of one kind has already caught on in a big way, and now dominates wide tracts of the legal landscape. Unfortunately, it is a kind of fee-shifting that shares the logic and neutrality of neither the English nor the American rule, while borrowing the litigation-stoking features of both. It is "one-way" shifting: the award of fees to winning plaintiffs but not to winning defendants.

The one-way fee, although perfected recently, was actually invented some time ago. A few such provisions were enacted in the last century, aimed at very rich and unpopular defendants: railroads and trusts. For many years the Supreme Court kept striking down these one-way laws, saying that they violated the constitutional rights of their targets and warning that once the principle was established a few wealthy institutions would not remain its only victims. Later it changed its mind and began upholding such rules. All its earlier warnings were then borne out.

Starting in the 1930s, picking up speed in the 1960s, and then going at feverish pace since the 1970s, lawmakers have loaded the statute books with these heads-I-win, tails-we're-even provisions. The usual practice was to proclaim a lopsided fee shift in new laws that were said to involve the "public interest." When you think of it, however, just about all the products of the legislation mills can be shipped under that self-congratulatory label. With the RICO law, to take one notable example, one-way fee shifts became available in many routine commercial disputes between businesses. Some have argued that the device is a suitable means of vindicating congressional policy in each and every law, the only practical problem being how to identify which side should be favored in each kind of case.

Courts have learned other creative ways to put just the right amount of English on the fee ball. One common interpretation is that a plaintiff has prevailed and should get fees if he wins on any issue or claim on his list, however minor, or drops his suit after the defendant alters his conduct in any way that could be interpreted as a concession. The defendant can prevail (without of course deserving fees) by stonewalling on all concessions and then winning on all contentions. "The determination of whether a litigant is a prevailing party," note the authors of one leading treatise, ". . . is guided by standards which differ markedly depending on whether the fee petitioner is a plaintiff or a defendant." Some courts began ruling that plaintiffs should get back attorneys' fees even when they *lose*, on the ground that by suing they had done a public service in helping to clarify legal issues, provide reminders of accountability, and so forth. The Supreme Court decided in 1983, amid much gnashing of molars from the "public-interest" bar, that that idea went too far.

All sides agree that one-way fee shifts to plaintiffs are meant to encourage litigation, and of course they have done just that. In the meantime, their widespread adoption has quietly undercut the chief practical argument against full, two-way fee shifting, namely that American courts are not used to calculating fees. Courts can no longer be thought to lack competence at setting proper fee levels; they do it all the time for victorious (and even hemi-demi-semi-victorious) plaintiffs. The only remaining step is to begin doing it for defendants as well.

In addition, of course, since Roman times and further back, fee-shifting has given rise to an elaborate body of law in the rest of the world, from which we might well borrow. Those countries have long since reduced the practice to a routine, governed by steady and predictable rules, to judge by a survey by Werner Pfennigstorf of European fee-shifting in the journal *Law and Contemporary Problems*.

European systems typically carve out a number of exceptions to the general fee-shifting rule. One is for criminal cases, perhaps because it is thought rough to pressure a criminal defendant to plead guilty if he has even an unreasonable belief in his own innocence. Another is for divorce: a marriage cannot be dissolved without positive court action, so that it might be said that neither spouse has unreasonably insisted on going to trial. There may still be a role for shifting fees, however, against the spouse whose demands were more out of line with the eventual court disposal of property and custody.

Litigants who raise superfluous issues or file needless motions may pay a partial or offsetting fee award even if they win the case on the merits. In split decisions, where each side wins on some issues of a case, the fee ruling can also be split (Pfennigstorf observes that this is a clarification rather than an exception to the rule). Some countries leave each side to pay its own costs after certain unusually close lawsuits, such as when a panel of judges is split on a case or a verdict is overturned on appeal. This custom, like many in fee-shifting, dates back to the Romans. European courts also maintain independent sanctions for bad conduct in litigation, which, like Rule 11, can be awarded against litigants who behave vexatiously even on the way to winning on the merits.

It is crucial that full fee recovery be denied to the litigant with an otherwise valid claim who demands vastly more than it is worth. Most countries treat such cases as outright defeats for the claim-inflater and assess fees against him, which plays an obvious (and extraordinarily important) role in discouraging Yankee-size damage claims. England gets the job done through a device that also has analogues elsewhere: the defendant can "pay into court" a settlement offer, and if the later verdict comes in below that offer the plaintiff who spurned it must pay whatever costs the defendant incurred afterward. Our own federal rules, by the way, include a device that somewhat resembles this one but has not been widely used in practice.

It has been objected that once juries know that costs will be paid by the loser, they will start fudging decisions to keep a sympathetic litigant from losing. The concern cannot be dismissed out of hand, but it should not be considered fatal. First, it is widely agreed that most juries try hard to follow legal guidelines in determining whether liability has occurred; the problem is that those guidelines are so amorphous and confusing that no consistent outcomes are possible, but changes in fee rules need not worsen that problem. Juries' damage calculations are more influenced by sympathy, but one of the sympathetic factors is currently the knowledge that winners have to pay their own costs; hence the tendency to blow up "soft" damages for things like pain and suffering to cover what is expected to be a huge lawyers' fee. Once it is known that costs will be awarded as a matter of right, that upwardly distorting influence will be removed.

To help set juries' minds at ease about sticking indigent plaintiffs with a fee shift and end Rule 11's confusion about which wrongdoer pays, it could be provided that fee shifts should normally be charged to the lawyer, with clients free to commit themselves by contract to reimburse him for such charges. That would ensure that lawyers do not litigate with impunity by lining up clients immune to judgment; yet, since lawyers would scramble to seek reimbursement agreements when they could, the more traditional principal/agent relationship, with the client in rightful control, could reestablish itself in most cases. Above all, contingency-fee lawyers who take an equity stake in legal claims should be put on the hook for at least some of the fee-shift risk, as befits true players rather than passive taxi drivers. The exposure would of course heighten the speculative nature of their activities, but they are gambling sorts and no doubt could easily spread the risk among their profits from their many clients who prevail, just as industrial manufacturers are said to be able to spread the costs of liability payouts among their many activities. Many European countries, incidentally, require litigants to post a deposit against the risk of having to pay costs after losing.

It would be interesting to see whether the contingency fee as such—that other venture in American exceptionalism—survived in its current form under a regime of full fee-shifting. Would prevailing lawyers settle for whatever hourly fee the court awarded from the opponent, or force their clients to chip in a supplementary payment as well? Either way, it would be hard for them to predemand a huge share of the award without running into some questions from clients, since if the claim wins they will already be getting what the court finds to be a reasonable hourly recompense for their work.

In the long run, one might even predict that fee-shifting would help curb the drift of American law toward vagueness and indeterminacy. Litigators in other countries do not seem to have formed themselves into a collective lobbying force against clear and objective law, the way so many of them have here. One reason may be that under a fee-shifting regime, needless legal uncertainty is not especially appealing to plaintiffs (who have something real to lose) or their lawyers. Here, every new outbreak of legal uncertainty is a much more unalloyed boon to speculative litigators. Fee-shifting encourages both lawyers and litigants to converge with their adversaries, both in the suit at hand and on the wider issue of what the law's demands should be.

America's trial lawyers and their allies carry on at length about how courts should hold people to the very strictest liability for any and all harm they may cause others, with "harm" and "cause" so broadly defined as to pass all understanding. Fee-shifting is strict liability for litigators themselves. It deters them from using compulsory process to harm fellow citizens, whether the harm be negligent, intentional, or by ill chance.

Indeed, strict liability for lawyering is much more benign and workable than the new forms of liability found elsewhere in the modern law. It need not, for example, result in speculative and open-ended damage calculations. The employer sued by a former employee for giving a bad reference, the corporate management sued by a stockholder for failing to disclose some news development, the movie star sued by the former paramour who quit a job to keep house for him, can only guess wildly as to what they might be made to pay. Not so the payor of the type of fee-shift practiced in the rest of the world. Those assessments can be based on purely historical out-of-pocket costs. They do not require thirty-year income projections. They do not cover emotional distress, loss of enjoyment of life, or unhappiness caused to family members, although all three are very real in litigation. They should seldom require outside expert testimony. They are not tripled. They are not punitive. And so they will be much more predictable and even insurable, and less disruptive to the planning of daily life, than almost any of the novel legal obligations that have been so freely created in recent years.

Symmetrical, two-way fee-shifting has begun its progress on these shores. It has been the rule since the 1920s in Alaska, which admittedly boasts an atypical legal culture. Arizona shifts fees for breach-of-contract claims. Florida shifts them for medical malpractice claims. A 1970 amendment to the Federal Rules of Civil Procedure made two-way shifting the rule for disputed discovery motions, as well as for the rare cases where a lawyer's bad faith can be shown.

Full two-way fee-shifting is the single most important and constructive legal reform that ordinary citizens can fight for over the long term. It is memorably simple, and fair, and not easily subverted once put into effect. It may also be the only reform that could render tolerable today's procedural system of push-button litigation on demand, if that system is one we want to keep. If the coercive power to drag others to court is not tempered by some levying of costs on those who use that power for ill, the injustice it visits on the innocent will inevitably lead to pressure to ration its use in some other way, when the victims of wrongful litigation finally rise up and organize themselves.

Plaintiffs with strong cases have everything to gain from fee-shifting, and will be the most fiercely fought-over allies in the coming battle for legal reform. Trial lawyers sometimes contend that in a system of two-way fee-shifting these plaintiffs would be so terrified of the fluke chance of losing that they would not dare to file their rightful suits. In reality, the vast majority of cases will as always be settled out of court, and the right of fee recovery will boost the settlement value of the truly strong cases. As Oxford's Patrick Atiyah reminds us, the British accident victim with a good claim can find a lawyer just as easily as the American. And the British complainant gets the full value of the claim, without having to deduct a huge lawyer's contingency. The only real pressure on the litigant with a good claim would be not to exaggerate its value, and that does not seem too much to ask. It is the heavily contingent unlikely-to-succeed wildcat litigators who would be discouraged by fee-shifting. And they are precisely the ones who should long ago have been driven from the courthouse. Lawyers typically proclaim their complete confidence in the merits of their clients' causes. By the horror with which they react to full fee-shifting, we will get a good idea of their sincerity.

16

☤

THE BALANCE OF LEGAL PEACE

There never was a good war or a bad peace.

—BENJAMIN FRANKLIN, *letter to
Josiah Quincy (1773)*

For all the many successes of American society, our system of civil litigation is a grotesque failure, a byword around the world for expense, rancor, and irrationality. America's litigation explosion has squandered immense fortunes, sent the cream of a nation's intellectual talent into dubious battle, reduced valuable enterprises to ruin, made miserable the practice of honorable professions, and brought needless pain to broken families. It has been a spiral of destructive recrimination, with no end in sight.

This practical failure is born of an underlying moral failure. Our law has ceased to attach moral significance to wrongful accusation. The fee-shifting practiced in all other major countries has a plain ethical meaning: accusation is a serious matter. Do not expect to offer excuses if you have accused wrongly. The apparatus of coercion is not there to be deployed at your whim.

The former American law embodied the same message through a series of indirect regulatory barriers that served many of the same ends as a direct financial levy. Hence the tenets of the old legal ethics: that the good lawyer did not go about looking for chances to litigate, that he tried to maintain a certain objectivity about the cause he advanced, remaining aloof from the enthusiasms of his client. Hence, too, the deep ambivalence of the older system of procedure, which created formal rights, yet gently dissuaded people from pressing them. The hinge of strife would swing, but it was not to be perfectly oiled. Hence the modesty of the old law in almost every area, deferring to objective triggers and private contractual choices even at the sacrifice from time to time of the preferences of those who ran the system. Hence finally the view of a lawsuit as something unfortunate, something with more losers than winners, a poor substitute for getting along with each other.

The legal thinkers and ethicists of an earlier day recognized that litigation had an inevitable role to play in life. Like the cutting of flesh in surgery, it was no disgrace when done for the best of reasons and with minimum damage to healthy tissue. As such, it could attract minds of the highest probity, humanity, and intellectual capacity. But it was hardly to be employed when prophylactics or gentler remedies might avert its trauma. And like surgery, it could become a horror in the hands of the truly bad, of those who had never acquired, or had thrown away, a moral compass.

To the makers of our modern law, this extreme caution and modesty seemed too many miles from Utopia. The law did too little to help remake society along more desirable lines. It permitted too much inertia. It was too kind to rights in possession and not kind enough to rights for which a case could be made.

They concluded that litigation was not a bad but a good,

not a costly sink but a bottomless fount of public benefits. They began to imagine that the best legal system is the one that imposes the most judicial correction; and since the way to get more judicial correction is to generate more denunciations to the authorities, they began to hail contentiousness as the mark of a good public citizen and dismiss acceptance and forbearance as a betrayal of victimhood.

This vision is at the ultimate origin of today's abuses. It is why the stirring up of fights can be conceived as a public spirited enterprise; why the reigning view of lawyers' ethical responsibility is all gas pedal and no brake; why it has been made so easy to start a suit and so hard to get one finished; why privacy is sacrificed to an ever-wider dragnet for incriminating matter; why opponents can blithely be denounced to whichever court and under whichever law appear most likely to condemn their actions; why fees are shifted often to those who file lawsuits and win, but hardly ever to the wrongly accused; why guesswork and guilt-finding, formerly kept so scrupulously separate by every system of justice that aspired to the name, have been allowed to combine into a poisonous mixture.

The ideology of litigation, in its contradictory and multiplicitous way, has something spurious to offer every political viewpoint. For radicals it offers an unending pantomime of class struggle and social upheaval, exposing the ultimate antagonisms between workers and bosses, consumers and producers, husbands and wives, in a perfect orgy of consciousness-raising and grievance. For democrats it promises to impose the social norms of common-man juries and bring private concentrations of wealth and power to heel. For conservatives it claims to mold antisocial defendants into lawabiding citizens through the forms of a cherished tradition of legal order. For boosters of economic prosperity it vows to correct inefficiencies in markets and bring ultra-advanced business techniques to the legal profession itself. For libertarians it purports to defend individual rights against the coercive impositions of the outside world.

It fails on every front. Endless litigation displays many of the painful side effects of social upheaval, but few of the looked-for benefits. It encourages self-seeking, but not to productive purpose; it forces people to knuckle under to social norms—at least those of this week's judge and jury—but only by destroying any chances left for harmony between the actual parties. It is the safest and stodgiest way of playing at revolution, the most invasive and coercive way of asserting a right to be left alone, the most divisive and alienating tactic for rallying community opinion. A litigation explosion is a civil war in very, very slow motion.

As such, it advances no coherent theory of individual rights or the common good. No philosophy that champions the rights of individuals should accept the irresponsible deployment of compulsory process against private citizens or the suppression of free contract, the cornerstone of personal autonomy in social interaction. No philosophy of community and mutual aid should welcome a regime of law that sets people against each other in adversarial bitterness at every turn. No philosophy of utilitarian growth and progress should favor paralyzing productive initiative by strewing the legal environment with concealed land mines of unpredictable jeopardy.

Nor is endless litigation any friend of the downtrodden and wretched. It impoverishes women and children in family breakups. It sends aggrieved workers to live embittered in their rooms rather than rejoin the world of work. It becomes an obsessive hobby into which distressed persons pour the energy with which they could have climbed out of their distresses. Yes, it does afflict the comfortable, if that is thought to be a worthy goal. It throws a fear into those with something to lose—although, come to think of it, nearly everyone has at least a child, car, pension, or garden plot that some litigator might find worth taking away from them. But litigation is equally a notorious weapon in the hands of wealthy and unscrupulous persons and enterprises for whom legal aggression is just another means of self-aggrandizement. Have-nots are seldom the ultimate winners in a war of all against all.

As a program to share wealth or less tangible benefits, anyway, lawsuits are absurdly slow, capricious, and inefficient: of the money they shift around, more than half gets dissipated in the process of transfer. And much of that winds up in the pockets of what when all is said and done may be the most prosperous body of professionals in the world. Piecemeal, arbitrary expropriations, after titanic struggles with the collecting agents, surely do more dollar-for-dollar damage to the spirit of enterprise than almost any scheme of predictable and proportionate taxation.

Up to a point, litigation can surely deter misconduct, just as the invisible-fist theory would have it. For fear of being sued, some drivers will keep a few extra lengths behind the car in front, which is a good thing. Tailgaters are also deterred by fear of being mangled in crashes: fear of colliding with people's fenders is even more effective in inducing caution than fear of colliding with their legal interests. Which does not mean society is better off every time a tailgater gets mangled, or taken to court. The fate of those who are justly sued can remind the rest of us that we ought to lead better lives, but in that respect it is no different from the dreadful example set by other personal disasters, such as cirrhosis of the liver.

And what of the promise that stepping up the level of litigation would bring about more justice by disposing of more human conflicts on the merits? Leave aside the question of what sort of merits could possibly be reflected in the random and inconsistent findings of guesswork-driven courts. Suppose for a moment that all courtroom determinations are accurate. Is it really worth any amount of additional lawyering to get the tiniest extra bit of substantive rights enforced? Does the substantive evil of denying someone a minor remedy to which some law entitles him always outweigh the procedural evil of tying up an opponent for years without explaining the case against him, or ruining him with legal fees? We all want our legal rights enforced when we are out of possession, of course, but we also want to keep our rights in possession out of eternal jeopardy and suspense. Both, not just the substantive right, are issues of fairness. Both pertain to real human beings. There is no reason for low substantive cards to trump high procedural ones.

But that is not the choice we actually face. Today's American law shortchanges both kinds of fairness alike. Because it invites defendants with weak cases to head for the labyrinth of discovery and motions practice and denies most winning plaintiffs a fee recovery, it does not in fact do a good job of helping plaintiffs with what used to be called open-and-shut cases. Plaintiffs with truly strong cases do not profit from the spread of vague, subjective legal standards and case-by-case judicial discretion, which may if anything embolden their opponents to put up resistance. They do not need to bring in low-grade evidence to confuse the issues, or shop around carefully for the right forum, law, or jury. They want to get to trial quickly, not wait while bad cases clog the dockets. Their cause suffers when public confidence in the legal system ebbs away and lawsuits come to be seen as something-for-nothing bids instead of quests for resolution.

But our law is not genuinely pro-plaintiff; it is merely pro-litigation. It is preoccupied with drawing forth the borderline and speculative claim, not the solid and unquestionable. Advertising and solicitation now as always concentrate on the marginal customer, not the one whose mind is already made up. Accusation-made-easy pleadings, home-delivery jurisdiction, negative-checkoff class actions, dial-an-expert testimony mills—all of these work to pull in participants who would not have bothered to sue had it been any real trouble.

Persons who press their legal rights to the limit should be discouraged from imagining that they are somehow performing a public service. We have all met the sorts of persons who invariably see trespass when a schoolchild cuts across their lawn, nuisance when the neighbors play their stereo too

loud on Saturday night, fraud when a mail order purchase is
not all they had hoped for. On the defendants' side, likewise,
we have all met persons who see no reason they should pay
the rent or send the child support check until a court forces
it out of them. Maybe the law should give both types of person
the adjudications they insist on. But it should not let them
set themselves up as general benefactors.

The litigious person might respond that he is just more
insistent on asserting his rights than the rest of us. He may
even hint that, in being less than enamored of his rights
assertions, we are more likely to be ourselves the sort of
insensitive people who trample others' rights. In real life,
however, the kind of people who take others to court a lot
as plaintiffs also frequently tend to find themselves taken
there as defendants. The same assertiveness is at work in the
kind of bullying that flouts authority and the kind that enlists
it. And the same live-and-let-live attitude is missing.

Civil law, when it works well, can protect us from many, if
hardly all, of the wrongs done to us in the outside world. It
should also protect us from the wrongs that can be done in
the courtroom itself: false accusation and false resistance to
just legal claims. Fee-shifting is the ultimate answer to the
problem of hit-and-run accusation, because it matches the
economic incentives to the practical and moral realities of
imposition. But a truly humane legal system could go further
to avoid what might be called the vice of oversensitivity. The
most useful burglar alarms are not those that go off at the
smallest vibrations; and the law might well seek to absorb
rather than transmit some of the inevitable shocks and stresses
of living in a world that is full of other people.

One familiar way the law can install padding around its
coercive machinery is by heightening its standard of proof.
The customary standard for proving a civil case is a mere
"preponderance of the evidence," or 50 percent plus a
smidgen. Imposing a tougher standard across the board would
not be easy, in part because it would penalize the first to file

in the many two-way disputes where either side can sue. (Although it would be a refreshing change to see the race to the courthouse replaced by a race to forbearance in which each side held back from striking the first legal blow.) Where the stigma or disruption value of litigation is high, however, there may be little alternative. The lawmakers of Michigan, specifically citing the need to keep children from being put through needless court fights, have provided that whoever wishes to reopen a settled custody case must prove by clear and convincing evidence that the child would benefit. Many states have raised the standard of proof in punitive claims, and at least one, Colorado, has set it where it belongs: at "beyond a reasonable doubt," the standard of criminal law.

It took centuries of struggle against arbitrary authority to establish the civil-liberty safeguards that protect criminal defendants from being railroaded to punishment. Today the forces of irresponsible accusation have turned instead to the civil law, which they like better anyway because they get to keep the proceeds. Reasonable persons can differ as to exactly how much due process should attach to civil jeopardy. What should not be in dispute is that to whatever extent odium is allowed to attach to civil charges, the targets should partake of at least some of the protections against being railroaded that are enjoyed by those accused of criminal wrongdoing. And where odium is the whole point—as with punitive and triple damages—the protections should be comparable to those on the criminal side of the law. Self-incrimination, junk evidence, complaints that do not specifically inform the defendant of the charges from the start, should all be out of bounds. And a disinterested prosecutor sworn to public norms, not a contingency-fee lawyer, should be the one to press the charges.

The most sorely missed protection of all is the kind of clear, objective law that lets people and enterprises know whether and when they are at risk of liability. It is always tempting to support a vaguely drafted new law when the vagueness does not seem to endanger—or, worse, when it seems to benefit—the side we think of as sympathetic or deserving of protection. This is the stirring of, at base, a temptation to despotism. Law is not law at all—it is merely the arbitrary imposition of power—when it refuses to give fair advance notice of how its coercions will be applied.

It is always when our sense of indignation carries us away that we are most likely to overlook due process and fair play. Moral outrage is the favorite propellant of litigious persons and of the legal culture that so caters to their predilections. Litigation buffs can reel off case histories of callous corporations, slovenly surgeons, pathological bosses, and hubbies-from-hell that would make anyone angry. Their typical method of arguing against fair play in litigation is to re-try in the public forum their favorite winning cases from the jury box.

But if the sword of indignation is to be admitted into our civil law, it should cut both ways. The outraged plaintiff today can ask for punitive or triple fines that may bankrupt his opponent. The outraged defendant cannot recover even singly, let alone in triplicate, for the harm to his reputation in being wrongly accused of fraud or sexual harassment or unfitness as a parent or the selling of tainted food. Even a rule to shift legal fees would give him, well, mere fees, when an attorney's bill might be the least of his losses.

Some boast that America is the most advanced of all nations in developing rights of redress. But in fact we are among the most backward, because our legal system does not redress the ills it inflicts itself. If our law, not content to draw the bounds of our tangible rights, insists on policing our general adherence to the Ten Commandments, let it not forget the eighth, the only one specifically addressed to the justice system: Thou shalt not bear false witness.

America is now reaping the harvest of a strange and ill-considered experiment in its legal system. We have deputized our immense professional body of lawyers to stir up grievance for profit. We have invented procedures that make it astonishingly easy for them to entangle other citizens in compulsory process. We have raised the stakes in their assaults to the point where the labors of a lifetime are time and again blasted in a moment by the chances of the courtroom. We have allowed the laws themselves to slide gradually into undefined, shadowy forms, their content worked out case by case after the fact depending on an advocate's prowess rather than proclaimed in advance for all.

No great abuse was ever ended without a struggle. The industry that has sprung up around contention and accusation is powerful. It will not lightly give up its control of the machinery of judicial compulsion, any more than other powerful classes will lightly give up the control of tanks in countries where wars are carried on by means less subtle than words. As individuals and in our larger associations, we are most of us terribly vulnerable to the perils of litigation. Yet as a society, we are in no sense helpless to move against its evils. All it takes is the will. The will may not be here yet, but it is coming. When it does, we will again make litigation an exception, a last resort, a necessary evil at the margins of our common life.

ACKNOWLEDGMENTS

For ten years Bill Hammett of the Manhattan Institute has carried on a farsighted program to support the writing of books on public affairs. This volume, like many before it, is a product of that program, which gave me not only long and patient financial backing but also a degree of freedom that few writers enjoy. The institute's staff also provided endless logistical help, intellectual stimulation and moral support. No organization I can think of has done so much on such a comparatively slender outlay to enrich the climate of debate in our country.

Many friends and colleagues read the manuscript and offered unstinting critical advice, above all Peter Huber. Richard Epstein, George Gilder, Charles Murray, Richard Neely, Jeffrey O'Connell, Mark Riebling, and especially Lynn Baker offered valuable written comments. The book was likewise improved by conversations with David Bernstein, Doug Besharov, Peter Brimelow, Gordon Crovitz, Mark Eldridge and the London hosts of the U.S./U.K. Conference on Legal Services Reform, Don Elliott, Maggie Gallagher, Mike Greve, Alex Kozinski, David Frum, Ed Kitch, Gary Lawson, Lee Liberman, Michael McConnell, Gene Meyer, Larry Mone, James Perry, Judy Pendell, George Priest and participants in his Yale Law School conferences on civil procedure, Leslie Spencer, Terry Teachout, Richard Vigilante, and many others, including participants in a series of Manhattan Institute conferences on legal issues. My thanks as well to the staff of the Brooklyn Law School library and to George Johnson for the use of their research facilities.

My publisher, Truman Talley, got me off to a good start by encouraging me to paint on a broad canvas. If not for Steve Pippin the book would not have been possible at all.

Notes

FOREWORD

"Distinctly medieval": Philip Shuchman, "Ethics and Legal Ethics: The Propriety of the Canons as a Group Moral Code," 37 *George Washington Law Review* 244, 263–66 (1968).

Five-to-four decision: Bates v. State Bar of Arizona, 97 S.Ct. 2691 (1977).

Harvard study: Peter Huber, "Malpractice Law—A Defective Product," *Forbes*, April 16, 1990.

Institute of Medicine study: "Malpractice Costs Cut Ranks of Those Who Deliver Babies," Associated Press dispatch, *The New York Times*, October 12, 1989.

Miami neurosurgeon premiums: Diana Henriques, "Just What the Doctor Ordered," *Barron's*, October 2, 1989.

New York City figures: Statement by Mayor Edward I. Koch before the Governor's Advisory Commission on Liability Insurance, February 21, 1986.

Patrick Atiyah quote: "Tort Law and the Alternatives: Some Anglo-American Comparisons," 1987 *Duke Law Journal* 1002, 1017.

International survey: "Tort Cost Trends: An International Perspective" (Simsbury, Ct.: Tillinghast, 1989).

Tie up anyone's bid for a year: Jeffrey Sheban, "Takeover Game in Britain Is Played With Rules That Would Halt U.S. Deals," *The Wall Street Journal,* November 3, 1989.

Survey on California employment verdicts: Reported in *The Wall Street Journal,* March 3, 1987. *Drug test award:* reported in *The Wall Street Journal,* August 8, 1989.

Survey of top lawyer incomes: Peter Brimelow and Leslie Spencer, "The Plaintiff Attorneys' Great Honey Rush," *Forbes,* October 16, 1989.

CHAPTER 1

Major Hopkins advertisement: Quoted in Murray Teigh Bloom, *The Trouble With Lawyers* (Simon and Schuster, 1968), p. 110. Bloom cites a 1964 column, "The Family Lawyer," syndicated by the American Bar Association.

Los Angeles case: Mayer v. State Bar, 26 P.2d 11. *Kentucky case:* Petition of Hubbard, 267 S.W.2d 743.

Obviously improper: Henry Drinker, *Legal Ethics* (Columbia University Press, 1953), p. 64.

How much new legal business: Jerome Wilson, "Madison Avenue, Meet the Bar," 61 *A.B.A. Journal* 586 (1975).

Absolute and compelling need: James G. Frierson, "Legal Advertising: Can It Become a Life Preserver for the Profession?," 2 *Barrister* 6 (1975).

Bates & O'Steen case: Bates v. State Bar of Arizona, 97 S. Ct. 2691 (1977).

Sokolove ads: David Stipp, "With Hard-Hitting Ads, Liability Lawyer Wins Clients—and Raises Colleagues' Ire," *The Wall Street Journal,* July 3, 1986.

Television ads: "Lawyer Ads Are Rising," *New York Times,* April 5, 1990.

L. A. Times ads: Reported in *The Wall Street Journal,* November 4, 1986; "The Stress Sweepstakes," *The Wall Street Journal,* February 4, 1987.

Philip Zauderer case: Zauderer v. Office of Disciplinary Counsel, Supreme Court of Ohio, 105 S.Ct. 2265 (1985).

"Political or ideological": In re Primus, 436 U.S. 412 (1978). Targeted letters: Shapero v. Kentucky Bar Association, 486 U.S. 466 (1988).

Northwest crash: " 'Priest' at Detroit Crash Suspected as Impostor," *The New York Times,* September 14, 1987; Wayne Green, "Bar Groups Take on Ambulance Chasers," *The Wall Street Journal,* September 28, 1988. The Red Cross charge was attributed to Texas Bar Association president James Sales.

Tanker-chasing: Jill Abramson, "A Slick of Lawyers Spreads from Valdez Oil Spill," *The Wall Street Journal,* April 13, 1989.

McCoy, Wells article: "In the Valdez Spill Lies Opportunity to Really Clean Up," *The Wall Street Journal,* April 10, 1989.

Biggest ambulance chase in history: Quoted in John Jenkins, *The Litigators* (Doubleday, 1989).

Refusing to talk: Martin Mayer, *The Lawyers* (Dell, 1968), p. 8. *Chivas Regal:* Patricia Bellew Gray, "Lawyer Harry Lipsig Makes a Killing Suing People of New York," *The Wall Street Journal,* March 16, 1988.

Out of the woodwork: Ellen Joan Pollock, "Lawyers Abandon Resistance to P.R. firms," *The Wall Street Journal,* March 14, 1990.

Dan Dorfman column: USA Today, November 6, 1987.

Meeting people's needs: "New Partner in the Firm: The Marketing Director," *The New York Times,* June 2, 1989.

Outstanding number of errors: Bill Richards and Barry Meier, "Lawyers Lead Hunt for New Groups of Asbestos Victims," *The Wall Street Journal,* February 18, 1987.

Henry Drinker quote: Legal Ethics, p. 211. *Pests of civil society:* William Blackstone, *Commentaries on the Laws of England* (Garland rep., 1978), v. 4, p. 135.

Come around to me: Finley Peter Dunne, *Mr. Dooley on the Choice of Law* (Michie, 1963), p. 36.

Drawing a line: Frierson, "Legal Advertising: Can It Become a Life Preserver for the Profession?"

But what of it?: Jethro Lieberman, *Crisis at the Bar* (Norton, 1978), p. 103.

Professional responsibility: Monroe Freedman, "Access to the Legal System: The Professional Responsibility to Chase Ambulances," in Monroe Freedman, ed., *Lawyers' Ethics in an Adversary System* (Bobbs-Merrill, 1975).

CHAPTER 2

Eisen case: Dennis Hevesi, "Three Lawyers Accused of Using Bribes and Faked Evidence," *The New York Times,* January 12, 1990; Wade Lambert and Wayne Green, "Personal-Injury Lawyers Charged With Fraud," *The Wall Street Journal,* January 12, 1990. A trial on the charges began in November 1990 and was expected to last several months.

New Jersey firm: "U.S. Court Rules Law Firm's Client Files Can Be Searched in Criminal Inquiry," *The Wall Street Journal,* August 4, 1989.

Miami lawyers: Joe Starita, "Insurance Mill Enriches Lawyers, Doctors," *Miami Herald,* October 9, 1988.

"Scrupulous fairness": Gordon Crovitz, "Contingency Fees and the Common Good," *The Wall Street Journal*, July 21, 1989.

Find a lawyer as easily in England as here: Patrick Atiyah, "Tort Law and the Alternatives: Some Anglo-American Comparisons," 1987 *Duke Law Journal* 1002, 1017.

Sharswood quote: George Sharswood, *An Essay on Professional Ethics* (T.&J. Johnson & Co., 1907).

Arch-tempter to the ambulance chaser: Quoted in Murray Teigh Bloom, *The Trouble With Lawyers* (New York: Simon and Schuster, 1968), p. 138.

Drinker quote: Legal Ethics (Columbia University Press, 1953), p. 65.

University of Iowa survey: Gilbert Cranberg, "In Libel, Money Isn't Everything," *The Wall Street Journal*, July 13, 1989.

Income survey: Peter Brimelow and Leslie Spencer, "The Plaintiff Attorneys' Great Honey Rush," *Forbes*, October 16, 1989. The Brimelow/Spencer article and accompanying tables are an invaluable resource in understanding the emerging litigation industry.

Richard Grand income: Laurence Bodine, "Your Best Defense? Advice from the Plaintiff Bar," *The Wall Street Journal*, April 2, 1990.

Well into seven figures: Patricia Bellew Gray, "Lawyer Harry Lipsig Makes a Killing Suing People of New York," *The Wall Street Journal*, March 16, 1988.

Ron Motley income: Karen Dillon, "Only $1.5 Million a Year," *The American Lawyer*, October 1989.

Eisen spokesman: "Three Lawyers Accused of Using Bribes and Faked Evidence."

FTC report: Cited in Gordon Crovitz, "Contingency Fees and the Common Good."

Alleged O'Quinn use of "runners": Wayne Green, "Bar Groups Take on Ambulance Chasers," *The Wall Street Journal*, September 28, 1988.

O'Quinn quotes: Dianna Solis, "O'Quinn Defeats Tenneco With Emotion," *The Wall Street Journal*, December 16, 1988.

CHAPTER 3

Minkoff suit: "Investor's Suit Settled by CBS," *The New York Times*, January 4, 1990.

Nothing self-evidently wrong with champerty: Philip Shuchman, "Ethics and Legal Ethics: The Propriety of the Canons as a Group Moral Code," 37 *George Washington Law Review* 244, 263–66 (1968).

ComputerLand case: "Selling Interests in Syndicated Lawsuits Raises Cash—and Questions over Ethics," *The Wall Street Journal*, October 20, 1988.

Court did away with rule on likely merit: Eisen v. Carlisle & Jaquelin, 417 U.S. 156, 94 S.Ct. 2140 (1974).

Class members need not feel aggrieved: Jack Friedenthal, Mary Kay Kane, and Arthur Miller, *Civil Procedure* (West, 1985), p. 734.

Bakker: "Bakker's TV Ministry Sued for $601 Million," *The New York Times,* April 26, 1987.

School sports: Lavin v. Chicago, 73 F.R.D. 438 (1979). See Deborah Rhode, "Class Conflicts in Class Actions," 34 *Stanford Law Review* 1183 (1982).

Only so much: Ajax, tr. John Moore (Univ. of Chicago Press, 1957), 11. 676–79.

Settling asbestos claims: Leslie Cheek III, comments at Brookings Institution conference on civil liability, Washington, D.C., June 1987.

No one so much as the plaintiff's lawyer: Satterwhite v. City of Greenville, 557 F.2d 414 (1977).

Drop the fiction: "Class Standing and the Class Representative," *Harvard Law Review,* (May, 1981), p. 1637.

CHAPTER 4

Home a better place: As You Like It, Act II, scene iv.

Ida Weitz case: Davis v. St. Paul-Mercury Indemnity Co., 294 F.2d 641 (4th Cir. 1961).

Most important principle: Coleman's Appeal, 75 Pa. 441, 458 (1874).

Hotel case: Fisher v. Fielding, 34 A. 714 (Ct. 1895).

Airplane in flight case: Grace v. MacArthur, 170 F.Supp. 442 (E.D. Ark. 1959).

Pennoyer v. Neff case: 95 U.S. 714 (1878).

Holmes opinion: Flexner v. Farson, 248 U.S. 289 (1918).

International Shoe case: 326 U.S. 310.

Florida court: Hanson v. Denckla, 357 U.S. 235 (1958).

Go to Virgin Islands: Hendrickson v. Reg O Co., 657 F.2d 9 (3rd Cir. 1981).

Bus parts: Duple Motor Bodies, Ltd. v. Hollingsworth, 417 F.2d 231 (9th Cir. 1969).

Florida journalist: Calder v. Jones, 104 S.Ct. 1482 (1984).

Telephone bids: Parke-Bernet Galleries, Inc. v. Franklyn, 256 N.E.2d 506 (N.Y. 1973).

Cleopatra: Taylor v. Portland Paramount Corporation, 383 F.2d 634 (9th Cir. 1972).

Prescription: Wright v. Yackley, 459 F.2d 287 (9th Cir. 1972).

Cornelison v. Chaney case: 545 P.2d 264 (Cal. 1976).

Irresistible New York method: Seider v. Roth, 216 N.E. 312 (N.Y. 1966).
Experienced injury lawyer's estimates: "How Much Is a Human Life Worth?,"
 Chicago Sun-Times, May 25, 1980, cited in Marshall Shapo, reporter,
 "Toward a Jurisprudence of Injury: The Continuing Creation of a
 System of Substantive Justice in American Tort Law" (Report to the
 American Bar Association, November 1984), p. 2–26.
New York City survey: Statement by Mayor Edward I. Koch before Gov-
 ernor's Advisory Commission on Liability Insurance, February 21,
 1986.
Refile in court with higher verdicts: Schimansky v. Nelson, 374 N.Y.S.2d 771
 (App. Div. 1975).
Tank-car spill case: "Wheel of Fortune," *The Wall Street Journal*, November
 16, 1987.
Earl Cowan case: Cowan v. Ford, 694 F.2d 104 (1982); 719 F.2d 785
 (1983); 713 F.2d 700 (1983).
Kathy Keeton case: Keeton v. Hustler Magazine, Inc., 104 S.Ct. 1473 (1984).
 See Peter Huber, "Courts of Convenience," *Regulation*, September/
 October 1985.
If forum selection is considered so important: Stacy Adler, "Forum Can Be
 Deciding Factor in Coverage Suits," *Business Insurance*, November
 21, 1988, p. 82.
Eastern Air Lines: Rosalind Resnick, "Bankruptcy Lawyers Lose a Foe in
 Florida," *National Law Journal*, February 19, 1990.
Texas concentration: Peter Brimelow and Leslie Spencer, "The Plaintiff
 Attorneys' Great Honey Rush," *Forbes*, October 16, 1989.
McDonnell Douglas: Douglas Besharov, "Forum-Shopping, Forum-
 Skipping and the Problem of International Competitiveness," in Wal-
 ter Olson, ed., *New Directions in Liability Law* (Academy of Political
 Science, 1988).

CHAPTER 5

Star Chamber quote: H.G. Hanbury, *English Courts of Law* (Oxford Univ.
 Press, 2nd ed., 1953), p. 82.
Sample custody pleading: Child Custody & Visitation Law & Practice (Matthew
 Bender, 1983), p. 25–14 (supplement).
Upon the facts: Walrath v. Hanover Fire Ins. Co., 110 N.E. 426, 427 (N.Y.
 1913).
Very first civil complainant: The case is reported in Genesis 3: 9–13.
Illinois case: Spangler v. Pugh, 21 Ill. 85 (1859).
Cannot clearly be discerned: Fleming James, Jr., and Geoffrey C. Hazard,
 Jr., *Civil Procedure*, 2nd ed. (Little, Brown, 1977), p. 87.

Rush of weak and ill-considered claims: O.L. McCaskill, "The Modern Philosophy of Pleading: A Dialogue Outside the Shades," 38 *A.B.A. Journal* 123 (February 1952). See also James Fee, "The Lost Horizon in Pleadings," 48 *Columbia Law Review* 491 (1948).

Thinking through a case: Moses Lasky, Memo for the Committee on Rule 8, 13 F.R.D. 275 (1952).

Pleading formalism: Roger Haydock, David Herr, and Jeffrey Stempel, *Fundamentals of Pretrial Litigation* (West, 1985), ch. 3.

Dioguardi v. Durning case: 139 F.2d 774 (2nd Cir. 1944).

Judge Silverman cases: Porter, under Nelson v. N.Y.U. Medical Center, 381 N.Y.S.2d 491 (1976); Friedman v. Tobias, 363 N.Y.S.2d 432 (1974).

It is a serious matter: A.W. Barron & A. Holtzoff, *Federal Practice and Procedure* s. 302, at 215 (Wright rev. 1960).

Cole Porter case: Arnstein v. Porter, 154 F.2d 464 (2nd Cir. 1946).

More time to prepare his defense: Robbins v. Jordan, 181 F.2d 793 (D.C. Cir. 1950).

Unison Industries lawsuits: Communication to author from Frederick Sontag, president, Unison Industries, February 1, 1990. See also David Collogan, "It's Just Not Fair," *Business and Commercial Aviation*, August 1989.

No apparent origin: Edward W. Cleary, "The Uses of Pleading," 40 *Kentucky Law Journal* 46 (1951).

CHAPTER 6

All inventors know about depositions: Tom Wolfe, "Land of Wizards," *Popular Mechanics*, rep. in Gay Talese, ed., *The Best American Essays of 1987* (Ticknor & Fields, 1987).

Custody interrogatory: Matthew Bender & Co., *Bender's Forms of Discovery*, Support and Custody (Rel. 33-4/86 Pub. 103 [v. 1–10]).

British rules: Jeremy Epstein, "English Discovery: Simpler and Cheaper," *National Law Journal*, November 28, 1988. The English case is Harmon v. Home Secretary, A.C. 280 at 308 (Keith, J.) (1983).

Fishing expedition: Fleming James, Jr., and Geoffrey C. Hazard, Jr., *Civil Procedure*, 2nd ed. (Little, Brown, 1977), p. 87.

Anything goes: Moses Lasky, Memo for the Committee on Rule 8, 13 F.R.D. 275 (1952).

1949 proposal: "Tactical Use and Abuse of Depositions," 59 *Yale Law Journal* 117, 133 (1949).

Margaret Bultman case: Heiner v. North American Coal Corp., 3 F.R.D. 64, 65 (W.D.Pa. 1942).

Hanst quote: Charles Maher, "Discovery Abuse," *California Lawyer*, June 1984.

IBM case: Nicholas deB. Katzenbach, "Modern Discovery: Remarks from the Defense Bar," 57 *St. Johns Law Review* 732, 733–34 (1983).

Sam Walton case: Christi Harlan, "Wal-Mart Is Fined Sum of $11,550,000 for Late Testimony," *The Wall Street Journal*, January 3, 1989.

Survey of lawyer objectives: William A. Glaser, *Pretrial Discovery and the Adversary System* (Russell Sage, 1968), pp. 58–63.

Ignore witness questions: Roger Haydock and David Herr, *Discovery Practice* (Little, Brown, 1982), p. 201.

More forceful personality: James Jeans, Sr., *Litigation* (Kluwer, 1986), p. 216.

Very ugly documents: DF Activities Corp. v. Brown, 851 F.2d 920, 923 (7th Cir. 1988).

Three hundred and eighty-one-page set of interrogatories: In re U. S. Fin. Sec. Lit., 75 F.R.D. 702, 707 (S.D. Cal. 1977), 74 F.R.D. 497, 497 (S.D. Cal. 1975).

One of today's compendiums: Douglas Danner, *Pattern Discovery: Medical Malpractice* (Lawyers' Co-op, 1985).

Taxi company: Edward Savell, "Basic Use of Discovery Procedures—Some Practical Problems," 3 *Forum* 197, 199–200 (1968) (A.B.A. Section on Insurance, Negligence and Compensation Law).

Snow in July: Frost v. Williams, 46 F.R.D. 484 (D. Md. 1969).

Sixty-four million pages in IBM case: Michael A. Pope, "Rule 34: Controlling the Paper Avalanche", in John G. Koelti, ed., *The Litigation Manual* (A.B.A. Section of Litigation, 1989), p. 75.

Responding as third party: Charles Maher, "Discovery Abuse," *California Lawyer*, June 1984.

Sears files: Kozlowski v. Sears, 73 F.R.D. 73 (D. Mass. 1976).

Computerized data base: Bell v. Auto Club of Michigan, 80 F.R.D. 228 (E.D. Mich. 1978).

Vaccine case: Graham v. Wyeth, 666 F. Supp. 1483 (Kan. 1987).

"Does not appear to save": Maurice Rosenberg, "Changes Ahead in Federal Pretrial Discovery," 45 F.R.D. 479 (1968).

Legal services: The Law and Direct Citizen Action, p. 14, quoted by Rael Jean Isaac, "Bringing Down the System Through 'Training'—The LSC Manuals and Training Materials," in *Legal Services Corporation: The Robber Barons of the Poor?* (Washington Legal Foundation, 1985), p. 102.

Little scribbles: Michael Allen, "Cleaning House: U.S. Companies Pay Increasing Attention to Destroying Files," *The Wall Street Journal*, September 2, 1987.

Coke formula: Diet Coke III, 107 F.R.D. 288 (1985); see also 696 F.Supp.
57, 170 (D. Del. 1988).

Probing this organ and that one: Schlagenhauf v. Holder, 379 U.S. 104
(1964).

Charlie Chaplin and Mary Astor cases: Kenneth Anger, *Hollywood Babylon*
(Dell, 1975), pp. 132, 278. See also G. Ragland, *Discovery Before Trial*
(Callaghan, 1932), p. 31, quoting a Los Angeles lawyer.

Legal services tips: The Law and Direct Citizen Action, prepared by the Institute for Social Justice, Advocacy Training and Development Unit,
Legal Services Corp., Washington, D.C. (November 1981), pp. 18,
20, 21, and "Litigation Strategies and Organizing," workshop prepared by Gary Bellow in *You Bet Your Job: Trainer's Notes* (legal
services video training program), quoted in Isaac, "Bringing Down
the System Through 'Training,' " pp. 93, 102–104.

ATLA campaign: Paul Barrett, "Protective Orders Come Under Attack,"
The Wall Street Journal, August 31, 1989.

Had the city by the throat: Patricia Bellew Gray, "Lawyer Harry Lipsig
Makes a Killing Suing People of New York," *The Wall Street Journal,*
March 16, 1988.

Hickman v. Taylor case: 329 U.S. 495 (1947).

CHAPTER 7

Marie and Anthony: The case is reported at 474 So.2d 1014 (La.App. 5th
Cir. 1985); 492 So.2d 1193 (La. 1986).

More time squabbling after divorce: Sally Burnett Sharp, "Modification of
Agreement-Based Custody Decrees: Unitary or Dual Standard?," 68
Virginia Law Review 1263 (1982), p. 1264.

Hotbed of litigation: Joan Wexler, "Rethinking the Modification of Child
Custody Decrees," 94 *Yale Law Journal* 757 (March 1985).

Elliot and Sharon: The case is reported at 432 N.E.2d 765 (N.Y. 1982).

Virginia court's optimism: Keel v. Keel, 303 S.E.2d 917, 920 (Va. 1983).

Repose needed above all: Wexler, "Rethinking Child Custody," p. 784.

Vehicles in the park: H.L.A. Hart, *The Concept of Law* (Oxford Univ. Press,
1961), p. 123.

Undue influence in will contests: David W. Louisell, Geoffrey C. Hazard,
Jr., and Colin C. Tait, *Cases and Materials on Pleading and Procedure:
State and Federal,* 5th ed. (Foundation Press, 1983), p. 98.

Lawrence J. Golden quote: Equitable Distribution of Property (McGraw-Hill,
1983), p. v.

Bass divorce: Eric Schmuckler, "Breaking up Is Complex to Do," *Forbes,* October 24, 1988.

Two hundred and ninety-nine criteria: see Robert F. Cochran, Jr., "The Search for Guidance in Determining the Best Interests of the Child at Divorce: Reconciling the Primary Caretaker and Joint Custody Preferences," 20 *University of Richmond Law Review* 1 (Fall 1985), note 81, citing Pearson, Munson & Thoennes, *Journal of Family Issues,* vol. 3 (1982), pp. 5–6.

Five reasons: Henry Aldrich (1647–1710).

Manufacturer liability guidelines: John Wade, "On the Nature of Strict Liability for Products," 44 *Mississippi Law Journal* 825 (1973). See Peter Huber, *Liability: The Legal Revolution and Its Consequences* (Basic Books, 1988), p. 43.

No contingency unprovided for: Harry W. Jones, "Some Causes of Uncertainty in Statutes," 36 *A.B.A. Journal* 321 (1950).

Alex Kozinski quote: "Hunt for Laws' 'True' Meaning Subverts Justice," *The Wall Street Journal,* January 31, 1989 [paragraph break omitted].

Ad hoc inquiries: Connolly v. Pension Benefit Guaranty Corporation, 106 S.Ct. 1018, 1026 (1986).

Age of majority: Laurence Tribe, "Childhood, Suspect Classifications, and Conclusive Presumptions: Three Linked Riddles," 39 *Law and Contemporary Problems* 8, 32–33 (Summer 1975).

Vague standards preferred: Duncan Kennedy, "Form and Substance in Private Law Adjudication," 89 *Harvard Law Review* 1685 (1976).

Framework to negotiate: Garska v. McCoy, 278 S.E. 357 (W.Va. 1981).

Government bound in all its actions: Friedrich Hayek, *The Road to Serfdom* (Chicago, 1944), p. 72.

It's that simple: Richard Epstein, "Simple Rules for a Complex World," *The Wall Street Journal,* June 27, 1985.

CHAPTER 8

What not to believe: Helen, tr. Richmond Lattimore (Univ. of Chicago Press, 1956), 11. 1617–18.

"As if my head were about to explode": Fredric Tulsky, "Did Jury's Award Consider Psychic's Loss of 'Powers'?," *National Law Journal,* April 14, 1986.

Irrelevant evidence can only hurt: Stephen A. Saltzburg and Kenneth R. Redden, *Federal Rules of Evidence Manual,* 4th ed. (Michie, 1986), p. 133.

Rex v. Culander & Duny: 6 *State Trials* (17 Charles II), 685, 697.

Biased in favor of admissibility: Jack Weinstein, *New York Law Journal*, October 23–24, 1975.

Hearsay rule faces "extinction": Faust Rossi, "The Silent Revolution," in John G. Koelti, ed., in *The Litigation Manual* (A.B.A. Section of Litigation, 1989), pp. 640, 641.

Foxhole with noncombatants: Quoted in Blake Fleetwood, "From the People Who Brought You the Twinkie Defense," *Washington Monthly*, June 1987.

Medical testimony going rates: Jon Hamilton, "New Twist on Malpractice Troubles," *Washington Post*, August 1, 1989.

Twenty thousand dollars per complainant: E. Donald Elliott, "Toward Incentive-Based Evidence: Three Approaches for Regulating Scientific Evidence," Working Paper #76, Yale Law School Program in Civil Liability, March 1988, p. 7.

Texaco case: see Richard Epstein, "The Pirates of Pennzoil," *Regulation*, November/December 1985, p. 23.

Frye case: Frye v. U.S., 293 F. 1013 (D.C. Cir. 1923).

Florida judge: Cited in Edward Imwinkelreid, "Science Takes the Stand: The Growing Misuse of Expert Testimony," *The Sciences*, (November/December 1986).

Aerobics to exploding bottles: Trial, February 1985, p. 92. "Two of our recent cases . . .": *Trial*, December 1985, p. 96.

Other examples: Trial, April–July issues, 1989. See Walter Olson, "The Case Against Expert Witnesses," *Fortune*, September 25, 1989.

Second expert at no extra charge: "Doctors Seek Crackdown on Colleagues Paid for Testimony in Malpractice Suits," *The Wall Street Journal*, November 7, 1988.

Jacobs's writings: Quoted in Frank Edwards, *Medical Malpractice* (Henry Holt, 1989), p. 53.

Jacobs's record: John Jenkins, "Expert's Day in Court," *The New York Times Magazine*, December 11, 1983.

Jack Weinstein quote: "Improving Expert Testimony," 20 *University of Richmond Law Review* 473, 482 (1986).

Philadelphia case: In re Paoli Railroad Yard PCB Litigation, Memorandum of Judge R.F. Kelly (E.D.Pa.), November 28, 1988, Master File # 86-2229, pp. 10–12, 23–24.

Auto accident and cancer: Warden v. Taylor, Tex., Harris County 281st Jud. Dt. Ct. No. 81-28711 (Aug. 10, 1987), reported in 21 *A.T.L.A. Law Reporter*, February 1988, pp. 20–21.

Class action: In re Richardson-Merrell, Inc. "Bendectin" Product Litigation, 624 F.Supp. 1212 (S.D. Ohio 1985), *aff'd*, 857 F.2d 290 (6th Cir. 1988), *cert. denied*, 109 S.Ct. 788 (1989); see also In re Bendectin Products Liability Litigation, 749 F.2d 300 (6th Cir. 1984).

Spermicide case: Wells v. Ortho Pharmaceutical Co., 788 F.2d 741 (11th Cir. 1986).

Washington obstetrics case: Richard Preston Blow, "Trial by Error," *Regardie's,* April 1989.

Vaccine: Gina Kolata, "Whooping Cough Vaccine Found Not to Be Linked to Brain Damage," *The New York Times,* March 23, 1990.

Cerebral palsy: Jane Brody, "Personal Health: New Research Discounts Long-Held Assumptions on Possible Causes of Cerebral Palsy," *The New York Times,* December 21, 1989. *EFM:* Lawrence K. Altman, "Electronic Monitoring Doesn't Help in Premature Births, a Study Finds," *The New York Times,* March 1, 1990.

Apples: Western Union v. DuBois, 21 N.E. 4 (Ill.). *Absconding agent:* Lowery v. Western Union, 60 N.Y. 198, 19 Am.Rep. 154. The cases in this discussion are taken from S. Walter Jones, *A Treatise on the Law of Telephone and Telegraph Companies* (Vernon Law Book Co., 1906), ch. 21.

Horse race: Western Union v. Crall, 18 P. 719 (Kan.). *Stockbroker:* Smith v. Western Union, 83 Ky. 104.

Gloria Grayson case: Grayson v. Irvmar, 184 N.Y.S. 2d 33 (1959).

Positive you haven't frightened someone: William Prosser and Young B. Smith, *Torts: Cases and Materials* (Foundation Press, 1967), p. 449.

Carmen Battalla case: Battalla v. State, 176 N.E. 2d 729 (Ct. App. N.Y. 1961).

Dold family case: Dold v. Outrigger, 501 P.2d 368 (Haw. 1972).

Doris Barnett case: National Law Journal, January 29, 1990.

Wide range of estimates: David S. Evans, "Hedonic Damages," *Viewpoint: The Marsh & McLennan Quarterly,* Fall 1989, p. 15.

Five different damage theories: Wayne Green, "Trial Strategies Often Focus on Rival Damages Theories," *The Wall Street Journal,* May 12, 1989. In October 1990 a federal court ordered Kodak to pay $909 million; the amount was below what had been expected, and Polaroid's stock fell sharply the next day.

Ruth Johnson case: National Law Journal, September 4, 1989, p. 34.

Coyne and McCoubray case: National Law Journal, January 29, 1990, p. S12.

Zalay case: "Former Hancock Salesman Wins Lawsuit," *The Wall Street Journal,* September 14, 1989.

A.B.A. recommendation: Ruth Marcus, "A.B.A. Panel Recommends Change for Injury Suits," *Washington Post,* January 12, 1987.

Carrying hyena gut: John Leubsdorf, "The Contingency Factor in Attorney Fee Awards," 90 *Yale Law Journal* 473, 501 (1981).

Rand study: George Eads and Peter Reuter, *Designing Safer Products,* Rand Corporation Publication R-3022-ICJ (1983).

CHAPTER 9

Dr. Warren case: Rosenthal v. Warren, 475 F.2d 438 (2nd Cir. 1973), 374 F.Supp. 522 (1974), 342 F.Supp. 246 (S.D.N.Y. 1972).

The law and manner of the Jat community: In re Dalip Singh Bir's Estate, 188 P.2d 499 (Cal. Ct. App. 1948).

Old Rhode Island marriage: In re May's Estate, 114 N.E.2d 4 (N.Y. 1953) (marriage of uncle and half-niece). *Bigamy prosecution:* Williams v. North Carolina, 317 U.S. 287.

Baby Lenore: Cases reported at 254 So.2d 813 (Fla. Dist. Ct. App. 1971), *cert. denied*, 409 U.S. 1011 (1972); see also 269 N.E.2d 787, 321 N.Y.S.2d 65 (N.Y. 1971).

Joseph Story quote: Conflict of Laws (8th ed., 1883), p. 38.

Babcock v. Jackson case: 191 N.E.2d 279 (N.Y. 1963).

Met in New York: Dym v. Gordon, 209 N.E.2d 792 (N.Y. 1965).

Met elsewhere: Tooker v. Lopez, 249 N.E.2d 394 (N.Y. 1969).

Only driver from N.Y.: Hepp v. Ireland, U.S. Dist. Ct., S.D.N.Y. (66 Civ. 2128, Frankel, J., 1970, unreported) (federal court applying New York law). See Willis L. M. Reese and Maurice Rosenberg, *Conflict of Laws: Cases and Materials*, 7th ed. (Foundation Press, 1978), p. 494.

New York retreat: Neumeier v. Kuehner, 286 N.E.2d 454 (N.Y. Ct. of App. 1972) (Ontario plaintiff and accident, New York driver).

Rhode Island case: Labree v. Major, 306 A.2d 808 (R.I. 1973).

Ouija board: Maurice Rosenberg, "Two Views of Kell v. Henderson," 67 *Columbia Law Review* 459, 465 (1967). Rosenberg put the comment in the mouth of a fictional character.

Massachusetts does not appear to have a strong interest: Labree v. Major, 306 A.2d 808, 816 (R.I. 1973). *Oregon case:* Fisher v. Huck, 624 P.2d 177, 178, 631 P.2d 339 (Ore. 1981).

Lord Chancellor's self-persuasion: W.S. Gilbert, *Iolanthe*, Act II.

Protecting its own residents: Neumeier v. Kuehner, 286 N.E.2d 454, 456 (N.Y. Ct. of App. 1972).

Kentucky case: Foster v. Leggett, 484 S.W.2d 827, 829 (Ky. 1972).

Plaintiff's move into state: Miller v. Miller, 237 N.E.2d 877 (1968); Gore v. Northeast Airlines, 373 F.2d 717 (2d Cir. 1967); Allstate v. Hague, 449 U.S. 302 (1981).

Missouri accident: Tjepkema v. Kenney, 298 N.Y.S.2d 175 (1st Dept. 1969).

Mozambique accident: Pancotto v. Sociedade de Safaris de Mocambique, S.A.R.L., 422 F.Supp. 405 (1976).

State applies its libel law although neither party lives in state: Keeton v. Hustler Magazine, Inc., 104 S.Ct. 1473 (1984).

Delaware drivers deserve Delaware law: Aaron Twerski, "Enlightened Territorialism and Professor Cavers—the Pennsylvania Method," 9 *Duquesne Law Review* 373, 382 (1971). See Cipolla v. Shaposka, 267 A.2d 854 (Pa. 1970).

Constitutional due process constraints: Home Insurance Co. v. Dick, 281 U.S. 397 (1930); John Hancock Mutual Life Insurance Co. v. Yates, 299 U.S. 178 (1936).

Count-the-contacts: Allstate v. Hague, 449 U.S. 302 (1981). *Kansas class action:* Phillips Petroleum v. Shutts, 472 U.S. 797 (1985).

Other state's law "better": Lichter v. Fritsch, 252 N.W.2d 360 (Wisc. 1977).

Neutrality as euphemism: Gunther Kuehne, "Choice of Law in Products Liability," 60 *California Law Review* 1, 30, 32 (1972).

Apply the law that will favor the plaintiff: Russell J. Weintraub, *Commentary on the Conflict of Laws* (Foundation Press, 1980), p. 346.

CHAPTER 10

Film-processing case: Mieske v. Bartell Drug Co., 593 P.2d 1308 (Wash. 1979).

Merely working out the implications: Patrick Atiyah, *An Introduction to the Law of Contract,* 4th ed. (Univ. of Oxford Press, 1989), p. 12.

Disagreeable consequences: Benjamin Franklin, *Autobiography* (Modern Library, 1950), p. 123.

Contracting out of first-year contracts: Richard Epstein, "The Social Consequences of Common Law Rules," 95 *Harvard Law Review* 1717, 1747 (June 1982).

"Terms of the trade": Because older courts tended to settle contract disputes in line with the prevailing custom of the time, place, and trade, the body of contract jurisprudence as a whole was a sprawling affair that could not readily be deduced from any particular abstract principles. That circumstance later allowed some Legal Realists and Critical Legal Studies adherents to argue that contract law was a mere display of raw judicial power.

Doubling-ryecorn case: Thornborough v. Whitacre, 92 Eng.Rep. 270 (1706), cited with another similar case in "Unconscionable Contracts: The Uniform Commercial Code," 45 *Iowa Law Review* 843, 847 (1960).

Covert tools: Karl Llewellyn, Book Review, 52 *Harvard Law Review* 700, 702 (1939).

Art of typography diverted: Delancey v. Insurance Co., 52 N.H. 581 (1873). Quoted in E. Allan Farnsworth and William Young, *Cases and Materials on Contracts* (Foundation Press, 1980), p. 467.

Unlikely fur depositories: The New York Times, March 26, 1972, business section, cited in E. Allan Farnsworth and William Young, *Contracts: Cases and Materials*, p. 455.

Checkroom case: Klar v. H. & M. Parcel Room, Inc., 61 N.Y.S.2d 285, *aff'd mem.* 296 N.Y. 1044, 73 N.E.2d 912 (1947).

"Brought to their minds": See, for example, the music-hall case Taylor v. Caldwell, 122 Eng. Rep. 309 (1863).

"Dragnet" provision: Specifically, each of a customer's payments would be applied proportionally to pay down some of the remaining balance on each item, so that none of the items would be paid off until the overall balance was reduced to zero.

Arthur Allen Leff quote: "Unconscionability and the Code—The Emperor's New Clause," 115 *University of Pennsylvania Law Review* 485, 556–58 (1967).

Williams v. Walker-Thomas Furniture Company case: 350 F.2d 445 (D.C. Cir. 1965).

Unlikely to survive into twenty-first century: Grant Gilmore, "Introduction to Havighurst's Limitations Upon Freedom of Contract," 1979 *Arizona State Law Journal* 165, 166.

Bartholomew Burne case: Burne v. Franklin Life Ins. Co., 301 A.2d 799 (Pa. 1973).

Nozko quote, Wyatt survey: The Wall Street Journal, April 24, 1990, p. 1.

Mississippi farm couple: Bank of Indiana v. Holyfield, 476 F.Supp. 104, 108 (1979).

Yarn case: Pittsfield Weaving Co. v. Grove Textiles, 430 A.2d 638 (N.H. 1981).

Washington electric company case: Royal Indemnity v. Westinghouse Electric Corp., 385 F.Supp. 520 (S.D.N.Y. 1974).

Death of contract: Grant Gilmore, *The Death of Contract* (Ohio State Univ. Press, 1974).

CHAPTER 11

Dallas fistfight: "How's Your Lawyer's Left Jab?," *Newsweek,* February 26, 1990.

Geoffrey Hazard quote: "Change Rules to 'Civilize' the Profession," *National Law Journal,* April 17, 1989.

Eugene Cook quote: Gary Taylor, "Texas Sets Its Sights on 'Rambo,' " *National Law Journal,* July 31, 1989.

Concession to the shortness of life: Reeve v. Dennett, 11 N.E. 938, 944 (Mass. 1887).

Nicholas Katzenbach quote: "Modern Discovery: Remarks from the Defense Bar," 57 *St. Johns Law Review* 732, 735 (1983).

Courtroom hubbub: Philip Schrag, "Bleak House 1968," 44 *New York University Law Review* 115 (1969).

Eight years of discovery and motions: Marrese v. American Academy of Orthopaedic Surgeons, 706 F.2d 1488 (7th Cir. 1983).

Bristle with discretion: Faust Rossi, "The Silent Revolution" in John G. Koelti, ed., *The Litigation Manual* (A.B.A. Section of Litigation, 1989), p. 640.

War over Redskins tickets: Mary H.J. Farrell, "When love dies, nothing tastes as sweet as . . . ," *People*, February 19, 1990, p. 83.

Hostility and bitterness: Harlem River Consumer Co-op, Inc. v. Associated Grocers of Harlem, Inc., 54 F.R.D. 551, 553 (S.D.N.Y. 1972).

Chicago survey: Wayne Brazil, "Civil Discovery: Lawyers' Views of Its Effectiveness, Its Principal Problems and Abuses," 1980 *American Bar Foundation Research Journal* 787.

Louis Harris poll: Presented at a conference sponsored by the Program in Civil Liability, Yale Law School, April 18, 1988.

Second nature to me: Brazil, "Civil Discovery," p. 846.

Cravath protractor: "Those Lawyers," *Time*, April 10, 1978, pp. 55, 59.

Injunction hearing: Lisa Belkin, "Bare-Knuckles Litigation Jars Many in Dallas," *The New York Times*, May 13, 1988.

Snakes: The Wall Street Journal, March 22, 1990.

Bickel & Brewer profits: Gary Taylor, "Dallas' Brash Young Upstarts," *National Law Journal*, January 22, 1990.

Run up opposition's costs: The Law and Direct Citizen Action, prepared by the Institute for Social Justice, Advocacy Training and Development Unit, Legal Services Corp., Washington, D.C. (November 1981), pp. 2, 11, cited in Rael Jean Isaac, "Bringing Down the System Through 'Training'—The LSC Manuals and Training Materials," in *Legal Services Corporation: The Robber Barons of the Poor?* (Washington Legal Foundation, 1985), pp. 99–100.

Small suits humming away, make them travel, hassle them to death: "Litigation Strategies and Organizing," workshop prepared by Gary Bellow in *You Bet Your Job: Trainer's Notes*, and "Mini FCC Packet" in California Legal Services, Inc., *Working With Community Organizations: Conference Materials*, p. 130, both cited in Isaac, "Bringing Down the System Through 'Training,'" pp. 99–101. The "Working With Community Organizations" materials were used at a conference held June 16–18, 1981 at Marcy, New York.

Robert Keeton quote: Trial Tactics and Methods, 2nd ed. (Little, Brown, 1973), p. 5.

Client's first reaction: American Law of Product Liability, 3rd ed., section 2, p. 22.

All-purpose theory: "Interviewing the Client," *American Jurisprudence Trials* 1, pp. 57–58.

North Carolina versus New Jersey crashes: "Crash Counsel," *Insurance Review,* April 1989.

Goose up the damages: Patricia Bellew Gray, "Lawyer Harry Lipsig Makes a Killing Suing People of New York," *The Wall Street Journal,* March 16, 1988.

Squeezed in a vise: "Interviewing the Client," pp. 62–63.

Pain and suffering checklist: American Law of Products Liability, 3rd ed., section 12, p. 51.

"My Day": Jeffrey O'Connell, *The Lawsuit Lottery* (Free Press, 1979), p. 20.

Nurture every twinge: O'Connell, *Lawsuit Lottery,* p. 22.

John Nemiah quote: "Psychological Aspects of the Injured," *Trial,* March/April 1971.

Workers'-comp seminar: Betsy Clarke, *Chronicles,* April 1989, p. 10.

Playing victimization for all it is worth: "Insult to Injury," *Disability Rag,* May/June 1986.

Trim the sails too much: David Berg, "Preparing Witnesses," in *The Litigation Manual* (A.B.A. Section of Litigation, 1989), pp. 466, 467.

Gloria Shanor quote: Michael Bradford, "Job Evaluations Can Trigger Termination Suits," *Business Insurance,* April 24, 1989.

That darn handbook: Susan Faludi, "At Nordstrom Stores, Service Comes First—But at a Big Price," *The Wall Street Journal,* February 20, 1990.

Cielsa, Galusha quotes: Chris Spolar, "Doctoring Billig's Recommendations," *The Washington Post,* March 10, 1986.

Policy against giving references: "Reference Preference: Employers Button Lips," *The Wall Street Journal,* January 4, 1990.

Scripted to Delaware case law: Gordon Crovitz, "Can Takeover Targets Just Say No to Stockholders?," *The Wall Street Journal,* March 7, 1990.

George Flynn quote: Stacy Shapiro, "Needless Papers May Haunt Manufacturers," *Business Insurance,* April 17, 1989.

Shredding campaigns: Michael Allen, "Cleaning House: U.S. Companies Pay Increasing Attention to Destroying Files," *The Wall Street Journal,* September 2, 1987.

Cleveland Plain Dealer: Betty Holcomb, "Should Reporters Torch Their Notes?" *Columbia Journalism Review,* January/February 1986.

Country lawyer: Quoted in Joseph Goulden, *The Million-Dollar Lawyers,* (Putnam, 1978).

Richmond, Short, Dranoff, Kolodny quotes: Andrew Patner and Wayne Green, "Matrimonial Attorneys Spar in Chicago," *The Wall Street Journal,* November 8, 1989.

Nasty tactics as art form: "How's Your Lawyer's Left Jab?"

CHAPTER 12

Coale quote: John Jenkins, *The Litigators* (Doubleday, 1989), p. 83.

Fine paper case: In re Fine Paper, 98 F.R.D. 48 (1983) (fee ruling after settlement of main class action); 751 F.2d 562 (1984) (appeal of fee ruling); 685 F.2d 810 (1982) (appeal of states after losing at trial in separate action); 840 F.2d 188 (1988) (appeal of Riordan on fees).

Plagiarism suits: H.L. Mencken, "Blackmail Made Easy," in *The Bathtub Hoax and Other Blasts and Bravos from the* Chicago Tribune (Knopf, 1958), pp. 186–91.

Special guardian quote: Murray Teigh Bloom, *The Trouble With Lawyers* (Simon & Schuster, 1968), p. 245.

Every time a company coughs wrong: "A Bondholder's Revenge," *Forbes,* August 24, 1987.

Feigned litigation: John C. Coffee, Jr., "The Unfaithful Champion: The Plaintiff as Monitor in Shareholder Litigation," 48 *Law and Contemporary Problems* 5, 17 (Summer 1985).

Thomas M. Jones survey: "An Empirical Examination of the Resolution of Shareholder Derivative and Class Action Lawsuits," 60 *Boston University Law Review* 306 and 542 (two articles) (1980).

RKO case: In re General Tire, 726 F.2d 1075, 1088 (6th Cir. 1984).

Coastal States Gas case: Weisberg v. Coastal States Gas Corp., 1982 *Federal Securities Law Reporter* (Commerce Clearing House) at 98,716 (S.D.N.Y. 1982).

Analysis of Jones figures: Bryant G. Garth, Ilene Nagel and Sheldon Plager, "Empirical Research and the Shareholder Derivative Suit: Toward a Better-Informed Debate," 48 *Law and Contemporary Problems* (Summer 1985), at 146.

Over-the-hill dragon: William Cary and Melvin Eisenberg, *Corporations,* 5th ed. (Foundation Press, 1980), p. 888.

Upon the anvil: Case reported at 244 S.E.2d 338 (W. Va. 1978).

Clark dissent: Arnstein v. Porter, 154 F.2d 464, 479 (2nd Cir. 1946).

Cost of defending major case: Laurence Bodine, "Your Best Defense? Advice from the Plaintiff Bar," *The Wall Street Journal,* April 2, 1990.

William Sanders estimate: Quoted in James Jeans, Sr., *Litigation* (Kluwer, 1986), p. 122.

Standard Brands Paint: Sonia Nazario, "Hard Line Pays as Firm Fights Nuisance Suits," *The Wall Street Journal,* December 9, 1988.

Dupont Plaza case: Linda Collins, "Growing Legal Bills Spur New Dupont Settlements," *Business Insurance,* July 17, 1989, and "Dupont Plaintiffs Oppose Defense Pact," *Business Insurance,* August 28, 1989.

Jeffrey Matz speech: "Actions for Damages: The Plaintiff's Perspective," delivered at the 1987 A.B.A. annual meeting in San Francisco, pp. 12, 45. A revised version of the speech appeared in the A.B.A. publication *The Brief*, Spring 1988.

Refac article: Edmund Andrews, "A 'White Knight' Draws Cries of 'Patent Blackmail,' " *The New York Times*, January 14, 1990.

Broadcast license objections: Walter Olson, "License Payola: It's High Time the F.C.C. Put a Stop to It," *Barron's*, December 1, 1986. See also Michael Greve, "Congress's Environmental Buccaneers," *The Wall Street Journal*, September 18, 1989.

Steven Brill account in The American Lawyer: Quoted in Nicholas Von Hoffman, *Citizen Cohn* (Doubleday, 1988), pp. 449–51.

Return of legal fees: Coffee, "The Unfaithful Champion: The Plaintiff as Monitor in Shareholder Litigation," note 77.

American Bar Foundation study: Cited in Jon Hamilton, "New Twist on Malpractice Troubles," *The Washington Post*, August 1, 1989.

CHAPTER 13

Breeden quote: Kevin G. Salwen and Laurie P. Cohen, "Getting Tough: SEC Under Breeden Takes a Harder Line on Securities Crime," *The Wall Street Journal*, May 10, 1990.

Psychiatric malpractice suit: Sara Charles and Eugene Kennedy, *Defendant: A Psychiatrist on Trial for Medical Malpractice* (Free Press, 1985), pp. xvii, 88, 97, 171.

First essential of due process: Connally v. General Construction Company, 269 U.S. 385 (1926).

All are entitled: Lanzetta v. New Jersey, 306 U.S. 451 (1939).

Dangerous to set large enough net: U.S. v. Reese, 92 U.S. 214, 221 (1876).

McBoyle v. U.S. case: 283 U.S. 25 (1931).

Contingency fee disallowed: Clancy v. Superior Court, 705 P.2d 347 (Cal. 1985), *cert. denied*, 475 U.S. 1121 (1986).

Vuitton case: Young ex rel. Vuitton et Fils S.A., 481 U.S. 787 (1987).

Punitive damages background: Richard J. Maloney and Stephen E. Little-john, "Innovation on Trial: Punitive Damages Versus New Products," *Science*, December 15, 1989.

Imwinkelreid quote: Edward Imwinkelreid, "Uncharged Misconduct," in John G. Koelti, ed., *The Litigation Manual* (A.B.A. Section of Litigation, 1989), pp. 728, 729.

Union Oil case: Spaeth v. Union Oil of California, 762 F.2d 865 (10th Cir. 1985).

Merrill Lynch case: Wall Street Journal, June 22, 1990.

GTE, Timothy Hutton cases: National Law Journal, January 29, 1990, pp. S11–S12.

Theodore Olson findings: Cited in Maloney and Littlejohn, "Innovation on Trial," p. 1396. See Andrew Blum, "Verdict Trends Remain Elusive," *National Law Journal*, January 29, 1990.

"Sound-alike" cases: "Beyond Bette Midler," *National Law Journal*, May 21, 1990, p. 6.

Holmes decision: U.S. v. Nash, 229 U.S. 373 (1913).

Obscene phonograph records: U.S. v. Alpers, 338 U.S. 680.

Hodge-podge as basis for jailing: Miller v. California, 413 U.S. 15, 43–44.

Boy Scout oath: Quoted in Gordon Crovitz, "Mother of Mercy, Will Drexel Be the End of RICO?," *The Wall Street Journal*, February 21, 1990.

Dirks v. S.E.C. case: 463 U.S. 646 (1983).

A.B.A. study: Cited in Gordon Crovitz, "RICO and the Man," *Reason*, March 1990.

Often disruptive and always agonizing: Medical Professional Liability and the Delivery of Obstetrical Care (National Academy Press, 1989), p. 44.

Advice not to take suits personally, and Philip Corboy quote: Charles and Kennedy, *Defendant*, pp. 186–88.

CHAPTER 14

Dr. Friedman case: Friedman v. Dozorc, 312 N.W.2d 585, 607 (Michigan 1981).

Illinois doctor: Berlin v. Nathan, 381 N.E.2d 1367 (Ill. App. 1978).

Most accident victims have some coverage: George Priest, "Understanding the Liability Crisis," in Walter Olson, ed., *New Directions in Liability Law* (Academy of Political Science, 1988).

Shearson/American Express v. McMahon case: 482 U.S. 220.

Third-party suits against employers: Dole v. Dow, 282 N.E.2d 288 (N.Y. 1972).

Suing managers: Grantham v. Denke, 359 S.2d 785, 787 (Ala. 1978); Fireman's Fund v. Coleman, 394 S.2d 334, 343 (Ala. 1980).

Employer as manufacturer of workplace: Bell v. Industrial Vangas, 637 P.2d 266 (Cal. 1981).

"Intentional": Blankenship v. Cincinnati Milacron Chemicals Inc., No. 81–42 (Ohio Supreme Court, filed March 3, 1982).

Steen case: Robert Reinhold, "Jurors Assess Monsanto $108 Million over Death," *The New York Times*, January 10, 1987.

Korean Air Lines case: Christi Harlan, "Punitive Damages in KAL Crash Case Could Set a Pattern for Future Trials," *The Wall Street Journal*, August 7, 1989.

Supreme Court cases on jurisdiction: Kulko v. Superior Court, 98 S.Ct. 1690 (1978) (father); World-Wide Volkswagen Corp. v. Woodson, 100 S.Ct. 559 (1980) (auto dealer); Rush v. Saychuk, 100 S.Ct. 571 (1980) (insurance policy).

Supreme Court cases on summary judgment: Celotex Corp. v. Catrett, 106 S. Ct. 2458 (1986) (factually unsupported); Matsushita Electric v. Zenith Radio, 106 S.Ct. 1348 (1986) (assess the credibility); Anderson v. Liberty Lobby, 106 S.Ct. 2505 (1986) (scintilla not enough).

Supreme Court cases on class actions: Zahn v. International Paper, 414 U.S. 291 (1973) (minimum dollar value); Eisen v. Carlisle & Jaquelin, 417 U.S. 156 (1974) (notification).

CHAPTER 15

Epidemic, deluge: "Not Practicing Safe Management," *National Law Journal*, April 10, 1989, p. 2.

From mosquito to shark bite: Stephen Adler, "Texas Law Firm Agrees to Pay Widow $4.3 Million After Suit for Malpractice," *The Wall Street Journal*, May 27, 1988.

Sewell & Riggs case: Wayne Green and Paul Barrett, "Jury Brings in $17.5 Million Verdict Against Firm in Malpractice Suit," *The Wall Street Journal*, January 10, 1990.

Coverage provided by lawyer groups: David Margolick, "At the Bar," *The New York Times*, November 18, 1988.

Exotic damage theories: John Bauman, "Proving Damages for Legal Malpractice," *Trial*, July 1989, p. 45.

And so proceed ad infinitum: Jonathan Swift, *On Poetry* (1712).

Cost of defending unfounded suits: Ronald Mallen, "Malpractice by Lawyers: Avoid Being a Statistic," *Trial*, July 1989, p. 40.

RICO and extortion value: Quoted in Lis Wiehl, "Lawyers Find New Ways to Sue Other Lawyers," *The New York Times*, June 16, 1989.

Obviously we are not responsible: Tom H. Davis, "A Plaintiff's Lawyer Looks at the Professional Liability of Trial Lawyers," in *Professional Liability of Trial Lawyers: The Malpractice Question* (A.B.A. Section of Insurance, Negligence and Compensation Law, 1979), p. 1.

Judge Shadur opinion: National Union Fire Insurance v. Continental Illinois, 113 F.R.D. 637, 641, 642, at ns. 12, 15 (N.D.Ill. 1987).

Ramsay Clark case: The Wall Street Journal, October 2, 1989. *Softball case:* Heimbaugh v. City and County of San Francisco, 591 F.Supp. 1573 (1984).

Medical school case: Cannon v. Loyola University, 784 F.2d 777 (7th Cir. 1986), *cert. denied*, 107 S.Ct. 880.

Judge Nangle opinion: Hasty v. Paccar, Inc., 583 F.Supp. 1577, 1578, 1580 (E.D. Mo. 1984).

Ida Hudson case: Hudson v. Moore Business Forms, 836 F.2d 1156 (9th Cir. 1988).

Lawyer, not law firm: Pavelic & LeFlore v. Marvel, 110 S.Ct. 456 (1989).

"Chill": Georgene Vairo, "Rule 11: A Critical Analysis," 118 F.R.D. 189, 197 (1988).

Policing frivolous-vs.-nonfrivolous distinction: Werner Pfennigstorf, "The European Experience with Attorney Fee Shifting," 47 *Law and Contemporary Problems* 37, 82 (Winter 1984). Much of this chapter's discussion of European fee shifting is based on Pfennigstorf's account.

Irrational to pay a debt in full: Arthur Allen Leff, "Injury, Ignorance and Spite—The Dynamics of Coercive Collection," 80 *Yale Law Journal* 1, 5 (1970).

Standards differ markedly for plaintiff and defendant: Mary Frances Derfner and Arthur D. Wolf, *Court Awarded Attorney Fees* (Matthew Bender, 1983), p. 8–14.

Court decided plaintiffs should not collect fees when they lose: Ruckelshaus v. Sierra Club, 103 S.Ct. 3274 (1983).

CHAPTER 16

Michigan custody rule: DeGrow v. DeGrow, 315 N.W.2d 915 (Mich. 1982).
False witness: Exodus 20:16.

INDEX